Peirce, James, and a Pragmatic Philosophy of Religion

Continuum Studies in American Philosophy

Series Editor: James Fieser, University of Tennessee at Martin, USA

Continuum Studies in American Philosophy is a major monograph series from Continuum. The series features first-class scholarly research monographs across the field of American philosophy. Each work makes a major contribution to the field of philosophical research.

After Rorty, G. Elijah Dann

America's First Women Philosophers, Dorothy G. Rogers

Feminist Epistemology and American Pragmatism, Alexandra L. Shuford

John Searle and the Construction of Social Reality, Joshua Rust

The Legacy of John Rawls, edited by Thom Brooks and Fabian Freyenhagen

Nozick, Autonomy and Compensation, Dale Murray

Peirce's Philosophy of Communication, Mats Bergman

Peirce's Pragmatic Theory of Inquiry, Elizabeth Cooke

Pragmatist Metaphysics, Sami Pihlström

Quine on Meaning, Eve Gaudet

Quine's Naturalism, Paul A. Gregory

Reality and Its Appearance, Nicholas Rescher

Relativism in Contemporary American Philosophy, Timothy Mosteller

Richard Rorty's New Pragmatism, Edward J. Grippe

Thomas Kuhn's Revolution, James A. Marcum

Varieties of Pragmatism, Douglas McDermid

Virtue Ethics: Dewey and MacIntyre, Stephen Carden

Peirce, James, and a Pragmatic Philosophy of Religion

John W. Woell

Continuum Studies in American Philosophy

In memory of my grandparents
Justus and Norma Kretzmann
James and Virginia Woell

Continuum International Publishing Group

The Tower Building	80 Maiden Lane
11 York Road	Suite 704
London SE1 7NX	New York NY 10038

www.continuumbooks.com

© John W. Woell 2012

All rights reserved. No part of this publication may be reproduced or transmitted in any form or by any means, electronic or mechanical, including photocopying, recording, or any information storage or retrieval system, without prior permission in writing from the publishers.

John W. Woell has asserted his right under the Copyright, Designs and Patents Act, 1988, to be identified as Author of this work.

British Library Cataloguing-in-Publication Data
A catalogue record for this book is available from the British Library

ISBN: HB: 978-1-4411-6800-9

Library of Congress Cataloging-in-Publication Data
Woell, John W.
 Peirce, James, and a pragmatic philosophy of religion/John W. Woell.
  p. cm. – (Continuum studies in American philosophy)
 Includes bibliographical references (p.   ) and index.
 ISBN 978-1-4411-6800-9 (hardcover) – ISBN 978-1-4411-1700-7 (ebook pdf) – ISBN 978-1-4411-1120-3 (epub) 1. Pragmatism. 2. Philosophy and religion.
 3. Religion–Philosophy. 4. Peirce, Charles S. (Charles Sanders), 1839–1914.
 5. James, William, 1842–1910. I. Title.
 B832.W64 2012
 144'.30973–dc23   2011046259

Typeset by Deanta Global Publishing Services, Chennai, India
Printed and bound in Great Britain

Contents

Acknowledgments	vii
Introduction	**1**
No Running in the Hall	1
The Hallway of Pragmatism	7
1. Realisms, Antirealisms, Nonrealisms, and Pragmatisms	**11**
The Confines of Rortian Pragmatism	12
At the Looking-Glass	14
Reading Pragmatism Analytically	23
2. Doubt, Skepticism, and Method	**37**
The Skeptical Hypothesis and Radical Skepticism	40
Responding Pragmatically to Radical Skepticism	50
Pragmatism and Hume's Problems	69
3. Thoughts, Things, and Theories	**73**
Kant and the Noumenon	75
Contemporary Kantians	85
Pragmatism-in-Itself	90
Peirce, James, and Logic	103
4. Inquiry, Metaphysics, and Rationality	**107**
Returning to Rorty	109
Peirce on Objects and the Limits of Inquiry	111

James and the Balance of Inquiry	125
A Narrow and Neutral Pragmatism	143
Conclusion	**147**
Philosophy Without Priestcraft	147
Epistemology and Religion	149
Pragmatism and Religious Belief	153
Back to the Hall	168
Notes	171
Bibliography	203
Index	213

Acknowledgments

Over the course of the nearly ten years from nascent idea to publication, I have accrued innumerable debts—both intellectual and personal. In the early years of this project in the School of Religion at the Claremont Graduate University, my fellow graduate students proved exceptional conversation partners and several faculty guided portions of the work. Rich Amesbury, Dan Ott, Derek Malone-France, Pat Horn and Randy Ramal endured more than their respective shares of my ramblings. David Ray Griffin and Patricia Easton influenced my thinking both directly and indirectly and helped me move from a budding theologian to a budding philosopher, though I cannot admit to being in full bloom in either category.

Financial support for the work was provided in the early years by a grant from the Claremont Graduate University and more recently by research and faculty development grants from the Kathleen Price and Joseph M. Bryan Family Foundation and Eleanor and Claude George Faculty Development Funds at Greensboro College. Both the institution and the Royce and Jane Reynolds Endowment provided further funds for conference travel to deliver elements of this project over the course of my years at Greensboro College. Many thanks are due to those whose generosity supports the work of so many.

Several have commented on pieces of this project as it has come into form. John K. Roth, D.Z. Phillips and Marjorie Hewitt Suchocki offered incisive comments on earlier versions of Chapters 1–3. Parts of Chapter 4 and the conclusion were presented to the members of the Society for Philosophy of Religion and the Highlands Institute for American Religious and Philosophical Thought. Bill Dean's comments on some early ideas on truth as satisfaction sent me scurrying for a stronger argument, which I have only begun to provide. To those faculty, friends, and audiences, I offer further thanks.

I have been fortunate as well to have had the company of many fine colleagues along the way. All who work in small colleges know how difficult finding the balance among teaching, service, and research can be; and several members of the Greensboro College faculty have played roles in helping me find space and support for this work through formal and informal writing groups, idea exchanges, and faculty seminars. In particular, my colleagues in the Department of Religion and Philosophy have proven engaged partners in conversation and have helped me learn and navigate the special challenges of the small college. Finding intellectual connections among a small and diverse faculty can be difficult, but I now know it can be done. W. Barnes Tatum, Paul Leslie, Rhonda Burnette-Bletsch, Rich Crane, Dan Malotky and Jennifer Bird along with the members of the Ethics across the Curriculum Summer Seminar in 2006 helped keep the ideas here in mind and keep the philosopher on task. Further thanks are due to the MERGE Faculty Writing Group at The University of North Carolina at Greensboro, who helped me push through the final stages of writing and editing, and my colleagues in Lloyd International Honors College, who helped provide the time and space for the final stages of production. Their energy and discipline proved invaluable.

Tom Crick, Sarah Campbell, and the staff at Continuum have been highly responsive and incredibly patient as this project has gone forward the past two years. Continuum's reviewers and readers have helped the project along and shaped its contents through their timely and detailed comments. Any issues with the prose or the arguments remain entirely mine.

Like any author, I owe a great deal to my family. My grandparents' influence and support continues to be felt long after their respective passings. My parents and parents-in-law have also proven indefatigable supporters of my career and work, and I owe them all great thanks. Through my many absences, weekends in the library and late evenings, my children maintained their cheer and manage to keep me as grounded as a philosopher can be. Finally, my wife's patience seems nearly bottomless, and her faith in me nearly boundless. Rebecca, I cannot repay, but I can acknowledge. Thank you.

Introduction

No Running in the Hall

Against rationalism as a pretension and a method, pragmatism is fully armed and militant. But, at the outset, at least, it stands for no particular results. It has no dogmas, and no doctrines save its method. As the young Italian pragmatist Papini has well said, it lies in the midst of our theories, like a corridor in a hotel. Innumerable chambers open out of it. In one you may find a man writing an atheistic volume; in the next someone on his knees praying for faith and strength; in a third a chemist investigating a body's properties. In a fourth a system of idealistic metaphysics is being excogitated; in a fifth the impossibility of metaphysics is being shown. But they all own the corridor, and all must pass through it if they want a practicable way of getting into or out of their respective rooms.

William James, *Pragmatism*[1]

Indeed, it was thought to be philosophy's business to decide whether any of our beliefs were "going somewhere," whether they were rational or irrational. It was thought to be philosophy's distinctive task to test whether our beliefs had the required foundations, whether our modes of discourse reflected reality. This was the Enlightenment ideal: all must be brought to the bar of reason to be judged there. So if philosophy of religion or ethics are to get somewhere, they must show us whether there is a God or what constitutes the good life.

D. Z. Phillips, *Philosophy's Cool Place*[2]

In remarks to Maurice O'Connor Drury, Wittgenstein once said of William James: "That is what makes him a good philosopher; he was a real human being."[3] For James and the pragmatists, a concern with the human was always near the forefront in their thinking, but Wittgenstein's remark reveals something deeper, a kind of intimacy between James's philosophy and his temperament. There is little doubt that James's use of personal language in his writing makes such a view plausible. James divides the world between the "healthy-minded" and the "sick souls" in the *Varieties*, between the "tough-minded" and the "tender-minded" in *Pragmatism*, and between the "cynical characters" and the "sympathetic characters" in *Pluralistic Universe*. In each instance, James attempts to situate his approach as mediating between these dispositions, implying that temperament and philosophy might be as intimately related as Wittgenstein suggests.

Concern with the human need not be so explicitly personal in order to be recognized as being important to pragmatism. Without referencing the kind of temperamental or dispositional remarks noted above, Joseph Margolis finds one of pragmatism's distinct advantages to be that it "is one of a very small number of Western philosophical movements . . . that . . . never exceed the natural competence and limitations of mere human being."[4] By situating inquiry within the scope of human action, Margolis claims that pragmatism maintains a humility that is uncharacteristic of much philosophy and keeps its concerns deeply grounded in human interests. Pragmatism thus avoids the problems of either transcendental metaphysics or materialistic empiricism and offers a functional view of the scope and shape of philosophical inquiry.

Taken in the proximity in which I have placed them here, the comments offered by Wittgenstein and Margolis might seem to offer to less sympathetic readers a concise picture of what was wrong with classical American pragmatism. The limitations of James as a philosopher might reveal the limits of classical American pragmatism itself even without the insertion of an indefinite article in Margolis's final phrase. Obviously, it would be a mistake to think that the former claim about James as a philosopher marks territory similar to that of the latter claim about pragmatism as a philosophical movement, but I want to argue here that Wittgenstein's remark about James reveals something that becomes more fully realized in Margolis's remark about pragmatism in general. Pragmatism maintains an abiding concern with the human or, to put it more robustly, with the full range of human experience.

In what follows, I advance a two-part thesis to contextualize the (seemingly) overwhelmingly obvious claim about pragmatism's concern with human experience in order to make its meaning more precise. The argument is intended to be both critical and constructive. It should illuminate both the readings of the classical American pragmatists and the issues in contemporary Anglo-American philosophy. It pushes through epistemological and metaphysical problems and into their impact on the philosophy of religion. It attempts both to limn the bounds of classical American pragmatism and to offer a particular application of some of its central insights. Finally, the argument attempts to bridge the supposed divide between Charles S. Peirce and William James by noting their philosophical agreement on matters central to pragmatism as a philosophical movement and their mutual concern with the religious as an element of human experience.

The two-part thesis, then, can be put simply: first, attempts at reading Charles Sanders Peirce and William James through the lens of contemporary debates surrounding realisms and their counterparts in late twentieth-century analytic philosophy serve to drive a wedge between Peirce and James where it least belongs; second, close attention to the role of inquiry and its consequences in belief formation in Peirce's and James's respective works provides a means for fully appreciating pragmatism's richness. To frame more closely the thesis in the terms offered by the two quotations from Wittgenstein and Margolis, Peirce and James both understand humans to be intentional beings, and attention to this theme reveals pragmatism to be more self-reflexively confined to "the natural competence and limitations of mere human being" than is often argued while locating these competencies and limitations differently than is often thought. Of course, this is the merest sketch of an argument and the loose marking of a context, and a bit more specificity can be had without moving into detailed argument.

The opening chapters argue that contemporary analytic construals of realism and its counterparts in epistemology and metaphysics provide poor resources for understanding early American pragmatism. A surprisingly diverse group of philosophers have seen the question of the metaphysical realism and Realism with regard to truth of Peirce and James (if not John Dewey as well) as needing to be settled—on one side or the other—before the real value of pragmatism can be assessed. Although more will need to be said by way of definition, I take Hilary Putnam's succinct summation of the basic forms of metaphysical realism to be sufficient here: 1) "the world consists of a fixed totality of mind-independent objects"; 2) "there is exactly one true and complete description of the way the world is"; and 3) "truth involves some sort of correspondence."[5] For reasons that I hope become clear in Chapter 1, the first of these forms is strictly *metaphysical* realism in that it makes a claim about the basic objects that exist in the world while the second and third are species of Realism with regard to truth in that they make claims (albeit claims that can be construed metaphysically) about the nature of truth. Clearly, it would take considerable suasion and some looseness around the meaning of "some sort of correspondence" to make the last of Putnam's three forms stick to the early American pragmatists and their understandings of truth. Just as clearly, though, Peirce's and James's stances toward the first form—the strictly metaphysical form—seem to hinge on what, precisely, each might mean by "mind-independent" as a modifier for "objects." This is a difficult question in Peirce and James and one on which this book attempts to shed some light.

The book proceeds to analyze primarily the question of "mind independence" in Peirce and James by examining the "competencies and limitations" they each thought human beings to have. Because a part of the argument is that the views of both realists and their counterparts are late twentieth-century artifacts in philosophy that depend upon particular understandings of these competencies and limitations drawn by René Descartes and Immanuel Kant, the argument moves, somewhat simultaneously, on two fronts. The second and third chapters examine the ways in which contemporary analytic philosophy uses concepts drawn from Descartes and Kant to understand central philosophical issues, both about metaphysical realism and Realism with regard to truth and about early American pragmatism and its views on objects and truth. Furthermore, these chapters explore the ways in which Peirce and James deal with the works of Descartes and Kant and offer readings of them that differ in significant ways from those required to understand the central philosophical issues of metaphysical realism and Realism with regard to truth. In sum, my argument is that neither metaphysical realism or metaphysical antirealism nor realism or nonrealism with regard to truth can be clearly formulated along pragmatist lines.[6] Thus, when the various issues surrounding contemporary realisms are used as a lens through which to read the early American pragmatists, such readings cannot help but distort our pictures of Peirce's and James's works and, fundamentally, pragmatism itself by not infrequently using these issues to drive a wedge between, most often, the hardnosed Peirce and the amorphous James.[7]

Constructively, I argue that early American pragmatism marks the competencies and limitations of human being through its understanding of the roles of inquiry and belief formation in human life. Considerable attention has, of late, been paid to fallibilism in early American pragmatism, but a straightforward—if tripartite—summation comes from Margolis's identification of three related themes: 1) fallibility with regard to any particular proposition of belief; 2) the possibility and likelihood of self-corrective inquiry in some finite interval; and 3) a metaphysical understanding of the role of inquiry and the inquiring self.[8] Although this attention to fallibilism is well placed, the additional norms that govern pragmatic inquiry are less well covered. Pragmatic fallibilism is but the flip side of a regulative conception of the relationship between truth and inquiry that governs the pragmatic elucidation of concepts.

These notions are then taken up in the final chapters of the book, which offer the more constructive argument, but not without its critical elements. Using the resources gained through the argument above, the second part of the thesis is supported by looking at the ways in which this reconstructed conception of inquiry provides a fairly thorough reinterpretation of logical reasoning. If the argument of the first chapters has been successful, then it will be difficult to see the early American pragmatists as offering resources for philosophy of either a broadly realist or broadly antirealist type. Turning my attention to the pragmatic method as a maxim of logic in Peirce and James and examining its role in their work, my argument is that pragmatism marks the competencies and limitations of human being in a way that is different from much contemporary philosophy.

Although it would take considerably more space than is available in this volume to articulate fully the consequences of the view of pragmatism I am pressing here, as a philosopher of religion, I am particularly concerned with the effects of pragmatism upon my field. Although I do not think that Peirce and James shared a religious worldview even in the very limited sense in which we can draw such views out of their writings, I do think that they shared an understanding of religion in general and of the philosophy of religion in particular. Attention to these more general understandings proves instructive as an application of the pragmatism outlined here. In particular, a pragmatic philosophy of religion pays close heed to the fallible and functional aspects of religious concepts and claims, while also recognizing their continued contestability across a variety of contexts. Without the added recognition of the importance of public contestability, which is required by pragmatism's emphasis on the regulative nature of the relationship between truth and inquiry, religious claims cannot be properly understood.

It might seem odd at first blush to place these religious concerns in such close proximity to the epistemological concerns surrounding pragmatism; however, the epistemological pieces of the argument come into glaring relief when specifically religious issues are addressed. Even the casual reader of Peirce and James cannot help but be struck by the deeply religious sensibilities of both authors. Although James chooses to wear his on his sleeve more often than does Peirce, the latter does more than merely swim in the prevailing religious milieu of his day. Not only has Peirce's "Neglected Argument" begun to receive some of the attention it surely deserves, but his work is also permeated by an abiding concern with the philosophical place of the divine in a logical and scientific system.[9] Although I would not go so far as to argue that either author engages pragmatism because of concerns with religious issues, that pragmatism maintains a concern with such issues seems clear. Recall that James's famous analogy of pragmatism as a hallway with many chambers opening off it includes references to both the fervent hopes of the believer and the construction of an atheistic metaphysics.

Whatever the pragmatic outcomes of such arguments might be, it seems clear that religious concerns lie close to pragmatism's heart.

It is therefore striking to see what might be, at best, the lack of or, at worst, disdain for such concerns among contemporary proponents of American pragmatism. Making note of the ways in which Rortian pragmatism diverges from its earlier forms has become a cottage industry, but one obvious feature of Rorty's pragmatism is its strident atheism. Given the predominant scientism and non-theism of analytic philosophy in the second half of the twentieth century and Rorty's place within it, this is hardly surprising. While some contemporary philosophers might view this charitably as benign neglect, when Rorty does turn his attentions to religious concerns, one is immediately struck by the stridently non-Jamesean (if not also non-Peircean and non-Deweyan) tone of his arguments. He is, frankly, dismissive.[10] What would be unremarkable simply among contemporary analytic philosophers is notable here only because of its contrast with those philosophers whom Rorty works admirably to rehabilitate on so many other fronts. That the early American pragmatists were not so dismissive suggests that there is nothing particularly or inherently *pragmatic* in treating religion this way.

I raise this here not because my intention is to take issue with Rorty's or any other contemporary pragmatist's views on religion in these prefatory remarks, but because I think Peirce's and James's concerns with religious issues are more than coincidental. Religious issues highlight the broadest outlines of the competencies and limitations of human beings and are thus illustrative of the broad pragmatic themes with which this book is concerned. Religious concerns are part of what make James a real human being. Issues such as the reality of God and religious truth are not just paradigmatic examples or particular applications of the principles of early American pragmatism; they make perspicuous its central themes. Not only is a pragmatic philosophy of religion possible and desirable, it is central to a fuller rehabilitation of pragmatism and to a fuller understanding of early American pragmatism's key insights. Thus, the connection between the two parts of this book's thesis and between the epistemological and religious issues will not, perhaps, seem so odd by the book's final chapters.

Such brief remarks on my part will not go far in convincing all readers that the two parts of the thesis do belong together, and there is certainly more to be said on this head. The body of the book remains in which to say it, but the present work is not designed to argue it too directly. My hope is simply that what follows will show that both contemporary pragmatists and contemporary philosophers of religion have been wrong to avoid one another so scrupulously. Peirce and James provide fine examples of the ways in which pragmatic epistemology and philosophy of religion can engage one another, though neither offers thorough prescriptions for such rapprochement. Such prescriptions lie beyond the scope here too, but this work might prove suggestive of directions each might head in order to eventually meet.

The Hallway of Pragmatism

James's vivid metaphor of pragmatism as a corridor in a hotel cited in the epigraph has proven to be as prophetic as it was descriptive. In the century since James's death, the corridor has certainly been extended, and its chambers remain innumerable but expanding. Arthur Lovejoy's early estimation of thirteen pragmatisms seems wildly conservative now—particularly since pragmatism's revival in the closing decades of the twentieth century. It is beyond the scope of the current work to examine all the varieties of American pragmatism and attempt a delineation such as Lovejoy's. Each chamber built since James's first revival of Peirce's earlier pragmatism in the waning years of the nineteenth century may be seen to have its own particular results, respective to its own particular field of inquiry. However, if we remain within the confines of James's metaphor, once a particular application has been made and philosophical conclusions have been drawn, the corridor that is pragmatism has been abandoned for the comforts of the chambers. The question that remains is whether the corridor has any distinctive features worth noting or if it is little more than a way of getting practicably from one chamber to another.

In this sense, the perspective of pragmatism and the perspective of the book are analogous to what is suggested by D. Z. Phillips in the final chapter of *Philosophy's Cool Place*. Prior to the claims of the above epigraph, Phillips contends that philosophy has often been conceived of as having a duty to get one somewhere. The history of philosophy shows that philosophical systems are constructed, torn down, and superseded by other systems thought to be better at getting us somewhere than the systems that preceded them. According to this view, philosophy is a foundational form of discourse that serves as the final court of appeal for the reasonableness of ideas. If these ideas are to get us anywhere, they must pass muster within an all-encompassing philosophical framework. Through the use of philosophical discourse we see where we are headed and how close we are to reaching our destination.

This judgment as to how close we are to reaching our destination is made through the use of one form of discourse—philosophical discourse—as the paradigm against which all other forms of discourse are judged. Phillips argues that philosophy must recognize that this paradigmatic use of philosophical discourse is the result of a value judgment that cannot be justified philosophically. Drawing on Wittgenstein, Phillips argues that this judgment comes when we fall prey to the temptation to think that ordinary words must have metaphysical meanings. Because philosophy is the home of the metaphysical vocabulary for talk of reality, all forms of discourse are thought to be subsumed by this philosophical form, and judgments regarding the success or failure of these non-philosophical forms of discourse can be made therein. Of this Phillips writes: "One of the deepest confusions in philosophy is to treat different spheres of discourse as though they themselves were hypotheses concerning a reality that is forever beyond them. But these spheres of discourse do not refer to reality either successfully or unsuccessfully. Rather, they determine in different contexts, what it means to talk of the real and the unreal."[11] There is some confusion in thinking that different forms of discourse are unified by offering diverse theories about a reality that lies outside their bounds. Failure to recognize this confusion leads either to the reduction of all forms of discourse to philosophical discourse or to the paradigmatic use of philosophical discourse as a means of judging the success of non-philosophical forms of discourse, which is really just a special form of this reductionism. However, if we recognize that different spheres of discourse are determinate of what talk of the real and the unreal comes to *in those contexts*, then there is little point in treating these spheres of discourse as reducible to philosophical discourse about reality. Furthermore, it becomes impossible to make the judgments required by the paradigmatic conception of philosophy because philosophical discourse and non-philosophical discourse might not have a common object—for instance, the real. Finally, we can recognize that these spheres of discourse are not attempts to get us somewhere—closer to reality—but expressions of the lives in which they occur, expressions in which "we learn to distinguish between truth and falsity, the real and the unreal."[12] Philosophy itself provides its own means for making these distinctions, but these means cannot provide the paradigm for the others.

Phillips's conclusion is not that philosophy has gone somewhere that it should not have, like ending up in Newark when one had set out for New York. Phillips's conclusion is that the task of getting somewhere in philosophy is itself confused because the destination for which it aimed is confused.[13] Although this is itself a philosophical conclusion, it is not the kind of conclusion that gets us closer to a destination—truth, reality, God.

The judgment "closer" is itself a value judgment that cannot be underwritten philosophically. In the end, what philosophy does is offer that perspicuous view within which the various elements of what one is investigating can be seen in their proper place. It goes nowhere itself. It provides only one means for understanding what certain concepts come to within the spheres of discourse in which they are used. For example, the philosophy of religion has long been concerned with showing whether or not there is a God. In contrast, Phillips's contemplative conception of philosophy that goes nowhere "contents itself with showing what it means to believe in God or to deny His existence."[14] To do this, one must turn to an examination of the consequences of the belief in the respective lives of the believer and the unbeliever to see what this belief amounts to—not in order to judge or to justify, but in order to understand.

This tour of Phillips's contemplative conception of philosophy is important for this work in two related ways. First, it is the conception, the method if you will, that I want to bring to the examination of the early American pragmatism of Peirce and James. I am not interested in going somewhere with pragmatism; rather, I am interested in understanding what the early American pragmatism of Peirce and James is. Second, as should be apparent from the discussion of James above, something like this contemplative conception of philosophy is operant within early American pragmatism itself with its emphasis upon appreciable effects.

James's metaphor of pragmatism as a corridor is relevant again here. Just as according to the contemplative conception of philosophy, philosophy underwrites neither the belief of the atheist nor that of the believer, so too does pragmatism allow philosophical space for the atheist and the believer alike. One can enter either chamber from this corridor. What becomes important in this sort of investigation is the place that beliefs, thoughts, and concepts have in people's lives. In a similar sense in which Wittgenstein and Rush Rhees emphasize the importance of a form of life for the proper understanding of discourse, Peirce and James emphasize the importance of conceivable consequences for the proper understanding of any concept, object, belief, or judgment. We will approach pragmatism in just this way, turning it upon itself in order to find what sort of meaning it might conceivably have when viewed simply as this corridor that leads nowhere necessarily but can seemingly lead just about anywhere. Rather than try to get somewhere with pragmatism, we will loiter in its hall.

There are two dangers of running in the hall of pragmatism in order to reach the chambers that open from it that this book seeks to avoid. The first danger lies in thinking that the application of the pragmatic method makes particular philosophical conclusions necessary. That is, we run the risk of believing that pragmatism tries to underwrite particular philosophical conclusions. The second danger lies on the opposite head in thinking that pragmatism can yield no larger philosophical conclusions whatsoever. That is, we run the risk of believing that pragmatism is so free-wheeling in its application and its anti-dogmatism that no conclusions can be drawn through its use. These dangers lie along the hallway like trapdoors that lead us unwittingly out of the corridor and into the chambers, but these dangers are conclusions reached through pragmatism and not necessary features of the pragmatic corridor. If we walk slowly through the corridor, we can be properly wary of these dangers and avoid them. Therefore, this book takes as its starting point, both in method and in philosophical perspective, the tasks of locating the corridor itself and of describing the features of that corridor.

In pursuit of this aim, I advance a dual thesis: that the pragmatic corridor does have distinctive features of its own and that these features have largely been misconstrued by those who read Peirce and James through the contemporary lens of Anglo-American analytic philosophies. Although advancing this dual thesis is to argue in some respects that the revival of American pragmatism in the latter third of the twentieth century has distorted (or, perhaps, remodeled) some features of the pragmatic hall, this argument is largely tangential to the main project here, which is to note the distinctive features of the pragmatic corridor rather than using it to go somewhere—hurriedly or otherwise.

If I might be permitted to continue stretching the metaphor of the hall, the following chapters might be taken to be the walls that line the corridor. They attempt to sketch some of the minimal boundaries of pragmatism in the interest of noting some of its basic features. The basic outlines are set through a series of closely related but nonetheless distinct claims about a pragmatic understanding of reality and our relationship to it and should, if successful, demonstrate that the rifts between Peirce and James are not as deep as they might first appear and that, with regards to their respective views of metaphysics and epistemology, they can be placed in surprisingly close proximity.

Chapter 1

Realisms, Antirealisms, Nonrealisms, and Pragmatisms

The accolades that Richard Rorty has garnered are a mark of both his originality and his boldness. His originality can be seen not only through a perusal of his own works, but through the amount of criticism that has been directed at his claims and the variety of quarters from which this criticism has come. Rorty has forced philosophers to reconsider many dearly held opinions and, at times, to justify their own existence as academic professionals. In fact, in his bolder moments, Rorty recommends that the notion that there is a discipline called "Philosophy," that philosophy is a "natural kind," ought to be abandoned in favor of thinking of philosophy as a literary enterprise that tells the various stories of certain problems and lines of thought through revisionist "intellectual histories."[1] When this prescription for philosophy in general, or philosophy departments in particular, is coupled with his unique views on traditional philosophical problems, it is little wonder that he has spurred so much debate.

Perhaps furthering the controversy surrounding Rorty is the fact that he seems entirely unfazed by the criticisms leveled at him. Hilary Putnam remarks that Rorty is not merely dismissive of a philosophical controversy that the discipline has taken seriously in the past but that "he *scorns* the controversy" once he has diagnosed it as arising from a philosophical picture that we ought to reject.[1] It often seems as if Rorty simply finds the problems with which philosophy deals to be uninteresting; thus, criticisms of his position fall on largely deaf ears. It is perhaps because of this mood of indifference toward not only the work of other philosophers who would continue to think of philosophy as a discipline that works on a set of problems, but also toward criticisms of his own work that James Conant, for one, sees the content of many of his replies to critics as "content which could be most economically expressed simply through a shrug of the shoulders."[2]

Although it seems odd for someone who has engendered so much controversy to be indifferent to the very storm that surrounds him, this seemed to be Rorty's attitude.

Because Rorty willingly admits that his use of other philosophers' opinions is "revisionist," it becomes increasingly difficult to find a criticism that will stick. That is, one cannot simply call into question the accuracy of his interpretation of, for example, William James's "The Will to Believe" because Rorty revels in what he sees as the impossibility of gauging such "accuracy." Furthermore, Rorty's tendency to respond with what would best be expressed with a shrug of the shoulders has allowed debates that may have begun around his work to continue despite his lack of interest in the issue at hand. In spite of—or perhaps because of—these difficulties with criticizing Rorty's own views and his readings of other philosophers, the enterprise has continued. Critics fire from all quarters, and, whether Rorty responds or not, the debates continue. Rorty even manages to serve as the focus of debates he did not originate.

The Confines of Rortian Pragmatism

By the time Rorty's *Philosophy and the Mirror of Nature* and *Consequences of Pragmatism* were published in 1979 and 1982 respectively, Michael Dummett's notion of "anti-realism" had been kicking around philosophy departments for fifteen years.[3] Likewise, philosophers had been doing work on pragmatism and in the pragmatic vein continuously since James had coined the term.[4] However, by combining Dummett's notion with his own reading of the early American pragmatists, Rorty managed to bring American pragmatism to the forefront among the analytic philosophers who had been in ascendancy since the linguistic turn. In doing so, a problem that had previously been relegated to the background came to the fore.[5] Lines were drawn, encampments set up, and the battle was on.

Rorty's suggestion in these works (and since) is that early American pragmatism, specifically that of William James and John Dewey, rejects the notion that our discourse entails being answerable to the world.[6] That is, neither James nor Dewey were committed to the notion that our claims have something to do with "the facts of the matter" nor were they interested in finding criteria that would help to evaluate the accuracy of these claims in light of "the facts of the matter." Human discourse is answerable to nothing but itself.

The person who adheres to these notions regarding discourse becomes an "ironist" because he or she recognizes "that anything can be made to look good or bad by being redescribed," and he or she renounces "the attempt to formulate criteria of choice between final vocabularies," vocabularies that we use to justify our actions but that cannot themselves be justified through any non-circular argument.[7] Talk about truth therefore ought to be replaced with talk about justification, which amounts to no more than what my audience will let me get away with.[8] The result is the replacement of "objectivity" with "solidarity," the imagining of the largest possible audience to which we could defend our claims. Rather than seeing this loss of objectivity as the lamentable first step toward complete relativism and nihilism, Rorty argues that it should lead us to a liberal politics that recognizes that "cruelty is the worst thing [we] do."[9] The futility of both metaphysical and epistemological enterprises conceived of as providing some insight into our relationship to "the way things are" pushes one necessarily into pragmatism. Pragmatism, according to Rorty, holds that the only means for the assessment of claims is the analysis of the way in which those claims function within discourse itself. Such an evaluation of claims is, in general, not a matter of understanding the relationships between concepts and a world beyond them; rather, it is a process of relating concepts and claims to each other and being able to defend one's claims to larger and more diverse audiences.[10] Discourse is both self-referential and self-justifying.[11]

Because Rorty has made these claims not only for his own position, but also for pragmatism more generally, many authors interested in American pragmatism have found Rorty's discussions of the relationship between human discourse and the non-human world to be a useful lens through which to view the work of the early American pragmatists. Taking this as a starting point has served to focus discussion on the metaphysical pictures (if any) offered by Peirce, James, and Dewey, which has led eventually and ineluctably to attempts to fit the early American pragmatists into the current rubric of categories with which much analytic philosophy operates. One way of doing this is to look at how the pragmatists deal with metaphysics and epistemology and then use these perspectives to answer the closely related questions, "Is early American pragmatism metaphysically realist or antirealist?" and "Is early American pragmatism Realist or Nonrealist with regard to truth?"[12] However, these questions, and the terminological baggage packed within them, are not as easily answered as one might hope; nor has any sort of consensus regarding their respective answers been reached. In spite of this difficulty and lack of consensus, these questions persist.[13]

At the Looking-Glass

The introduction of the technical nomenclature "metaphysical realism," "metaphysical antirealism," "Realism with regard to truth," and "Nonrealism with regard to truth" as a sort of lens through which to view early American pragmatism has served to focus the discussion regarding early American pragmatism's relationship to contemporary philosophy. However, because there are difficulties with these terms, some clarity regarding their meanings needs to be introduced before we can understand how they have been used to read Peirce and James in particular. My intent here is to rein in both my own use of the terms thus far and the numerous philosophical positions denoted by these terms, such that some clarity regarding their application to early American pragmatism can be achieved. That is, we will be looking *at* the looking-glass used for philosophical reflection on the work of the pragmatists themselves.

Realism in general

Crispin Wright notes in *Realism, Meaning, and Truth* that use of the term "realism" has its own history. Originally used to formulate a position opposed to idealism, the term has since come to mean something significantly more complicated through the debate with antirealists, philosophers who espouse neither realism nor idealism. Wright notes in his "Introduction" that realism holds two central doctrines. First, there is an objective world "almost entirely not of our making, possessing a host of occasional features which may pass altogether unnoticed by human consciousness and whose innermost nomological secrets may remain forever hidden from us."[14] Second, in spite of this essential feature of the world, human beings are "by and large and in favorable circumstances, capable of acquiring knowledge of the world and of understanding it."[15] These two tenets of realism are generally formulated with particular enemies in mind. The first tenet is an obvious response to idealism, which, stated generally, holds that there can be no world independent of our cognitive capacities and modes of investigation. Rather, the world is much as we conceive of it because our cognitive capacities and modes of investigation help make the world what it is. The second tenet is an obvious response to skepticism, which, again stated generally, holds that although—or in some instances because—there is a world independent of human conceptions of it, there is no "adequate warrant for regarding our routine investigative practices as apt to issue in knowledge of or reasonable belief about the world."[16] Perhaps if idealism and radical skepticism had remained fashionable in philosophical circles, these tenets would suffice to describe the position now referred to as "realism." However, as Wright capably notes, the enemy is no longer the idealist or the skeptic.[17]

The new enemy of realism, at least since Michael Dummett coined the term, is the "anti-realist," who differs from the idealist in two specific ways. First, according to Wright, the contemporary antirealist attempts to avoid the type of general, overarching formulations regarding either his or her own position or that of the realist. This may be seen as simply a matter of style, but it has substantive consequences. The antirealist forces the realist to defend his or her position piecemeal, taking on not the general tenets noted above, but specific conclusions reached by the realist with regard to supposedly "'effectively decidable' statements."[18] The idealist would see the realist's conceptions of reality itself as objective and somehow hidden from us (at least in part) and of truth as some sort of privileged relation between a statement and a fact as a total misconception of the natures of reality and truth respectively. The antirealist, on the other hand, simply attacks the efficacy of the realist's arguments. Second, this disagreement between the realist and the antirealist with regard to the efficacy of the realist's arguments leads to a disagreement between the antirealist and the idealist. Although the idealist's arguments would counter the realist's, the antirealist would see the idealist's arguments as vulnerable to the very same attacks.

In Dummett's work, the cardinal rule for both realism and idealism is the principle of bivalence, according to which "every statement—so long as it is not too vague—is determinately either true or false."[19] By contrast, the antirealist is wed to no such rule and is allowed to take the obvious vagueness of our everyday discourse at face value. Since Dummett's original attack on the principle of bivalence, some realists have eschewed the principle in the strict sense noted in favor of a version of realism that can take account of the vagueness of everyday language. A realist of this ilk may continue to hold that the principle of bivalence holds for descriptive or declarative statements while admitting that most ordinary discourse, which includes imperative, exclamatory, and interrogatory sentences, need not adhere to this strict principle.[20] Furthermore, many realists—most notably John Searle and Hartry Field—have eschewed the notion that realism, as a strict ontological doctrine, requires any particular set of claims with regard to issues of truth and falsity. That is, they would deny Dummett's central contention that realism is wed to the principle of bivalence because realism as an ontological doctrine has no necessary consequences for issues of truth and falsity.

All this is simply to suggest that realism, although originally engaged in debate with idealism and skepticism over the general tenets noted above, has slowly evolved through its debate with antirealism into something more specific and more restricted in scope than the position marked by these general tenets. It is also important to note at this point that although the realism marked by these tenets could be traced back through the history of philosophy and attributed to any number of philosophical schools (empiricists, scholastics, Aristotleans, and others), realism and antirealism in their current forms belong largely to the Anglo-American analytic tradition.[21] This more specific and more restricted form of realism, which is opposed to antirealism rather than idealism, is now most often referred to as "metaphysical realism" in order to distinguish it from the more general form of realism. In addition, just as realism has evolved through its debate with antirealism, so too has antirealism evolved to attack more than the principle of bivalence, and it now has its own metaphysical species, "metaphysical antirealism," which holds to the falsity of the tenets of the metaphysical realism to which it is opposed.

The three tenets of metaphysical realism

Because there are numerous ways to describe the major tenets of metaphysical realism, perhaps our best course is to use the words of one of its proponents.[22] In "Realism and Relativism" Hartry Field, a self-proclaimed metaphysical realist, sketches the three tenets that metaphysical realism takes to be true:

T1) The world consists of a fixed totality of mind-independent objects.
T2) There is exactly one true and complete description of the way the world is.
T3) Truth involves some sort of correspondence.[23]

In order to get from this synopsis of metaphysical realism to the delineation of the four positions with which this section is concerned, one need not go far. In fact, each position is marked by its claim that one or more of the above tenets is true or false.

Metaphysical realism accepts the first tenet as true outright. This form of realism is "metaphysical" in that it is the affirmation of an ontological claim regarding the furniture of the universe. As John Searle has put it: "[R]ealism is an *ontological* theory: It says that there exists a reality totally independent of our representations."[24] Like Searle, Michael Devitt holds that this claim is purely metaphysical—it is necessary to keep the realist cart in front of the epistemic horse.[25] A metaphysical realist, as I will continue to use the term, simply accepts that Tenet 1 is both a metaphysical (non-epistemic) claim and a true claim at that. A metaphysical antirealist, on the other hand, agrees with the metaphysical realist that Tenet 1 is a metaphysical claim but holds that it is false.

On the face of it, Searle might seem to imply that metaphysical realism is not committed to Tenet 2. In fact, he states baldly that it is a mistake "to suppose that realism is committed to the theory that there is one best vocabulary for describing reality, that reality itself must determine how it should be described."[26] This is a denial that realism, so defined, requires a particular theory of language. Searle's denial that realism provides a theory of language is a denial that metaphysical realism has necessary epistemic consequences and is not, therefore, necessarily a denial of Tenet 2. Rather, it is an attempt to preserve Tenet 1 as metaphysical. If Tenet 2 were to be considered a metaphysical and not an epistemic tenet, then Searle's denial of epistemic consequences for Tenet 1 would not need to undercut Tenet 2. In its proper light, his denial that realism provides a theory of language can be seen simply to be the further bolstering of the claim that Tenet 1 is a metaphysical tenet. However, the possibility of equivocation about whether Tenet 2 is metaphysical or epistemic points to further problems regarding it.

The question of whether Tenet 2 is metaphysical or epistemic meets of no easy answers in the writings of either metaphysical realists or metaphysical antirealists. In fact, there is a general lack of agreement over what the premise means and what other claims it entails. For example, Hilary Putnam, who is clearly not a metaphysical realist, claims that this second tenet of metaphysical realism amounts to the claim that "it makes sense to think of a God's-Eye View (or, better, a 'View from Nowhere')."[27] However, Searle, among others, denies that metaphysical realism entails such a claim, given that "the whole idea of a view is already epistemic."[28] Therefore, metaphysical realism, if it is to remain metaphysical, cannot espouse such a view. Again, Searle need not be seen as denying Tenet 2 but only Putnam's construal of it as an epistemic claim. However, the difficulties with Tenet 2 do not end there.

Michael Hymers notes that Tenet 2 and Putnam's use of it against Field seem to entail claims regarding the possibility of an ideal theory.[29] This would be a problem not only for an argument against the metaphysical realist, who may not (as Searle is) be committed to this possibility, but also for

Putnam whose argument undercuts the very notion of an ideal theory. Michael Williams objects, claiming that: "We have little or no idea what it would be for a theory to be ideally complete and comprehensive in the way required, or of what it would be for inquiry to have an end."[30] In spite of his sympathies toward Putnam elsewhere, Williams argues here that no cogent epistemic account of an ideal theory can be given. At the same time, in spite of his own espousal of metaphysical realism and general antipathy toward metaphysical antirealism, David Lewis shares Williams's suspicion of the notion of an "ideal theory" but argues that it does not make sense in light of the possibility of a number of complete descriptions of the world.[31] Lewis objects that it is metaphysically possible under metaphysical realism for there to be more than one correct, complete description of the world, and thus there is no single ideal theory. Like Searle's denial that metaphysical realism entails the claim that a "God's-Eye View" makes sense, Williams's and Lewis's denials that the notion of an ideal theory makes sense provide two means for the metaphysical realist to sidestep Putnam's attack on metaphysical realism. First, if Putnam's attack relies upon such a notion in order to undercut it, then the realist is justified in thinking Putnam's argument to be weak at best or self-contradictory at worst. Second, if Putnam's attack is actually an attack on the notion of an ideal theory and the metaphysical realist is not wed to such a possibility, then the metaphysical realist can easily evade this criticism by showing that his or her own position does not rely on such a notion.[32]

If the metaphysical realist need not admit that either the "God's-Eye View" or an ideal theory makes sense, then it seems that the metaphysical realist need not be wed to Tenet 2. Furthermore, if the notion itself can be questioned on either metaphysical realist or metaphysical antirealist grounds, then it is difficult to see why either metaphysical realists or their antagonists need to take a position with regard to Tenet 2. Thus, the truth or falsity of Tenet 2 would not seem to mark the difference between the metaphysical realist and the metaphysical antirealist. Both the metaphysical realist and the metaphysical antirealist are free to deny that there is exactly one true and complete description of the way the world is either as a "God's-Eye View" or as an ideal theory.[33] In addition to this, both are free to assert that these notions—if Tenet 2 does indeed rely upon either of them—do not make sense and, thus, that Tenet 2 does not make sense. Taking such a position would free the metaphysical realist or the metaphysical antirealist from asserting either the truth or falsity of Tenet 2.

My suggestion here, then, is that Tenet 2 cannot serve as a watershed issue between the metaphysical realist and the metaphysical antirealist for two reasons. First, some metaphysical realists, such as Field, do accept that sense can be made of the claim and that such a claim is true; other metaphysical realists, such as Searle, see such a notion as epistemic and, therefore, inessential to the metaphysical issues of metaphysical realism; and still other metaphysical realists, such as Lewis, deny that a claim of this sort makes any sense whatsoever. Thus, unlike Tenet 1, which is held to be true by all metaphysical realists and thereby helps define metaphysical realism itself, there is no real agreement among metaphysical realists over Tenet 2. Second, in the treatment of Tenet 3, which is to follow, it will become apparent that Tenet 2, if taken as epistemic, can be agreed to by a metaphysical antirealist who is yet a Realist with regard to truth, or denied by the metaphysical realist who is a Nonrealist with regard to truth. That is, Tenet 2 may be closely linked to Tenet 3 if taken in this epistemic manner; or, as I have suggested above, Tenet 2 may be closely linked to Tenet 1 if taken in a metaphysical sense rather than in an epistemic one; or Tenet 2 may not have a sense at all. Each of these positions, with regard to Tenet 2, is open to either the metaphysical realist or the metaphysical antirealist. This difficulty with Tenet 2 need not be resolved here but does suggest that Tenet 2 need not be true for the metaphysical realist, be false for the metaphysical antirealist, or be given a sense by either. In the end, Tenet 2 is entirely dispensable to drawing the distinctions with which this section is concerned.[34]

Before we can see clearly how all this works itself out, we must look closely at Tenet 3, which makes the rather general claim that truth involves some sort of correspondence. Given metaphysically realist commitments to Tenet 1, this correspondence must be between statements (or claims, beliefs, or whatever) and the mind-independent world.[35] It is important to note here that "some sort of correspondence" does not necessarily mean "correspondence theory of truth." The latter is more specific than the former. This is quite simply the suggestion that the truth of a claim is in no way dependent upon any speaker whatsoever but is dependent entirely upon the goings-on of the mind-independent world, upon the obtaining of some mind-independent state of affairs.[36] That is, a realist notion of truth is radically non-epistemic.

William Alston notes in his *A Realist Conception of Truth* that one can hold that Tenet 3 is true in this general sense without developing a correspondence theory of truth. Alston claims that his "alethic realism" is a "minimalist account of truth" in that it does not require that one develop a robust correspondence theory of truth like those of Russell and the early Wittgenstein. His alethic realism is minimalist in comparison to full-blown correspondence theories in four ways. First, Alston's realism with regard to truth avoids giving an account of the structure and status of propositions in the sense required by a full-blown correspondence theory. Second, alethic realism does not delve into the investigation of how a proposition is made true by a particular fact or what sort of "identity in content" must obtain in order for the former to be made true by the latter. Third, Alston's position does not aspire "to say just what correspondence amounts to." That is, the "ontological task" of describing in what correspondence consists is shirked by Alston. Fourth, a full-blown correspondence theory attempts to define truth, whereas alethic realism does not.[37] In this regard, one can be a Realist with regard to truth without holding to a full-blown correspondence theory.

For Alston, Tenet 3 would be seen as simply the general contention that truth is expressed in a privileged sort of relation between a particular mind-independent state of affairs and a particular claim regarding that state of affairs. Alston enumerates what is entailed by this third tenet when construed generally and applied to the statement "grass is green:"

> It is not required for the truth of the statement that I, or anyone else, or any social group know that grass is green or be justified or rational in believing it. It is not required that science be destined, in that far-off divine event toward which inquiry moves, to arrive at the conclusion that grass is green. It is not required that it have been rendered probable by some body of empirical evidence. So long as grass *is* green, then what I said is true, whatever the epistemic or other status of that proposition, belief, or statement vis-à-vis any particular individual or community. Truth has to do with the relation of a potential truth bearer to a *reality* beyond itself.[38]

A truth-relation on this conception is simply the relation between a truth-bearer and the world that is what it is independent of it, and this more general form of "correspondence" need not be spelled out in a full-blown "correspondence theory of truth." Put more directly, all that assent to the truth of Tenet 3 requires is to assent to the notion *that* truth involves some kind of non-epistemic correspondence between the mind-independent world and a claim about it; it does not require one to assent to some particular notion of *what* correspondence between this world and this claim need involve.[39]

Although it may seem difficult to see how Tenet 3 could be worked out in any satisfactory sense independent of Tenet 1, such a position is not entirely inconsistent. Richard Kirkham notes that an absolute idealist, while claiming that no states of affairs obtain mind-independently and thus that

Tenet 1 is false, could still assent to the truth of Tenet 3: "If he were, he would be saying that one condition for the truth of a belief (or sentence or whatever) is never met, so there are no truths. This would be an odd position to take, but not an inconsistent one."[40] Our metaphysical antirealist, who would agree with the idealist that Tenet 1 is metaphysical and false, would also be free to accept Tenet 3 as true but would also have to admit, like the idealist, that there are no true claims. Furthermore, as William Alston and Paul Horwich have noted in elaborating their own views with regard to truth, accepting that Tenet 3 is true need not bind one to a particular description of "the furniture of the universe."[41] Alston claims that "Though a particular realist or nonrealist [antirealist] metaphysical position . . . has implications for what propositions are true or false, they have no implications for what it is for a proposition to be true or false."[42] According to Alston, one's metaphysical picture has no bearing on *what* truth is, only on *which* claims are true because truth itself is radically non-epistemic. The example given by Kirkham and the claim made by Alston are simply different means to the same dual point: assent to the truth of Tenet 3 does not require assent to the truth of Tenet 1, nor does assent to the truth of Tenet 1 entail assent to the truth of Tenet 3.[43]

Claiming Tenet 3 to be false would not be inconsistent with claiming Tenet 1 to be true. In fact, in positing his "redundancy theory of truth," Hartry Field claims to be doing precisely this. Field accepts Tenets 1 and 2 (in some metaphysical sense) but rejects Tenet 3. According to his redundancy theory, to say that a claim is true is simply to pay it the compliment "I assent to this claim." On such an account, truth is not a property but a disposition or attitude towards a particular statement. Truth is, therefore, epistemic. However, Field continues to describe himself as a metaphysical realist. This need not puzzle us; Field is simply claiming that although the world consists of a fixed totality of mind-independent objects and there is exactly one true and complete description of that world, truth is not the expression of a relationship between a state of affairs in that world and a claim that is independent of it. Truth, for Field, is the satisfaction of particular scientific criteria in every possible world with the same laws as the natural world such that a properly situated language user would assent to the claim itself.[44] Thus, even Field admits that the truth or falsity of Tenet 3 is independent of the truth or falsity of Tenet 1 and that assent to the truth of one of these claims need not imply assent to the truth of the other.

The result of this tour of Tenet 3 should be obvious. If assent to the truth or falsity of Tenet 3 is independent of assent to the truth or falsity of Tenet 1, then something other than metaphysical realism must be involved here.

Therefore, it is my suggestion that we follow a modified version of Kirkham's nomenclature in calling those who hold that Tenet 3 is both radically non-epistemic and true "Realists with regard to truth" and those who hold that Tenet 3 is both radically non-epistemic and false "Nonrealists with regard to truth."[45] The positions themselves, then, are "Realism with regard to truth" and "Nonrealism with regard to truth."

Two issues, four possibilities

Realism with regard to truth and Nonrealism with regard to truth are both doctrines about truth, not about what exists. Metaphysical realism and metaphysical antirealism, on the other hand, are both doctrines about what exists, not about truth. Having left Tenet 2 behind for the reasons specified above, we now have the following taxonomy for the positions:

- Metaphysical realism: it is true that the world consists of a fixed totality of mind-independent objects.
- Metaphysical antirealism: it is false that the world consists of a fixed totality of mind-independent objects.
- Realism with regard to truth: it is true that truth involves some sort of non-epistemic correspondence between statements and the mind-independent world.
- Nonrealism with regard to truth: it is false that truth involves some sort of non-epistemic correspondence between statements and the mind-independent world.

These basic, discrete positions can be, and often are, combined with those concerned with both metaphysical issues and issues regarding truth such that four possible combinations arise out of these discrete positions. One could be a metaphysical realist and a Realist with regard to truth. One could be a metaphysical realist and a Nonrealist with regard to truth. One could be a metaphysical antirealist and a Realist with regard to truth. One could be a metaphysical antirealist and a Nonrealist with regard to truth.

We can fill in this picture by reviewing the relationships of those discussed thus far to these four possibilities. William Alston has espoused, minimally, metaphysical realism/Realism with regard to truth by admitting that there is "the thinnest sort of significant connection between alethic realism and metaphysical realisms."[46] Michael Devitt, whose views we will visit elsewhere, also falls under this head. His Realism with regard to truth is much like that of Alston in that he assents to the notion that "correspondence truth . . . is in no way epistemic."[47] Hartry Field has argued for both metaphysical realism and Nonrealism with regard to truth. Kirkham's "odd but not inconsistent" idealist would qualify as a metaphysical antirealist but a Realist with regard to truth. Finally, Richard Rorty, with whose work this chapter began, is most often seen as the paradigmatic metaphysical antirealist/Nonrealist with regard to truth, and the reasons for this will be discussed below.

Reading Pragmatism Analytically

With this basic understanding of the terminology through which late twentieth-century analytic philosophers have attempted to read early American pragmatism in hand, it becomes much easier to understand how the various issues surrounding realism have been not only the frame through which pragmatism has been viewed, but also a central issue in thinking about pragmatism more generally. Recalling James's remark (cited in the Introduction to this book) that pragmatism narrowly considered is no more than a method, and more widely considered is this method plus a conception of truth, truth—and thus Realism or Nonrealism with regard to it—would seem to lie very near the heart of pragmatism itself. Further metaphysical issues regarding the realism of pragmatism might be yet more deeply rooted, reaching as far back as what Murray G. Murphey dubs "The First System" in his excellent study of Peirce. There, Murphey notes a deep tension between Peirce's anti-phenomenalist response to Kant in which he rejects the distinction between the phenomenal object and the *Ding an sich* and Peirce's semi-phenomenalist—if not idealist—position that whatever is, is thought of.[48] Rorty's revival of pragmatism in the final quarter of the twentieth century serves only to focus attention on issues already operant in discussions of early American pragmatism; however, Rorty manages to focus attention on these issues by consistently citing pragmatism as being at least the backdrop for his own antirealism and Nonrealism.

Rorty claims both that it is false that the world consists of a fixed totality of mind-independent objects and that it is false that truth involves some sort of correspondence. He is in agreement with the metaphysical realist in thinking the former to be *only* an ontological doctrine, and he agrees with the Realist with regard to truth in thinking the latter to be *only* a nonepistemic notion. In fact, his denial of the tenets of metaphysical realism and Realism with regard to truth are made together: "'Truth' in the sense of 'truth taken apart from any theory' and 'world' taken as 'what determines such truth' are notions that were . . . made for each other. Neither can survive apart from the other."[49] Rorty argues that we can avoid the problems of metaphysical realism and Realism with regard to truth (the two are necessarily conjoined for Rorty) only by taking up the notion that "the world" is just the name for those objects that inquiry is leaving alone. This latter notion, however, is not simply the innocuous renaming of a conception; it is, more importantly, the rejection of the notion of "the world" in the sense in which the metaphysical realist would use it. It is the world of the metaphysical realist that is "well lost" and with it the possibility for non-epistemic Realism with regard to truth.[50]

Rorty provides the link between the above discussion of contemporary analytic philosophy and early American pragmatism because he makes these claims while standing on the shoulders of William James and John Dewey. For example, when he "loses" the world, Rorty does so citing Dewey: "I think that the realistic true believer's notion of the world is an obsession rather than an intuition. I also think that Dewey was right in thinking that the only intuition we have of the world as determining truth is just the intuition that we must make our new beliefs conform to a vast body of platitudes, unquestioned perceptual reports, and the like."[51] Rorty thus denies the tenability of both the metaphysical realist's conception of the world and the Realist with regard to truth's non-epistemic conception of truth, posits his own radically epistemic conceptions of the world and truth, and does so while making an implicit claim about Dewey's own philosophical opinions in this regard. It is this third move that brings together the discussions and criticisms of Rorty, currents in contemporary analytic philosophy, and early American pragmatism. By proclaiming his own metaphysical antirealism and Nonrealism with regard to truth while claiming similar positions for James and Dewey, Rorty is arguing that James and Dewey—indeed, pragmatism itself in its more interesting aspects—espoused metaphysical antirealism and Nonrealism with regard to truth. Much of this is because, in Rorty's reading of pragmatism, pragmatism made the turn toward discourse and away from metaphysics years before much of the rest of the philosophical world. Rorty reads pragmatism as entailing the view that "there are no constraints on conversation save conversational ones—no wholesale constraints derived from the nature of objects, or of the mind, or of language, but only those retail constraints provided by the remarks of our fellow inquirers."[52] Pragmatism, then, is simply an early pivot in what eventually becomes the linguistic turn.

Reading against Rorty

If Rorty can be said to have opened a philosophical can of worms by combining his arguments on topics within contemporary analytic philosophy with his implicit claims regarding the early American pragmatists, then it can also be said that several hungry fish have taken the bait. In addition to those who have argued directly against Rorty, H. O. Mounce, Nicholas Rescher, and Richard Gale have each argued that his implicit claims regarding early American pragmatism are not only inaccurate but also incoherent. Both Mounce and Rescher argue that Peirce offers a metaphysical realist picture that has important implications for theories of truth; Richard Kirkham offers a metaphysically antirealist and Nonrealist view of Peirce; and Richard Gale has argued for a "divided" William James, whose Promethean metaphysical antirealism and Nonrealism with regard to truth battle without resolution with his mystical metaphysical realism and Realism with regard to truth.[53] Although these four come at Rorty's reading of early American pragmatism differently, they all use Rorty's reading as a point of contrast and look at Rorty's views as a direct rival to their own projects.

Mounce and Rescher argue differently but come to the same two-part conclusion: first, that Charles Sanders Peirce was in fact a metaphysical realist; and second, that Rorty's position, drawing as it does on Dewey in particular, leads necessarily to relativism and subjectivism in the same ways that James's and Dewey's positions did in the first part of the century.[54] The difficulty, as both Mounce and Rescher see it, begins with confusion over Peirce's claims in his earliest essays on pragmatism over the relationship between the human mind and the non-human world.

According to Mounce, the "Classical Pragmatism" espoused by Peirce has scientism and the notion of an order that transcends the human mind at its root. Mounce argues that Peirce should have recognized that his argument against Kant's thing-in-itself led to "Anti-Realism or Subjective Idealism" and was, moreover, fallacious. Mounce's reasons for this are worth considering. On the one hand, Mounce sees Peirce as accepting Hegel's argument against Kant's conception of the noumenon according to which one cannot draw a limit to knowledge without knowing what lies on the other side.[55] Mounce argues that Hegel's argument is fallacious in that it trades in an ambiguity around "drawing a limit." On Mounce's reading of Kant, Kant is not "drawing a limit" in the sense of bringing one into existence; rather, Kant is "drawing a limit" in the sense of acknowledging one. In order to bring a limit into existence, one "presumably knows what lies on either side of the limit." In order simply to acknowledge a limit that already exists "in the nature of the case," one need not know *what* lies on the other side, but only that there "is something on the other, without having sufficient evidence to know what that something is."[56] Although there is very little textual evidence for seeing a Hegelian influence on Peirce's rejection of the Kantian noumenon, Mounce insists that Peirce's early thought is marked by an at least implicit acceptance of the view that "nothing exists except in relation to the human mind."[57] In turn, this leads Peirce to reject the contrast between "conscious inference or hypothesis" and "immediate perception or awareness of the world," which would make all ideas and concepts relative to the human mind insofar as inferences or hypotheses would be all to which our ideas and concepts could refer. Peirce's thought on this head is in deep tension, then, with what Mounce sees as an "instinctive preference for Realism" inherited from his father, Benjamin.[58] His attempted way out of this difficulty is similar to Hegel's, insofar as Peirce continues to hold that "the Real transcends what you or I happen to think here and now" while not transcending thought or experience more generally.[59] In order to maintain this view, Peirce eventually distinguishes between the inferences open to theoretical investigation and those "beyond the jurisdiction of criticism."[60] In so doing, Peirce is suggesting that whatever convergence might take place in inquiry as it is pursued is explicable because inquiry is guided by what is independent of inquiry; namely, the real. Thus, by the 1890s, on Mounce's reading, Peirce is explicitly adhering to Tenet 1 above.

Furthermore, according to Mounce, Peirce argues for the reality of natural laws, which have characteristics of the mental but do not "exist only in the *human* mind" and transcend their particular instances.[61] Peirce's realism is thus a form of objective idealism, which Mounce finds compatible with a thoroughgoing realism. Such "Realism" helps Peirce avoid the subjectivism and relativism that Mounce claims plague later pragmatists in that there is something—a world operating in accordance with natural laws—that exists in complete independence of the human mind. In order to support this reading, Mounce notes that Peirce must distinguish between practical certainty and theoretical inquiry and argue for the primacy of the former. We are practically certain because of the reality of natural laws, but theoretical inquiry allows us to investigate their exact nature. These theoretical formulations are revisable, and some of our practical knowledge will require revision in light of the theories developed. Nonetheless, such inquiry cannot negate practical certainty, for then "we should no longer know what counts as being certain in theoretical inquiry" because "we should lose our grasp on meaning."[62] Our practical certainty with regard to natural laws—that they exist and can be investigated—is a presupposition of the theoretical investigation itself. There must be some "characteristics of the mental" in such laws in order for them to be investigated, but because the human mind is "in part *constituted* by laws or tendencies," these laws cannot be the mind's creation.[63] The characteristics are, at least, obedience to law or habit, which is implicit and practical and thus beyond investigation. We can investigate which laws govern which behaviors of which objects, but there can be no investigation of the "*existence* of law," which would imply the possibility of a law's discovery. In turn, on Mounce's reading, Peirce's conception of truth is set within the context of inquiry regulated by such natural laws and is therefore also realist, thus adhering to Tenet 3 above. Mounce thinks it a result of historical contingency that the subjectivist aspects of pragmatism have been emphasized and have "achieved a full flowering in the work of Rorty."[64]

Rescher, on the other hand, while seeing Peirce's philosophical position as metaphysically realist in much the same way as Mounce does, argues that Peirce's realism is best seen in his use of pragmatism as an "individual-transcending reality principle."[65] Although it is difficult to find an *argument* supporting the notion that this qualifies Peirce as a metaphysical realist, Rescher clearly believes that this "individual-transcendence" puts Peirce solidly in the camp of the Realist with regard to truth. Rescher argues that Peirce's method puts us on the path to the discovery of truth but is not in fact a theory about truth. Nonetheless, it is realistic in that it requires that there be a world to which our inquiry refers and is answerable *independent* of the particularities of inquiry itself. On Rescher's reading, this aligns Peirce with Rescher, Susan Haack, and other "pragmatists of the right" who "tend to follow Peirce into an adherence to metaphysical realism." Such pragmatists view inquiry not as engendering reality, but rather as yielding "products that are crucially conditioned by its independent operations."[66] Thus, Peirce's Realism with regard to truth leads directly to a metaphysical realism according to which there must be one mind-independent reality toward which all "properly conducted" inquiry is directed. James and Dewey, on the other hand, do not fare so well. Rescher considers theirs to be a "pragmatism of the left," which finds itself "inexorably drawn to James's approach of 'what works for the satisfaction of people's variable wishes and preferences.'"[67] It thus ends in Rortian (antirealist and Nonrealist) subjectivism and relativism.

When Rescher moves to expanding on what such a pragmatism of the right looks like, he does so by exploiting what he sees as the key insight of objective inquiry—namely, that "all real things are necessarily thought of as having hidden depths that extend beyond the limits, not only of experience but also of experientiability."[68] Rescher finds a reality that transcends the capacities of experience more generally a necessary postulate of our thinking. He claims that such a reality "constitutes the 'object' of our cognitive endeavors in both senses of this term—the *objective* at which they are directed and the *purpose* for which they are exerted."[69] According to Rescher, such a commitment is required for the classical doctrine of truth as correspondence to fact, which "only makes sense in the setting of a commitment to mind-independent reality."[70] This commitment is not evidential but functional and, Rescher holds, justifiable in pragmatic terms as a regulative postulate for inquiry. As in his direct discussion of Peirce, Rescher sees the necessity of a mind-independent reality—that is, the necessity of metaphysical realism—as flowing from a commitment to Tenet 3.

When he turns to a more direct argument for this, Rescher makes six related points. The first is simply the explicit statement of the relationship between truth and reality already noted: "By virtue of their very nature as truths, true statements must state facts: they state what really is so, which is exactly what it means to 'characterize reality.'"[71] The second point is that Rescher holds that the only sensible distinction that can be made between appearance and reality is the one between a reality radically mind-independent in the sense of being beyond experiencibility and the particular experiences of individuals. The third is that intersubjective communication requires common epistemic access to a real world of independent things. Fourth is that reference itself can be explained in terms of the common independent objects to which we refer. Rescher's fifth point is that fallibilism in the pragmatic vein requires acknowledgment that truth always outstrips inquiry, a reason he believes to rest on the second reason. The final justification is provided by the causal relations that must necessarily exist between the world and our experiences of it. In the end, Rescher argues that these pragmatic considerations amount to a "'transcendental argument' of sorts, namely, one that argues from the character of our conceptual scheme to the unavoidability of accepting its inherent presuppositions."[72]

Although there is little time and space in which to argue in detail against Mounce's and Rescher's points here, two notions will be highlighted in the following chapters which, I believe, would count considerably against a reading of pragmatism as metaphysically realist and Realist with regard to truth. The first is that pragmatism claims explicitly that it is committed to the notion of a reality that is independent of particular inquiries and experiences without being independent of inquiry and experience more generally. In the only sense in which "reality" is pragmatically elucidatory, reality must be available for experience and inquiry. We can go on to *define* reality in whatever way we might like, but its import for inquiry and experience is only provided through its susceptibility to investigation. The second is that pragmatism does not, even in the kind of minimal sense in which Rescher offers it, define truth as correspondence with reality and treat this definition as the same kind of common sense presupposition as Rescher does. To the extent that such a notion is meaningful, it arises as a result of pragmatic inquiry and not as a presupposition.

Both Rescher and Mounce are correct in noting that there is an important relationship between truth and inquiry expressed by the biconditional "H is true if and only if it would be believed at the end of prolonged inquiry."[73] They are also correct in noting that there are regulative notions that cannot be asserted but which nonetheless govern inquiry. However, to suggest that some inferences are beyond criticism more generally or that inquiry requires something beyond its general limits in order to operate properly is, I will argue, to import content from contemporary debates that Peirce and James were happy to do without and to make such content constitutive of pragmatism itself.

Although Richard Kirkham does not offer a sustained reading of Peirce and is unclear with regard to Peirce's metaphysics, he does claim that Peirce is properly Nonrealist with regard to truth and metaphysically antirealist for two reasons. First, Peirce makes the seemingly obviously Nonrealist claim that truth is "'the opinion which is fated to be ultimately agreed to by all who investigate.'"[74] Kirkman puts the biconditional above in his own way: "A proposition is true if and only if it would be agreed to by everyone who investigates the matter with which it concerns itself" and offers that it is a definition of truth itself.[75] Such a statement clearly rejects the Realist doctrine that truth involves some sort of correspondence between a statement and a mind-independent world. Nonetheless, Kirkham believes there to be a way out here for Peirce in much the same way as Rescher does.

Peirce could, despite whatever misgivings he might have, hold to a conception of reality such that reality were independent of investigation and would determine the conclusion at which such an investigation would arrive. Kirkham views Peirce's preference for the scientific method as providing one way in which to view this possibility. Through the method of science, independent investigators inquire into the nature of an objective reality, which affects all investigators in the same way, through its causal and uncontrolled interactions with the senses. As independent investigators pursue these inquiries, they are driven "to beliefs that accurately reflect" this reality and "*ipso facto* driven to agree with one another."[76] On such a view, were Peirce to have pursued it, the mind-independent world would be the common object of investigation and would be indirectly but no less causally responsible for the agreement of those who investigate it. In the instances in which it occurs, then, we could safely replace "is true" with "accurately reflects objective reality" and have a consistently Realist view of truth. We would receive from Peirce the "pragmatism of the right" that Rescher so desires insofar as such a view would hold closely to each of the six pragmatic reasons Rescher offers for our requiring the presupposition of a mind-independent reality.

However, according to Kirkham, Peirce turns his attention away from this possibility and offers an account of reality that is dependent upon this Nonrealist account of truth. Despite the many instances in which Peirce insists that reality is independent of inquiry, Kirkham notes that these instances actually claim only that reality is independent of any one mind or subset of minds while not being independent of all minds. Kirkham quotes Peirce's claim, "'Everything, therefore, which will be thought to exist in the final opinion is real, and nothing else'" and attributes to him an idealism that is objective insofar as what is real is "constituted by the minds in the community" rather than by individuals, but is an idealism that runs athwart both Tenet 1 and Tenet 3 nonetheless.[77]

On Kirkham's reading of Peirce, we wind up not only with a theory that espouses Nonrealism with regard to truth because of its emphasis on the convergence of opinion among the community of inquirers, but also with an idealism that is a form of metaphysical antirealism because of its emphasis on the internal relationship between this final opinion and the determination of the real itself. Despite his having offered a way clear for Peirce, Kirkham sees Peirce's having abandoned metaphysical realism as having abandoned the "theoretical equivalence" posited between truth and consensus and the "plausible equivalence" between truth and correspondence.[78] Worse yet, for Peirce, his emphasis on the agreement that is to come when investigation reaches its end is hypothetical but is supposed to have *actual* consequences upon present investigations. Given the co-determination of the true and the real on Kirkham's reading, this implies a "reverse-chronological" causal influence not only from the final conclusion to the present investigation, which is temporally implausible, but also from the "hypothetical domain to the actual domain." Thus, Kirkham wonders if Peirce's view "is even intelligible."[79] When put together, the two claims regarding truth and reality, respectively, amount to the claim that the final opinion regarding the object of the final opinion is "truth" and the object of that final opinion is "reality." However, because both are dependent upon the ongoing process of human investigation in general, neither is what it is mind-independently because both are developing through mind-dependent investigation. Thus,

Kirkham's claim regarding Peirce seems justified despite a certain lack of charity in it.

Although a direct response to Kirkham's approach is not necessarily forthcoming, several arguments in the succeeding chapters will offer a means through which such a response might be made. I believe that the key to undermining both Kirkham's claims regarding Peirce's failure to adhere to either metaphysical realism or Realism with regard to truth and Kirkham's claims regarding Peirce's adherence to metaphysical antirealism and Nonrealism with regard to truth is to show that the project in which Peirce was engaged is neither a version of the "metaphysical project" that would attempt to offer a final definition of the relationship between truth and reality nor a version of the "essence project" that would attempt to offer an equivalency of the sort Kirkham mentions that would define truth itself. Peirce is engaged in many ways in showing that the concepts with which both projects operate falter when seen in their appropriate contexts. Furthermore, Peirce's project is that of pragmatically elucidating the concept of truth by showing its function in inquiry, and is, at one level at least, metaphysically neutral. Again, subsequent chapters will take up this reading of Peirce.

When approaching William James, one's way is fraught with peril. Responses to his Lowell Lectures of 1906–1907, published first in journal form and later as *Pragmatism*, sought rather immediately to paint him with a subjectivist brush, one through which his work could be seen as portraying human action as world-making and human conceptions as truth-making. A world independent of the human self recedes.[80] James's response to these early critics was to posit stridently his realism, seething to Charles Strong, "It seems as if the whole world had conspired to insist that I *shall* not be a realist, in spite of anything I . . . say to the contrary."[81] Even the most sympathetic of contemporary readers of James are forced to admit that a number of his claims regarding metaphysics and truth seem to indicate, at best, equivocation on the matters and, at worst, incoherence.[82] Although perhaps not so sympathetic, Richard Gale's reading of James offers little hope for resolving entirely the difficulties inherent to James's thought as long as one remains within the Jamesian corpus, claiming that James's philosophy is deeply—and, perhaps, irremediably—torn between James's Promethean and mystical selves.[83]

On the one hand, James's Promethean self gives way to the scientism and progressivism of his day, turning us all into world makers and committing itself fully to ontological relativism. In this Promethean mode, reality is consistently remade according to the interests of the agent, and James recognizes the concept-relativity of any world the inquiring agent might attempt to bring into focus.[84] Thus, it is not merely perspectives upon the world but the worlds themselves that are mind-dependent, which clearly places James in the antirealist camp. Although James's Promethean self occasionally capitulates to giving lip-service to both metaphysical realism and Realism with regard to truth, Gale argues that his attempts to do so are incoherent—both because they are incompatible with his criticisms of Realist conceptions of truth and because they are incompatible with the empiricism and humanism that drives James's Promethean side.[85] Thus, so far as his Promethean self is concerned, James remains the antirealist and Nonrealist that Rorty paints him to be.

In reading James in this way, Gale argues that James engages in the worst of antirealism and Nonrealism—namely, a doctrine that ends in near complete relativism and subjectivism because the worlds constructed by human beings are interest relative. Worse yet, the interests that individuals have at one point in time will inevitably shift at another, and each successive set of interests creates its own particular world, which is then abandoned in favor of another and so on. The worlds themselves cannot be fully united, and the individual is forced to make consistent qualifications that his or her particular claims and concepts are being made and used at one time qua this world and at another time qua that world. The result, Gale claims, is clear: "By effecting this sharp separation between the worlds and making their very actualization consist in being accorded reality by the interests of a Promethean subject, James gives *carte blanche* to each of his many selves to assert itself with a clear conscience."[86] In the end, Gale accuses James of "Poo-bahism" in that the Promethean subject is required to make qualifications of the sort above when he acts as his moral self, scientific self, or whichever self he might inhabit at that particular point. Even when these qualifications are merely implicit, James's pragmatism devolves into an assertion of each individual's unconstrained right to believe and use ideas in whichever way he or she might wish and have them, not unreasonably, count as true.

On the other hand, Gale offers that James's Promethean self is balanced by his mystical self. This mystical self, revealed most fully (as one might expect) in *The Varieties of Religious Experience*, requires that there be a single objective world just beyond our concept-dependent ken with which the mystic manages to be in touch. The mystic's grasp of the ultimate objective reality is passive and unmediated by concepts—received in a "cognitive revelation"—and the claims based upon such experiences are "nonrelativized reality-claims."[87] Because James's mission in this mystical mode is to allow for the truth of such claims, he is forced to deal with these claims in non-Promethean, and therefore non-pragmatic, terms. Insofar as James seeks to unify the manifold of this experience, he is forced to admit a unified world that underlies the mystic's experiences and is independent of the conceptual apparatus of the mind. James's mystical self is thus inclined toward metaphysical realism, and granting the mystic's claims their status as nonrelativized reality claims requires a fair amount of Realism with regard to truth—although James is rightly loath to offer a detailed account of how this might work.

On Gale's reading of James, then, James grants the mystic access to an objective, concept-independent reality that James's Promethean self cannot grant—either metaphysically or epistemologically. Although Gale admits there are ways of reading James that might have him side with either his antirealist and Nonrealist Promethean self or with his realist and Realist mystical self, he finds such readings not to be based within the Jamesian corpus and leaves James's attempts at unification short of their mark. It is not that James's work does not fit these parameters for Gale; rather, it is that James's work fits them all at different places and times. James's philosophy as a whole falls prey to the same "Poo-bahism" as his many Promethean selves do, as he switches between his Promethean and mystical selves largely without realizing that he is doing so.[88]

What is interesting about Gale's study of James is that it manages to frame several distinct issues that plague contemporary readings of James and then draw a broad and not unpopular conclusion about James's work on the whole. Two of the three issues are, obviously, James's stances with regard to Tenets 1 and 3 above. On the one hand, Gale reads James's insistence on a Nonrealist pragmatic account of truth according to which what is true is what is good for us to believe as driving his Promethean self into world-making metaphysical antirealism in accordance with which there is no world (or are no worlds) beyond those made by our interest-relative selves. On the other hand, Gale reads James's mystical self to be inconsistent with his insistence on pragmatism, searching as it does for a mind-independent world to which the non-conceptual experience of mysticism is tied. For such claims regarding access to an objective, mind-independent world to be true, they would require a notion of truth and meaning that is not tied to James's Promethean self but to his individual-transcending mystical self. Thus, Gale reads these claims as requiring that Realism with regard to truth be presupposed and James's mystical self as denying his own pragmatism.[89] James thus espouses all four possible views without acknowledgment.

The final issue that Gale illuminates with regard to James is the difficulty with which contemporary philosophers approach James's corpus. James is widely known for having committed himself to a variety of doctrines throughout his life and philosophical career, and he frequently did so without specifying the relationships among these. When, for example, he states explicitly (in *Pragmatism*) that pragmatism recommends itself apart from his radical empiricism, it is difficult to know what to make of this claim. James began touting radical empiricism as early as "The Will to Believe" in 1897 and reintroduced the world to Peirce's pragmatism the following year. Clearly, the two ideas grew around the same time. Despite the explicit separation there, which is similar to the separation he makes between his will-to-believe doctrine and his pragmatism, David Lamberth chooses to see pragmatism and radical empiricism as inexorably linked.[90] Although Lamberth recognizes the need to separate readings of James from issues in contemporary analytic philosophy as framed by Rorty and his opponents, the question regarding James's metaphysics winds its way into a question regarding the pragmatic conception of truth. The issue for both Gale and Lamberth, then, is what one ought to make of the relationships among James's many views. Gale's conclusion is relatively clear—namely, that James's many views cannot be made consistent with one another and that the search for a unifying or systematic understanding of James is futile. Lamberth's conclusion is also relatively clear—namely, that James's many views can be reconciled with one another if sufficient attention is paid to the metaphysics that preoccupies the final twelve years of his life, radical empiricism with its monistic pure experience and functional account of knowing.

On this head, the account that follows in subsequent chapters runs a bit closer to Lamberth than to Gale but without the emphasis on radical empiricism. Implicit and occasionally explicit in the book is an attempt to disentangle pragmatism from the many entanglements it finds in both Peirce's and James's works. In disentangling these, I argue that James is more systematic and less divided than Gale would have him be, but I do this by restricting pragmatism as a principle of logic more than Lamberth would. As stated in the introduction, the study here is animated by the questions of what pragmatism itself is and of whether such pragmatism is significantly different for Peirce than for James. In order to make this argument, we need not only free pragmatism from the contemporary shackles of the debates among metaphysical realism, metaphysical antirealism, Realism with regard to truth, and Nonrealism with regard to truth, but also from the not insignificant connections pragmatism has to other doctrines espoused by these two pragmatists.

Metaphysical and epistemological disagreements

This foray into the debate surrounding Rorty's work and his reading of American pragmatism is instructive in both a general and a more specific way. First, this discussion shows the general terms in which the debate between Rorty and his critics is framed. By and large, the argument concerns whether or not it is possible to construct a metaphysical and epistemological picture that provides an adequate explanation of the connection between mind-dependent concepts and the mind-independent world such that subjectivism and relativism are overcome. The critics of Rorty (whom I have noted in the preceding discussion) have said that such a construction and explanation is desirable, possible, and necessary, while Rorty and his supporters have said that such a construction and explanation is neither desirable nor possible nor necessary.[91] Second, this discussion shows that readings of early American pragmatism are now often framed in terms of this debate such that much current work on Peirce and James is done with reference to Rorty's reading of American pragmatism on this very issue. The argument between Rorty and his detractors is often concerned with whether or not Rorty's reading of American pragmatism with regard to this connection is correct, and—whatever the answer to this question may be—what this does for early American pragmatism's most famous output, the pragmatic theory of truth.

This chapter has gone to some length in pursuit of a single point: different philosophers read the early American pragmatists differently with regard to the questions of their metaphysical realism or metaphysical antirealism and of their Realism or Nonrealism with regard to truth. Philosophical discussion of Peirce and James has been focused on this point largely because of the work of Richard Rorty, who makes seemingly antirealist and Nonrealist claims while standing on the shoulders of James and Dewey. Metaphysical realism and Realism with regard to truth affirm the bifurcation of the world into the mind-dependent and the mind-independent. Their opposites, metaphysical antirealism and Nonrealism with regard to truth, argue that these claims are false and therefore implicitly affirm this division. The seemingly innocuous notion that an external object is, as Peirce says, "not affected by any cognitions, whether about it or not, of the man to whom it is external" has been exaggerated in "the usual philosophical fashion" to serve as the basis for positions imbued with theoretical content, which have, in turn, been used to read the early American pragmatists.[92] That there is considerable disagreement over the application of these four notions to Peirce and James should by now be clear. The project of the remaining chapters will be to find the sources of this disagreement and offer a means not so much for resolving as for dissolving it. Not only is it dangerous to read contemporary, post-linguistic turn positions into a philosophical movement that developed well before the linguistic turn, but doing so also shifts the focus from the hall that is pragmatism rather than illuminating it.

In making the first part of this argument—that reading pragmatism through a contemporary lens requires importing content the pragmatists were happy to do without—the following chapters draw occasionally on material from both Peirce and James that might seem to come from "beyond the hallway" as it were. This appearance reflects the reality. In making the larger point regarding pragmatism's rejection of tenets through which the contemporary debates are framed, it does become necessary to move into other areas of these philosophers' works. Nonetheless, insofar as doing so makes the largely critical point that Peirce and James rejected such tenets rather than making a more positive claim about pragmatism itself, I believe this move to be warranted. At the same time, the claims made in the final chapter and the conclusion are made within the confines of the hallway and are not intended to advance a constructive thesis beyond that warranted by Peirce's and James's pragmatism. In what follows, I will strive, wherever possible, to maintain some perspicuity with regard to pragmatism itself.

Chapter 2

Doubt, Skepticism, and Method

When thinking of philosophical doubt, it is tempting to think of it as the province of the first-year collegian. Say, for example, a student comes home for winter break after her "Introduction to Philosophy" course and, after telling her mother that she is now a vegan and will not partake of the Christmas ham, goes on to tell her that she has learned over the course of the semester that there are no good defeaters for her doubts that there is a Christmas ham in the oven, or an oven, or a house, or any other external object. The student has become a skeptic. Unable to meet the conditions that would allow her to claim knowledge of an external world, she finds herself free to doubt the existence of ordinary objects because any claims to knowledge about these would be equally tenuous. In the end, she finds it plausible that we are all simply brains in vats hooked up to some supercomputer run by an evil scientist. This scientist programs the computer to send the proper stimuli to our brains, causing us to think that we are seeing, touching, smelling, hearing, and tasting Christmas hams, ovens, houses, and other external objects. All the while, however, we are simply brains bathing in some nutrient solution hooked up to a supercomputer in a lab. The mother, being of a more practical bent, simply nods and says, "That's nice, dear. Would you please set the table?" and hopes that her daughter will eventually outgrow at least her skepticism, if not her veganism as well.

When confronted with radical skepticism, many philosophers react like the mothers in the holiday melodrama. They think that such skeptical concerns ought to be outgrown; no mature philosopher would entertain such ideas, particularly if that philosopher wants to remain employed. If philosophers are not inclined to refute skepticism through argumentation, then they often simply suggest that the crippling effects of such skepticism are reason enough not to take it too seriously. If the young collegian cannot be silenced, she can at least be ignored, made to sit at the philosophical kids' table until she is ready to admit the existence of the Christmas ham, even if not ready to partake of it.

Although this attitude towards skepticism is easy enough to take and has the support of any number of reputable philosophers, the history of philosophy would seem to reveal that skepticism refuses to be so banished.[1] The "philosophical kids' table" has been variously occupied by reputable philosophers from Empiricus to Montaigne and Hume to more contemporary occupants such as Goodman and Nagel.[2] However, it is not the mere litany of serious philosophers who have espoused skeptical views that should inspire us to take philosophical skepticism more seriously than the mother does her daughter's. Even those who would dismiss skepticism as "uninteresting" or "irrelevant" still seem to find it philosophically important. That is, there is something cogent to skepticism that compels us to take it seriously.

Michael Williams suggests in *Unnatural Doubts* that we are drawn to philosophical skepticism against the pleas of our common sense. Williams credits Hume for recognizing that the skeptical position is plausible and appeals to our intuition in a way that philosophical responses to it do not: "In Hume's eyes, there is simply no hope of our reaching a reflective understanding of human knowledge that will explain to us how we come by the knowledge we are ordinarily so ready to claim. To try for such a philosophical understanding is to engage the skeptic on his own terms and, thus engaged, the skeptic always triumphs."[3] To engage in argument with the skeptic is to grant the plausibility of the skeptic's thesis. Because such plausibility cannot be revoked once granted, the skeptic's questions nag at any philosophical system that begins here.

For Hume, these theoretical problems lead to a tension between philosophy and common life; if we were as skeptical regarding the existence of the external world as we rightly should be given the state of affairs in philosophy, we would be unable to live our lives in the world. Such skepticism would be crippling if let out of the study. Although notoriously a pessimist with regard to the possibility of refuting skepticism philosophically, Hume was also famously an optimist with regard to our practical affairs. We seem, on Hume's view, to be wired in ways that make it impossible to give up inductive reasoning or suspend belief in the world of common sense. Our inabilities to sustain skeptical doubt when we go about our everyday affairs are reason enough to continue going about our everyday affairs without skeptical doubt.[4] However, such optimism is not as deep as the pessimism that counters it. For Hume, philosophical skepticism is simply more natural than the philosophical theories that would undercut it and allow us to ignore skepticism entirely in our everyday lives. Williams writes: "[T]he force of the skeptic's insights, though attenuated, is never entirely extinguished.

The asymmetry thus favors the skeptic: though in philosophy, commonsense certainty is powerless against skeptical doubt, in everyday life skeptical doubt plays faint, discordant descant to the dominant themes."[5] If the skeptic cannot be entirely refuted, as Hume claims, then the skeptic has a foothold not just in our philosophical lives, but also in our ordinary lives. If we are reflective people, we carry skeptical doubt around with us even if we are not constantly mindful of it.

None of this is to suggest that we are forced to agree with Hume's assessment of our situation. We need not be like the young college student. We can disagree with the assessment that answers to skepticism regarding the external world are less intuitive or less convincing than the skeptical position itself and plunge headlong into the formulation of answers to the skeptical challenge. Indeed, some have thought it their very duty as philosophers to provide a compelling case against such skepticism, wresting it from the mind of the budding philosopher.[6]

What is important for this project is the recognition that skepticism is not simply a problem that has been, or should be, philosophically outgrown. Of most interest here is the way in which two forms of skepticism, stemming from the respective works of Descartes and Hume, have entered the contemporary scene and have continued to plague philosophical discourse. The mechanism for explaining the nature of radical skepticism may have changed, but the problem remains the same. Cartesian skepticism and contemporary "brains-in-a-vat" skepticism each call into question the very reliability of our knowledge-forming faculties even under the best possible circumstances. It is in this sense that this form of skepticism is "radical," even in relation to the Pyrrhonian skepticism of Ancient Greece and the *nouveau Pyrrhonisme* of seventeenth-century Europe. Hume's mitigated skepticism is a reaction to the radical skepticism of Descartes that shifts the ground on which the skeptic and his or her opponent might engage each other. Refusing to answer radical skepticism on its own terms, Humean skepticism counters with the practical optimism of our seeming successes in common life.

The first section of this chapter will explain the treatment of Descartes' version of the skeptical problem through a more contemporary and occasionally pragmatic lens, and will argue that Hume's version of the skeptical problem is the more difficult one for pragmatism. The second section will look specifically at Peirce's and James's respective responses to skepticisms of both the Cartesian and Humean varieties. The argument of the second section is that in responding to philosophical skepticism, Peirce and James use a more multifaceted approach than is commonly acknowledged and that this approach is intimately tied to a more comprehensive understanding of the nature of inquiry than is commonly argued. In the end, Peirce and James take on skepticism in a novel way by arguing against the conception of "ideas" common to Descartes and Hume, which vitiates the naturalness of skepticism, and arguing for the continuity of experience, which undercuts the asymmetry between philosophical reflection and common life.

The Skeptical Hypothesis and Radical Skepticism

Radical skepticism maintains prominence as the epistemological problem *par excellence*. Descartes offers an inventive skeptical hypothesis through the mechanism of the malicious demon, which allows us to doubt that the apparent proper function of our faculties is any guarantee of their veracity with regard to the world of ordinary experience. However, because Descartes entertains this hypothesis methodologically, as a means of finding his way to certain, bedrock propositions that cannot be doubted, he fails in many ways to realize its full import. While quickly dispatching what he took to be Descartes' "antecedent skepticism," Hume recognizes that it bequeaths "consequent" and "mitigated" skepticisms, which create four related problems for those who would respond to the skeptical challenge to knowledge. By dealing first with the skeptical hypothesis framed by Descartes and then with its consequences as highlighted by Hume, this section will attempt to make perspicuous the problem with which Peirce and James attempt to deal and the novel route they take in doing so.

Descartes and the skeptical hypothesis

In the first of his *Meditations*, Descartes offers three distinct formulations of the skepticism under consideration here.[7] The first very simply calls into question the reliability of our senses. The second calls into question the reliability of our mental powers in distinguishing between dreaming and being awake in order to undermine the reliability of both the physical senses and our mental faculties. The third again calls into question the reliability of our mental powers but does so by asking us to imagine that the proper functioning of our faculties—both waking and dreaming—is illusory, an elaborate trick being perpetrated on us by some malicious demon that is nearly equal in power to God and is capable of deceiving us universally not just about what we experience, but also about how we experience it.

Although the three formulations are quite distinct, each thought experiment rests on the same three-fold foundation. First, because these scenarios are not inherently self-contradictory, they are at least logical possibilities. Second, because these scenarios are themselves about the reliability and veridicality of our experience, no evidence from our experience can be brought to bear against them. Third, because no non-question-begging evidence can be brought to bear against them, they are, in the end, real possibilities. The conclusion of each argument, then, is the radically skeptical one that we have no non-circular argument for thinking these scenarios to be false. According to Descartes, this provides us with "grounds for doubt about all things."[8]

Although Descartes' solutions to the skeptical scenarios he constructs are not germane to this project because they are not directly employed by any of the positions to be considered here, Descartes' reasons for constructing these scenarios are worth reviewing. Descartes opens the "First Meditation" by explaining that he once realized that he had accepted a number of falsehoods and based an entire edifice of beliefs upon them. He goes on to say that this led him to think that it was necessary to demolish everything and start over from the foundations.[9] In order to do this, he did not need to show all his opinions to be false but only to show all these opinions to be doubtful. For the purpose of rejecting all of his opinions, Descartes finds it necessary only to show that the foundations of these opinions are shaky at best: "Once the foundations of a building are undermined, anything built on them collapses of its own accord."[10] If we can be given reasons for doubt regarding these foundations, then we have reason for doubt regarding the edifice that stands upon them.

John Clayton helpfully notes the ways in which the Cartesian project becomes embedded in our larger thinking about rationality. According to the Cartesian procedures, we must start by destroying the beliefs that we currently hold in order to begin afresh with only those beliefs that are impervious to doubt. In tearing down the edifice of belief upon which we ordinarily rely, Descartes, says Clayton, "is your worst nightmare as a neighbor." What for the ordinary homeowner might be mildly troubling and problematic, is for Descartes reason to scrape the lot and dig out the footings: "No sooner has he bought the house next door than he begins worrying that it may be haunted. Then one day he mutters that roofs have been known to leak and infers from this datum that his roof must be unreliable."[11] He quickly removes the roof, and floor by floor dismantles the house, levels the ground, and digs for bedrock. "With a worrying air of Gallic self-satisfaction, he then proceeds to lay new foundations and to begin rebuilding his house.

You offer to help, but he refuses all assistance."[12] The epistemological upshot of such a project is to find a single reliable means upon which to base all reasoning. Avoiding error is paramount, and recognizing others—both present and past—to be unreliable workers leaves us to work unencumbered and provides us with "a sure guide to truth, justice, and virtue."[13] We become responsible for our own philosophical homes should we be diligent and enterprising enough to look after them.

Although we have moved in many ways beyond the foundationalist Cartesian project that was the result of Descartes' own engagement with skepticism, we remain saddled with his legacy. D. A. Pritchard offers the contemporary summary of radical skepticism, according to which we no longer require the demon used by Descartes to provoke his profound doubts to think of the manipulation of our faculties. We require no more than advanced technology. Following Hilary Putnam and others, the "malicious demon" has been replaced by the "evil scientist," the thinking self has been replaced by the "brain in a vat," but the implications are entirely the same. According to the brains-in-vats hypothesis, we could be brains in vats of nutrient solution hooked up to a supercomputer, which is controlled by an evil scientist. We are fed stimuli, to which we respond, and these responses lead to appropriate responses on the part of the supercomputer such that we "feel" as if we are actually doing all the things the computer makes it appear we are doing. We are in the *Matrix*. In such a scenario, we could be in a situation in which we are deceived regarding all our experiences because we are deceived regarding the function of our mental faculties. Our manipulation is total, and the deception is complete.

Pritchard refers to the brains-in-vats hypothesis as "'SH' (the skeptically hypothesis)" and summarizes its consequences with regard to "O," "some 'ordinary' proposition that one would typically take oneself to know and which entails the falsity of" SH:

1. I know O.
2. I do not know not-SH.
3. If I do not know not-SH, then I do not know O.[14]

The general doubt inculcated by SH undermines all specific propositions of which we are ordinarily taken to have knowledge. We are left with doubt about whether we are ever correct in thinking that we have experiences of the kind we think we are having, in making judgments, in coming to logical conclusions, and so on. The apparent proper function of our faculties can provide no foundation for the construction of the edifice of certain knowledge.

Richard Popkin recognizes that this is the great contribution of Descartes to philosophical skepticism. Although in the arguments about the reliability of senses and the force and vivacity of experiences Descartes relied upon arguments that use the proper function of our faculties in order to undermine their reliability in general in much the same way that the *nouveaux Pyrrhoniens* did, in this final scenario the proper function of our faculties is manipulated without our knowledge. Popkin writes: "The possibility of our being constantly deceived by some evil agency raises doubt about even the most evident matters and any standards of evidence we may have."[15] Descartes altered the direction of the skeptical attack such that the target was no longer simply our knowledge but our very means of knowing. Of this Popkin says: "It is not that Descartes was denying or doubting the self-evidence of our mathematical or most certain knowledge, but rather he was showing that as long as we might be demonically infected, what appeared self-evident to us might be false."[16] Our faculties may be so controlled that their manipulation does not appear to us to be manipulation at all. Because of SH, proper function is impossible to distinguish from improper function.

The skeptical hypothesis, whether of the Cartesian or contemporary variety, is novel in the way in which it extends earlier skeptical arguments. Michael Williams notes historically at the beginning of *Unnatural Doubts* that despite earlier traditions among the ancients and the early moderns, "what has become for us the paradigm of a skeptical problem cannot be identified with any certainty in skeptical writings prior to those of Descartes."[17] What Descartes introduced onto the philosophical scene was a doubt that knows no bounds. Unlike the skepticism of the Pyrrhonians and *nouveaux Pyrhonniens*, SH asks us not to withhold judgment, but to recognize that all our judgments are made on insufficient evidence and thus incapable of becoming knowledge. It introduces the possibility that we could be wrong about everything in spite of the proper function of our faculties.

Furthermore, as Clayton points out regarding the account that takes SH seriously, we are not simply justified but more reasonable when we see that this sense of being wrong forces us to doubt all our opinions at once.[18] The result of this is as Akeel Bilgrami notes: "Cartesian skepticism was different and more radical from Ancient skepticism in claiming that if we put into question that we have *knowledge* of the external world, then the existence of the external world can be put into doubt."[19] This kind of radical error is important to SH because it is this kind of error that throws all our opinions into doubt. We could be wrong about everything.

Hume, symmetry, naturalness, and asymmetry

Although Descartes deserves considerable credit for the novelty of his skeptical hypothesis and the consequences of such skepticism, he was, quite obviously, not a skeptic with regard to human knowledge. For Descartes, radical skepticism was a *method* that one used in order to arrive at indubitable propositions by recognizing the marks of such propositions once they were properly isolated in the mind. It seems unlikely that Descartes ever entertained the worry that skepticism might be true.[20] However, the skeptical hypothesis escaped the philosophical system that originally imprisoned it within its walls and—like any escapee—quickly accumulated a host of nefarious characters that kept it from easy capture. Four are worthy of note: the argument from symmetry, the naturalness of skepticism, and two kinds of asymmetry—that between philosophical simplicity and complexity, and that between the theoretical and the practical. We have David Hume to thank for bringing each of these to the fore as they apply to radical skepticism.

When we begin to reflect upon the world philosophically, we begin to ask questions that we would not ask in our everyday affairs. Because our everyday life is organized around the satisfaction of particular interests, there is no room for the kind of general reflection that would lead to skepticism there. However, when we reflect philosophically, we forget these particulars and engage in attempts to find justification for those things we take for granted in our everyday lives. In philosophical reflection the focus is broad, and the search is for generalities. Williams credits Hume for recognizing that philosophical reflection is unique in that through it "we try to get a grip on the 'foundation' of our beliefs and inferences, to understand in some highly general way how they can have the status we ordinarily, and unthinkingly, grant them."[21] Through philosophical reflection we try to justify, generally and philosophically, our ordinary practices. Such reflection led Hume to believe that when we free our reason from the practical affairs of life and turn it toward these general questions regarding our ordinary beliefs and inferences, reason acts alone. The consequence of this reflective turn is that we are met only with contradictions. When we reflect philosophically, we find, as Williams notes, that although "knowledge is supposedly the product of reason, the senses, or both, neither reason nor the senses is properly intelligible, and the two sources of knowledge are anyway in conflict with each other." The conflict arises from the bare consideration of sense data as simple as the oar in water. Thus, according to Williams, Hume recognized that whether we think about knowledge as either the product of reason or the product of the senses "we are led inevitably to skepticism."[22] Because reason looks for general principles, the particular justifications that we use in our everyday affairs are irrelevant here. Philosophical reflection requires that we find some general criteria for the justification of every particular belief and inference and eventually reveals that this cannot be had. To think philosophically in this way is to be skeptical.

Reaching back to at least the Pyrrhonians, the symmetry that arises in philosophical thinking was widely recognized. Once we enter the study and begin to examine appearances or judgments against themselves or each other, we quickly come to realize that proper philosophical justification for taking the authority of one over another is unlikely to come. Sextus Empiricus argues that all that is needed to induce Pyrrhonian skepticism is the mere comparison of appearance to appearance, judgment to judgment, or appearance to judgment. He takes this, and the resultant symmetry, to be the very heart of skepticism: "Scepticism is an ability to place in antithesis, in any manner whatever, appearances and judgements, and thus—because of the equality of force in the objects and arguments opposed—to come first of all to a suspension of judgement and then to mental tranquility."[23] For Empiricus, the equality of force, the symmetry, offers reason enough for the suspension of judgment. Once one begins to examine judgments in this manner, one quickly recognizes how broadly such symmetry applies, which quickly leads to skepticism.

James Franklin argues that the symmetry that arises from consideration of the skeptical hypothesis is in fact its strongest and most compelling feature, and that arguments that attempt to take away this symmetry in favor of some realist hypothesis necessarily fail.[24] Once one enters into philosophical reflection, one is struck as Empricus was by the symmetry among rival hypotheses. In the confines of the study, the skeptical hypothesis seems no less likely to be the case than any rival hypothesis that might be raised against it. Because Descartes thought that he could identify the marks that would separate the true from the false, the problem of symmetry did not plague his skeptical method in the way that it does the skepticism that follows Hume. When we realize that we do not find the marks of clarity and distinctness that Descartes thought to be the guides for separating truth from falsity, Hume claims that we "can look upon no opinion as even more probable or likely than any other."[25] If we can give no reason to find one view more probable than another, then there is a logical symmetry between even the radical skeptical hypothesis and any rival. Hume is not necessarily claiming that such radical skepticism holds sway, but merely that it can claim as much philosophical ground as any rival hypothesis.

Erik Olsson applies this symmetry to the simple outline of the skeptical problem offered by Pritchard to note the parity between one's knowing some common sense proposition that one claims to know and one's not knowing that the skeptical hypothesis is not the case. The skeptical hypothesis is problematic because it is the kind of scenario that "is phenomenologically indistinguishable from everyday life." In principle, it bears no marks that might differentiate it from any common sense proposition: "It is logically possible that what we perceive is entirely an illusion, and there does not seem to be any reason to prefer the normal view to the illusion hypothesis; they are entirely symmetrical."[26] Without the marks that Descartes thought he could find, we are—at best—left on equal footing with the skeptic when we enter the philosophical study. The conclusion can only be that we know hardly anything at all and that if we do, we are unable to identify it definitively.

Hume makes clear that once we enter the philosophical study, skepticism arises quickly not only because of the symmetry one perceives between the skeptical hypothesis and its rivals but also because of one's natural tendencies in such reflection. Once such skepticism begins, it becomes difficult to stop: "As the skeptical doubt arises naturally from a profound and intense reflection on those subjects, it always encreases [sic], the farther we carry our reflections, whether in opposition or conformity to it."[27] To see how natural skeptical doubt can be made to appear, we need only return to Descartes' "First Meditation". When Descartes sets about undermining all his previous opinions, he begins in the most natural of ways. He recognizes first that his senses often deceive him in particular isolated instances. Thus, knowledge acquired through the senses is called into question. He then recognizes that his mind and reasoning often deceive him through dreams; he thinks himself to be having an experience that he is not in fact having. What is discovered upon waking is the general dubitability of experience more generally. As Hume notes regarding the existence and character of external objects of experience, it takes only "the slightest philosophy" to overturn the certainty we thought we had.[28] There seems to be nothing unnatural about these first two scenarios; they derive their sense from simple reflection on our everyday lives.

At first blush, Descartes' malicious demon hypothesis seems to up the ante considerably from these first two skeptical hypotheses. Descartes' final scenario asks us to imagine the *super*natural, that we are being systematically deceived by a malicious demon. The demonic mechanism used to engender this final level of doubt, a level at which we could be entirely deceived without ever recognizing it, need not make the doubt itself unnatural.[29] If we think of the doubt as arising from our manipulation by some supercomputer or virtual-reality machine, this becomes clear. Under such conditions, the scenario is merely extraordinary; it is no more than an unusual assemblage of readily available materials.³⁰ The doubt that arises is doubt about everything at once. What began naturally and simply ends radically, but we have not strayed as far as it may seem. We have simply followed our reflections to the broader and more general levels with which philosophy deals and carried our natural inclinations toward skepticism along with us.

Because of the systematic nature of the deception in the skeptical hypothesis, we find ourselves on epistemological sinking sand. The scenarios seem to be coherent enough to be logical possibilities; and, given that there is no obvious importation of highly developed theoretical concepts, either the malicious demon or the brains-in-vats hypotheses seem to be natural enough to be real possibilities. Intuitively, then, there is no more reason to find these scenarios dubitable than there is to find our common knowledge indubitable, and symmetry and naturalness work hand in hand. Barry Stroud notes that the power of skepticism arises from the fact that it can be expressed in terms of "platitudes we would all accept."³¹ Even the most radical of skeptical doubts can be couched in simple, compact arguments that seem to appeal only to our common sense and appear not to rely on theoretical imports.

Although symmetry and naturalness with regard to the skeptical hypothesis are largely damning when we enter the philosophical study, attempts to combat the skeptic are saddled by an asymmetry that makes the weapons we might employ in combat ill-suited to the task. The problem of asymmetry does not arise purely from philosophical reflection, but only from attempts to combat the natural skepticism that comes there. Hume contends that the asymmetry between the skeptical hypothesis and its rival makes the skeptic ultimately unanswerable. Whereas the skeptic need only appeal to intuition, his or her opponent is forced to counter with theory.³² The apparent simplicity of the skeptical argument is opposed by the grand complexities of a theory of knowledge. Williams notes this in Hume: "No doubt Hume's sense of the devastating simplicity of skeptical argument, in contrast to the baroque edifices of philosophical theory, does as much as anything to convince him that the skeptic is theoretically unassailable."³³ A refutation of skepticism relies upon theories of knowledge (or, more contemporarily, theories of meaning) that do not arise necessarily from our common sense view of the world, but the skeptic's doubts do arise from reflecting on this common sense view. Thus, the philosopher who would refute the skeptic starts with a heavy disadvantage.

Hume goes yet one step further with his contention that attempts to combat skepticism fall prey to this asymmetry. He claims that the defense of human knowledge grants the skeptic's point that human knowledge is something in need of defense. If we really thought that skepticism were incoherent, there would be no need of a defense of human knowledge. As Wittgenstein remarks in *On Certainty*: "When one hears Moore say, 'I *know* that's a tree,' one suddenly understands those who think that has by no means been settled."[34] Williams notes that for Hume, "the first fatal step on the road to skepticism is taken *as soon as we ask the basic epistemological questions*, and the urge to ask them belongs to human nature itself."[35] That is, when we enter the philosophical study with the desire to defend our claims to knowledge, this gives the skeptic a foothold; and the more elaborate our defense of human knowledge, the stronger that foothold becomes. For Hume, unlike Descartes, the skeptic wins in the study, and attempts to defeat the skeptic serve only to concede victory. Thus, the epistemologist is engaged in a paradoxical enterprise: by engaging in a theoretical defense against a seemingly intuitive problem, the epistemologist concedes the naturalness of the skeptic's doubts; by engaging in a defense of human knowledge, he or she grants the skeptic's argument that human knowledge requires such a defense. The former puts skeptical doubt on par with our cherished and supposedly indubitable beliefs; the latter gives skeptical doubt the upper hand. The two conspire to create a picture of epistemology that is paradoxical at best and pessimistic at worst.[36] Peter van Inwagen summarizes the result of the combination of such skepticism with such pessimism: "There is no way to tell whether or not this tale is true, and it is perfectly conceivable that we are all wrong about almost everything— for if the tale were true, we should all be wrong about almost everything."[37] Symmetry, which might allow for some optimism or at least whimsy, gives way to asymmetry, which provides grounds for pessimism or, at worst, nihilism, when we set about trying to defeat the skeptic.

Hume attempts to combat this pessimistic outcome by arguing for a natural optimism according to which the dictates of our common life might help us overcome the pessimism of the philosophical study. Unfortunately, the pessimism that arises from recognition of the asymmetry between responses to skepticism and the skeptical hypothesis itself arises not merely in the philosophical study; a similar asymmetry exists when we attempt to combat skeptical problems with practical considerations.

Hume offers the seemingly optimistic possibility for combating skepticism with the living of one's life. After noting the symmetry of the skeptical hypothesis to any common sense proposition, the naturalness of skeptical reasoning, and the asymmetry between skeptical reasoning and epistemological theory, Hume argues that the radical skeptic might be confinable to the philosophical study. Though he would carry the day there, Hume warns that the Pyrrhonian must not think his or her arguments impact common life: "The great subverter of *Pyrrhonism* or the excessive principles of skepticism is action, and employment, and the occupations of common life."[38] It seems that practical considerations offer us a means for—at the very least— silencing the skeptic while we go for billiards, backgammon, and a pint. We find a psychologically satisfying response to skepticism in the mere living of our lives. This is, despite skeptical considerations, what we do.

Nonetheless, Hume recognizes the inadequacy of the practical response to the skeptical hypothesis. Once we engage in philosophical reflection, which we can ill avoid, we are led naturally toward skepticism. Once we have engaged such skepticism, we return to our common life changed— "carelessness and in-attention alone can afford us any remedy."[39] The remedy merely treats the symptom and cannot cure the disease. While we might willingly and capably ignore the skeptic in going about our practical affairs, philosophical reflection has revealed the deep instability of even our practical understanding of our common life. Regarding Hume's attempts to juxtapose philosophical reflection with common life, Williams concludes: "The asymmetry thus favours the sceptic: though in philosophy, commonsense certainty is powerless against sceptical doubt, in everyday life sceptical doubt plays faint, discordant descant to the dominant themes."[40] To the extent that skepticism arises naturally, we must carry its conclusions into our common life—albeit in a back pocket.

Although Descartes capably creates the hypothesis from which we get the radical skepticism with which we must deal, such skepticism attains its most profound form in the work of David Hume. Hume reveals skeptical symmetry, naturalness, and asymmetry in a way that requires future philosophical work to deal with these features of the skeptical problem. It is, then, the Humean form of skepticism that we must keep in mind when dealing with doubt, skepticism, and method in the works of Peirce and James. Fortunately, locating these features of radical skepticism also provides us with a way forward: one could combat the skeptic by denying the symmetry of the skeptical hypothesis and the ordinary proposition; one could combat the skeptic by denying the naturalness of skeptical doubt; one could combat the skeptic by denying that philosophical argumentation and theory are asymmetrically related to the skeptical hypothesis and do not start from a disadvantage. Finally, one could also combat the skeptic by denying the asymmetry between the reflections of the study and the living of one's common life. In what follows, I argue that although pragmatism is usually understood as combating skepticism from this last position, Peirce and James worked variously along all four lines of attack, and a full understanding of pragmatism's response to skepticism requires recognizing how these weave together.

Responding Pragmatically to Radical Skepticism

When approaching radical skepticism from the perspective of early American pragmatism, it is important to note the pragmatists' agreement with Hume that radical skepticism is a specifically *philosophical* problem and that one way to avoid it, despite its apparent naturalness, is to avoid engaging it philosophically. Of course, this creates the second problem of asymmetry above, where our living our common lives seems incapable of fully eradicating philosophical doubt. Nonetheless, the pragmatic response has frequently been seen in specifically this light.

The pragmatic dismissal of skeptical problems is often viewed as the same kind of simplistic response as James's "solution" to the metaphysical debate about the squirrel with which he opens "What Pragmatism Means." Having gone camping in the mountains, James returned from a "solitary ramble" and found everyone in camp embroiled in "a ferocious metaphysical dispute" centered upon a squirrel—"a live squirrel clinging to one side of a tree-trunk while over against the tree's opposite side a human being was imagined to stand."[41] The person "tries to get sight of the squirrel by moving rapidly round the tree, but no matter how fast he goes, the squirrel moves as fast in the opposite direction, and always keeps the tree between himself and the man, so that never a glimpse of him is caught."[42] James is called upon to decide whether the man goes round the squirrel or not, and responds by offering some possible distinctions regarding what we might mean by "go round" "in one practical fashion or another."[43] James's distinction relativizes the notion of "go round" such that the settlement of the dispute is dependent upon the sense in which one might employ the term—for example, north, south, east, and west; or before, right, behind, and left.

At first blush, James's "solution" to this "metaphysical" problem rings hollow in at least two respects, but it offers more than it seems. First, James's appeal to the "practical fashion" in which his camping companions meant "to go round" would seem to neglect the seriousness of the metaphysical debate. There is a dismissive tone to the "solution," which dissolves the debate rather than providing an actual solution. Second, even if we allow that James has offered a solution to the problem, it seems not to be a very good one. His solution simply points to the different senses of "to go round" and thereby dissolves the dispute itself. This would seem to open up the possibility that the dispute will now take the form of an argument regarding which of these senses of "to go round" is right. Taking James's response in this way would have him falling prey to both asymmetry problems at once, the second and the first.

These initial reactions are misguided in the same way that thinking radical skepticism to be the province of the first-year collegian is. First, James's method of resolving the dispute by dissolving the bone of contention is legitimate. James simply points out that neither side understands what the other side means and that the dispute itself is dependent upon this misunderstanding. Once such understanding is in place, the debate can either cease or continue with the two sides on common ground. Second, James's resolution of the problem through a practical distinction only misses the mark if one requires that there be only one correct definition of the term or if one admits that we need arguments about which sense is correct. If the only solutions to such disputes were metaphysical, then there would be little hope for resolution at all.

If we look only at Peirce's many cursory dismissals of Cartesian "paper" doubt, the view of the pragmatic response as a quick dismissal that could fall prey to the second asymmetry problem in particular seems to have a great deal of merit. The pragmatists often offer reasons for dismissing skepticism that seem to follow this rather simple line of thought: because we cannot find a way in which the truth of the radical skeptical hypothesis would make a real difference to our practical affairs, such skeptical scenarios are necessarily falsified by the very living of our lives. Our need to live our everyday lives trumps whatever philosophical problems may arise from such skepticism.

Erik Olsson argues that the pragmatic response works best when it simply never allows the skeptic's doubts to get off the ground. Olsson reads William James—unlike Peirce—as conceding too much. On the one hand, Olsson argues, based on "The Will to Believe," that it seems difficult for James to deny that the skeptical hypothesis might be as genuine an option for the skeptic as the religious hypothesis is for James without some further argument than is present. In that essay, and the others in the volume, James seems to make the genuineness of the option—particularly its liveness—too dependent on either personal or philosophical temperament. On the other hand, Olsson accuses James of allowing for the possibility that the skeptical option might be genuine for some person while also attempting to combat the skeptic from a purely practical perspective.[44] Olsson cites Mounce's argument regarding certainty in the practical sphere grounding certainty in the theoretical sphere noted above, which he also offers with regard to James. Recall there that Mounce argues that the very idea of theoretical certainty requires a commitment to practical certainty. The word "certainty" itself is a "practical instrument." Thus, when we fail to recognize this, Mounce writes, "Scepticism is the inevitable consequence of confining oneself *simply* to the theoretical sphere."[45] By offering a reminder of the importance of the practical, Olsson and Mounce both see James as attempting to combat the skepticism that arises in the study with the living of our common lives.[46] In other words, James's response suffers from the dual maladies of the symmetry problem and the second asymmetry problem.

At the same time, Olsson argues that Peirce offers a more cogent three-part response that keeps the skeptic from gaining a foothold. Peirce concedes little. Peirce argues that we must start philosophy from the same position we start all inquiries in our ordinary lives and attacks the skeptic's premise of "I do not know that I am not deceived." On Olsson's reading, philosophy is a particular and, perhaps, peculiar kind of practical inquiry but differs only in its generality from the kind of thinking we do in our ordinary lives and remains, much as Mounce argues, grounded in the practical. When we start doing philosophy, we do so with the same beliefs we "employ in our normal inquires and deliberations."[47] Furthermore, in beginning philosophical inquiry in the same place in which we begin all inquiry, Peirce suggests that no part of our prior mass of cognition entails that I might not know that I am not systematically deceived. In most instances, my denial that I am systematically deceived exists as an "implicit belief," to which I am committed through my "explicit belief" in some ordinary proposition. Although "I may fail in my doxastic performance to live up to my commitments," that is not the same as embracing the doubt of the skeptic.[48] Finally, Olsson notes Peirce's more general view of doubt according to which genuine doubt is the motive for inquiry. The skeptical hypothesis cannot rise to the level of genuine doubt because "surprise is caused by novel experience" and no experience could cause me to embrace such systematic deception.[49] To take these three related arguments in turn, we can see Peirce as responding to the second asymmetry problem, the symmetry problem, and—to the extent that genuine surprise only arises in our living our lives—the second asymmetry problem again.

Although such pragmatic responses to radical skepticism resemble Hume's, they do so in a slightly inverted way. Whereas Hume claimed that radical skepticism's naturalness and unanswerability conspire to force us to leave it in the study while we go about our common lives, the pragmatists seem to be claiming that the fact that we do leave such skepticism in the study while we go about our common lives defeats it in both our common lives and in the study. If such skepticism cannot be lived, it must be false. However, such a view of pragmatism's response to skepticism would make the pragmatists little more than confused (or just lousy) Humeans in this regard, and this is decidedly not the case. This view of the pragmatists' dismissal of skepticism makes it ring as hollow as James's dissolving of the seemingly intractable debate regarding the squirrel. If we really thought that skepticism could be so easily conquered, we would have dismissed it long ago.[50]

Although it is not always clear that they did so, the early American pragmatists not only took the challenges of skepticism seriously, but also took up the gauntlet of responding to the skeptic philosophically. It is true that the pragmatists dismiss skepticism, but it is not true that they do so lightly. From Peirce's 1867 and 1868 articles in *The Journal of Speculative Philosophy* through Dewey's "Gifford Lectures", pragmatism took very seriously the challenge of radical skepticism. The pragmatists responded by showing that the doubts of the skeptic traded in terms dictated by an epistemological picture of our interaction with the world that was inherited from Descartes and has continued to dominate epistemology. Because of the conjunction of skepticism with modern epistemology, the sensibility of one directly affects the sensibility of the other. If either falters, then so does the other. Thus, that the pragmatic attack on skepticism is more than the simple rejection of the practical import of the skeptic's doubts can best be demonstrated by conjoining the pragmatists' direct attacks on the skeptical doubts raised by Descartes and Hume with their attacks on the epistemology proposed for the quieting of such doubts.

Isolated ideas and natural doubts

Because the exposition of the pragmatic response to skepticism is dependent upon locating the proper philosophical context of the skeptical challenge, a brief detour will be required before this section's main line of argument can be taken up. By looking first at possible strategies for the dismissal or defeat of skepticism and the philosophical context of the skeptical doubts entertained by Descartes (and still at work today), we can then turn to the ways in which the early American pragmatists avoid the skeptical problems of Descartes and Hume by elucidating the ways in which the pragmatists saw the problem of skepticism as tied to an epistemological picture that they reject. James's citation of the scholastic adage in his tale of the squirrel is relevant again here. The intractable debate between the skeptic and the anti-skeptic is one in which discussion has been worn "threadbare", and one in which several distinctions must be made for its resolution. Three such distinctions will be made in what follows: first, between the refutation of skepticism and the avoidance of skepticism; second, between two senses in which skepticism can be dismissed as optional; and third, between the apparent naturalness of skeptical arguments and the *unnaturalness* of their theoretical underpinnings.

The skeptic need not be given the last word if we can find a way to avoid both the paradox and the pessimism of epistemologies that would respond to her. Here, the distinction between avoiding and refuting skepticism is relevant; to avoid skepticism is not to offer a definitive refutation of the skeptic. A definitive refutation would require the construction of a theoretical viewpoint from which the skeptic's doubts could be seen to be unnecessary because they violate the given theory of knowledge. Descartes offers one such refutation. Others have seen fit to undermine the skeptic's position without constructing an elaborate epistemology in its place. Skeptical doubts may continue to be natural; they just happen to be refutable because they are internally flawed in some way. Arguments have been constructed to show that the skeptical position is incoherent, self-defeating, unintelligible, or nonsensical.[51] Through such tactics, the skeptic is refuted because the skeptic is faced with insurmountable logical problems in relating that position. However, this method of definitive refutation continues to cede the naturalness of the skeptic's doubts and oppose them with theory. Although these theories are negatively applied to reveal problems with the skeptical position, they suffer the same fate as Descartes' theory; they succumb to the first asymmetry problem and thus to pessimism.[52] Attempts at a definitive refutation of skepticism cannot help but fail.

Given skepticism's apparent naturalness and the problems with refutations of skepticism, it would seem that Hume was right; the skeptic is unassailable. However, Williams makes clear in his discussion of skepticism that there are two ways to go about dismissing the skeptic without engaging in the defense of human knowledge that grants the skeptic's point. These two paths result from two distinct ways of understanding the skeptic's problems. One may view the skeptic's concerns as natural but "optional" in that the division between our philosophical and common lives allows us to not take up the philosophical reflection that results in skeptical problems. We need never enter the study. Williams writes, "[W]e don't *have* to respond to skepticism because it makes no difference whether we do or not."[53] Because even the skeptic admits that his or her arguments would result in paralysis or neurosis if brought to bear on our common life, the need to lead a common life allows us to ignore the skeptic. As noted above, however, such an approach seems likely to fall prey to the second asymmetry problem. We are naturally reflective, and once we engage such reflections, we cannot seem to shake the feeling that they have revealed some deep instability in our common knowledge.

This way of dealing with skepticism has its obvious practical benefits, but it hardly takes skeptical problems seriously. With what may be a nod to the view of the pragmatic dismissal of skepticism pointed to above, Williams deems this a "bluff pragmatism."[54] It is a bluff in that it fails to take seriously the seemingly obvious connection between our philosophical and common lives to which Hume pointed. Through our natural desire to be reflective, we are driven to take up the philosophical position. Once there, Williams notes, "Skepticism is the position to which we are *all* led if we have a sifting humor and the nerve to follow it to the bitter end."[55] To think in the terms in which, according to the skeptic, we must think, is to be skeptical. To lead our common lives while ignoring this skepticism is to lead our common lives while ignoring our own reflective nature. In the end, the dismissal of skepticism for simply practical reasons not only fails to satisfy the philosophical skeptic; it also fails to satisfy us.

Williams is quick to point out that this practical way of opting out of the temptation to refute skepticism is not the only way. Indeed, it is Williams's task to show us that there is another way to avoid skepticism without succumbing to the desire for a definitive philosophical refutation that leads to the first asymmetry problem and, thus, to pessimism. One may avoid skeptical problems if one can undermine Descartes' contention, which is later reinforced by Hume, that skeptical problems arise *naturally* when one reflects on one's life. If one can show that the skeptic's doubts are context-bound and that the context to which they are bound is not that of reflection in general, then the skeptic's doubts can be avoided.[56] Both Descartes and Hume held that one is led to skepticism by the mere act of reflecting on one's life in order to justify one's commonly held beliefs; if we quite naturally and ineluctably become skeptics, then skepticism is an intuitive problem. However, if Descartes, Hume, and others who assume skepticism to arise naturally through reflection can be shown to be espousing a theoretical view that does not arise naturally, then we may have a means for avoiding skepticism that is neither asymmetrical and pessimistic nor unsatisfying.

In *Philosophy and the Mirror of Nature*, Richard Rorty offers his contested account of the internal relationship between early modern epistemology and radical skepticism.[57] When Descartes hit upon the notion that the sensory grasp of particulars was a mental discernment rather than simply a sensory given, this allowed him to contend that ideas need have no connections to any sensory given. An idea for Descartes is that which arises in the mind and becomes the immediate object of mental action. This notion later gives Locke the liberty to use "idea" to mean "'whatsoever is the object of the understanding when a man thinks'" or "'every immediate object of the mind in thinking.'"[58] On Rorty's account, an idea, for Descartes or Locke, requires nothing else for its existence; it is entirely self-contained and can therefore be examined as a singular object. It matters not on such an account whether the idea arrives from the senses or from reflection; all ideas have the same independent status as ideas.

These independent ideas that are objects in themselves require some new location for their existence, and Descartes provides one with his conception of mind. Although Rorty notes that other notions and functions roughly corresponding to the modern conception of mind had been proposed by previous philosophers, Descartes had hit upon something quite different, "the notion of a single inner space in which bodily and perceptual sensations . . . mathematical truths, moral rules, the idea of God, moods of depression, and all the rest of what we now call 'mental' were objects of quasi-observation."[59] Just as the eye can perceive and observe external objects in the world, the mind can perceive and observe internal objects in this new arena. Thus, our experience of the world is once removed from the world itself; as minds, we are able only to observe and entertain ideas, which form a "veil" between us and the world outside of us.

Descartes then needs a distinction between that which operates behind the veil and that which operates in front of it. What operates behind the veil is a kind of feeling that is simply thinking itself, the entertainment of ideas by the mind. What operates in front of the veil is a wholly different kind of feeling that presents to the mind what the mind itself feels. Thus, we have a distinction between the operations behind the veil and the operations in front of it. The conscious mind operates behind the veil while what is not conscious operates in the extended world of physical bodies; the two series of events are distinct.[60] The mind and its contents are thus at least imaginable, if not understandable, apart from the body. Each now has its own realm, its own set of objects, and its own procedures for investigation. They may run parallel courses, but either can be imagined without the other.

This distinction between the world of "inner space", which was the province of the mind, and the world of "outer space", which was the province of the body, makes possible the kind of skepticism that Descartes uses in his "First Meditation" and conquers through his discovery of the *cogito*. The division itself makes necessary a theory of knowledge that explains the relationship between these two worlds such that the objects of the inner world can correspond accurately to those of the outer world. By "carving out inner space" Descartes created "the problem of the external world," and "the idea of a 'theory of knowledge' grew up around this latter problem—the problem of knowing whether our inner representations were accurate."[61] According to Descartes, we recognize intuitively that we possess the faculty of inner sense through the clarity and distinctness of the impression of that idea. What remains to be argued is whether or not this intuition offers us any clue as to the world that lies outside the mind, and Descartes held that it is only through a thorough investigation of the mind itself that we may come to find such clues.[62] To the extent that we cannot find such clues, we are faced with the problem of symmetry pointed to above.

That Descartes' solution does little to satisfy most skeptics simply points to the symbiosis between Cartesian skepticism and Cartesian epistemology. Rorty notes: "The Cartesian mind simultaneously made possible veil-of-ideas skepticism and a discipline devoted to circumventing such skepticism."[63] That such skepticism continues to exist should lead us to the recognition that epistemologies that attempt to overcome such skepticism, although no longer Cartesian in nature, are still Cartesian in spirit. The use of the Cartesian conception of mind is alive and well wherever the "problem of the external world" is found. If the Cartesian conception of mind as the space behind the veil in which ideas are our sole objects of observation is not necessary, then both Cartesian epistemology and radical skepticism can be avoided.[64]

By showing the skeptic's doubts to be informed by a philosophical picture that is not necessarily the reflective interpretation of our common view of the world, Rorty offers us a means for the avoidance of skepticism and the traditional epistemologies that would oppose it. He shows that skeptical, Cartesian doubt swims in the waters of Cartesian epistemology and is not, as either Descartes or Hume would have it, *natural.* Williams's skeptic, bluff pragmatist, and refuter of skepticism are all in the grip of a picture that sees skeptical doubt as natural. They agree with Stroud that the skeptic's doubts can be phrased in terms of "platitudes we would all accept."[65] Rorty makes clear the particular ideas at the root of such skepticism and shows that they are not necessarily "platitudes we would all accept" or ideas that would occur to us *naturally* upon reflection. Rather, the notion of mind and the problem of radical skepticism conspire in a highly developed epistemological project and cannot be divorced from a context that takes the notion of mind and its veil of ideas to be unavoidable. The remainder of this chapter will be dedicated to showing that the pragmatists were neither in the grip of this picture nor of the opinion that the skeptic's doubts were expressible in such platitudes. The early American pragmatists are neither skeptics nor bluff pragmatists nor refuters of skepticism. They, like Williams, expose the skeptic's doubts as unnatural because these doubts are tied to a theoretical view of our relationship to the world from behind a "veil of ideas," and this view need not be accepted.[66]

Peirce, James, and the continuity of thought

If we look only to the places in which the early American pragmatists address Cartesian skepticism directly, that they took skepticism at all seriously seems a difficult case to make. Consider the following comments of Charles S. Peirce in reference to Descartes' methodological doubt:

> Philosophers of very diverse stripes propose that philosophy shall take its start from one or another state of mind in which no man, least of all a beginner in philosophy, actually is. One proposes that you shall begin by doubting everything, and says that there is only one thing that you cannot doubt, as if doubting were "as easy as lying" . . . Do you call it doubting to write down on a piece of paper that you doubt? If so, doubt has nothing to do with any serious business. [67]

Such cursory dismissals occur throughout the writings of Peirce and James and serve simply to further the view of their responses to skepticism as being "bluff pragmatism." To throw everything into doubt, to posit that we could be wrong about everything in order to find only those things of which we are absolutely certain, serves no practical purpose in our normal quest for knowledge. If such doubt is possible, it is also inappropriate.

As Williams notes, this response to skepticism is little more than a knee-jerk reaction, and it falls to the second asymmetry problem through which we attempt to quell doubt by living our lives. To think that this is all that the pragmatists have to offer is to read superficially. The early American pragmatists did indeed take skepticism seriously and rightly saw that the only means for its avoidance was the avoidance of the theoretical picture that gives such skepticism its sense. However, what makes such a thesis difficult to maintain is that the early American pragmatists rarely address skepticism or its radical incarnation directly and that, when they do, their comments are in the spirit of those outlined above. Furthermore, what the pragmatists do have to say about proposed defeaters of skepticism seems at times to put them more in the skeptical than in the anti-skeptical camp. James disdains the "tender-minded" rationalist or absolutist and praises the "tough-minded" empiricist with the skeptical attitude in *Pragmatism*.[68] If James's comments were paired with Peirce's above, it would seem that any picture of the pragmatists' relationship to radical skepticism would be convoluted at best and incoherent at worst.

The pragmatists were neither skeptics nor anti-skeptics in the senses outlined in the previous section. We will here be using the distinctions made above in order to argue that the pragmatists avoid skepticism by showing skepticism to be optional because the skeptic's doubts are unnatural. This, in turn, allows the pragmatists to avoid both the problem of symmetry and the two forms of the problem of asymmetry. The pragmatists saw skeptical problems as being tied to a philosophical conception of our cognitive situation that they rejected: the conception of mind as the inner space in which ideas are represented to our intuitive faculties, which are unrelated to the world outside of the mind. These ideas, present in Descartes and Hume, remain deeply imbedded in contemporary philosophy.[69]

In his early articles in *The Journal of Speculative Philosophy,* Peirce is at pains to repeal what had by his time become dogmatic claims regarding "certain faculties claimed for man."[70] If we look carefully at these essays, we see that they are no less than the attempt to dismantle the early modern conception of mind to which Rorty points. In order to overcome the skepticism introduced by Descartes, Peirce sees it as necessary to deny that we are endowed with a faculty that allows us to recognize an intuition that is determined only by itself and not by any previous cognition. That is, could there be an intuition that we intuitively recognize as arising in us without the intervention of any outside forces? If so, then, as Descartes noted, this intuition would bear upon itself the marks of truth arising directly from our nature.[71] Such cognitions would be indubitable. That we fail to find such marks makes our ideas dubitable and creates the problem of symmetry. However, rather than seeing this skeptical outcome as natural, (as Hume does), Peirce argues that every cognition must in some way be dependent upon others and must be judged based upon its connection to these others.

Peirce explains, using several examples, that there can be no thought that is not continuous with others and that all thought must therefore be mediated by other cognitions. Our ability to differentiate waking experiences from dreaming, the existence of a blind spot on the retina, the recognition of pitch, and the perception of space all serve to show the importance of the continuity of thought.[72] For Peirce, what is called into question by the importance of continuity is the very possibility that we have private ideas or thoughts—a notion central to the Cartesian account: "We have, therefore, a variety of facts, all of which are most readily explained on the supposition that we have no intuitive faculty of distinguishing intuitive from mediate cognitions . . . Moreover, no facts require the supposition of the faculty in question."[73] If what we are thought to know by self-contained intuition can be explained through reference to other cognitions, then the notion of private intuition proves superfluous to any epistemological theory.

After rejecting the notion that we have the intuitive faculty of distinguishing between a pure and a mediated cognition and the notion of an intuitive self-consciousness, Peirce continues his attack on the entrenched epistemological picture by attacking our supposed ability to distinguish between subjective and objective elements of experience through an intuition.[74] "The subjective element is not necessarily immediately known, but it is possible that such an intuition of the subjective element of a cognition of its character, whether that of dreaming, imagining, conceiving, believing, etc., should accompany every cognition. The question is whether this is so."[75] Peirce offers a brief *reductio* to show that the distinction between the various cognitive capacities of consciousness might be attributable to the objects experienced rather than to a capacity of the mind. The differences between the subjective and the objective elements of experience are marked not by our ability to discern between them, but by differences in the objects being considered. Neither believing nor conceiving requires an "intuitive recognition of subjective elements of consciousness."[76]

For Descartes, the idea of an idea and the idea of a sensation (ideas of two different objects) were qualitatively indistinguishable except through the discerning capacity of the mind. Without this discerning capacity, we are saddled with the problem of symmetry. Peirce takes on Descartes' dream example and argues that "the very fact of the immense difference in the immediate objects of sense and imagination, sufficiently accounts for our distinguishing those faculties; and instead of being an argument in favor of the existence of an intuitive power of distinguishing the subjective elements of consciousness, it is a powerful reply to any such argument."[77] According to Peirce, it is not a faculty of mind that allows us to discriminate in these cases but differences in the very things being considered that gives rise to the distinction between the subjective and the objective elements of experience. The difficulties of such discrimination further support both the observation that no such intuitive faculty must exist and Peirce's notion that such discriminations are simply inferences.[78] It seems, therefore, that the discrimination of the subjective and the objective elements of experience is neither necessarily given nor necessarily intuitive.

Peirce's consideration of the fourth question, "Whether we have any power of introspection, or whether our whole knowledge of the internal world is derived from the observation of external facts," bears significant resemblance to Kant's "Refutation of Idealism" in the *Critique of Pure Reason*, but it heads in the opposite direction.[79] Whereas Kant is at pains to prove that there is an external world having already constructed and demonstrated the intuitive existence of the internal world, Peirce is at pains to demonstrate that any inner world that may be supposed is only known through inductive inferences from the external world: "There is a certain set of facts which are ordinarily regarded as external, while others are regarded as internal. The question is whether the latter are known otherwise than by inference from the former."[80] Peirce again is considering whether there is any direct perception of the internal world "not derived from external observation."[81] Here, he holds that although the conjunction of certain conceptions to particular sensations is indeed an operation of the mind, the derivation of the concept of mind from this requires an inference from the attachment of a predicate to something external. Thus, knowledge of the mind so derived is not purely self-reflexive. In addition, the emotions are also products of our interactions with the world and can provide no support for the notion that we can have introspective knowledge. Any knowledge of the mind must, for Peirce, be derived through inferences involving things not simply present to the mind. There can be no bare self-contemplation.

All this bears upon the early modern conception of the mental in that what Peirce is denying is that there can be a faculty of mind that makes possible the supposedly intuitive distinctions that Descartes would enforce. Each and every operation of the mind that is supposed to be explicable and obvious simply through examination of one's mental faculties turns out to be impossible without the consideration of the non-mental: "[C]onsequently, the only way of investigating a psychological question is by inference from external facts."[82] To begin one's philosophical project through the contemplation of an internal world without recognizing that such considerations are not merely intuitive is to invite error. Peirce's argument throughout this article is that the supposition of purely internal faculties discovered by introspection is unnecessary. We need not begin philosophical contemplation with self-examination, and to do so invites skepticism. That each of the faculties that make mind (in the Cartesian sense) necessary can also be explained through reference to the non-mental serves to open the door for the rejection of this conception of mind and the epistemologies built on it. Peirce is arguing that when Descartes begins his philosophical quest, he has already come to assume unnecessary and problematic philosophical notions. This is obvious when one looks to Peirce's follow-up article in *The Journal of Speculative Philosophy*, which begins with Descartes.

Peirce opens the 1868 essay, "Some Consequences of Four Incapacities," with a direct attack on Descartes and the Cartesian method. He notes that the spirit of Cartesianism is alive in philosophy through four suppositions: first, that philosophy must begin with universal doubt; second, that "the ultimate test of certainty is to be found in the individual consciousness"; third, that all argumentation depends upon "a single thread of inference depending often upon inconspicuous premisses"; and fourth, that Cartesianism renders certain things inexplicable, "unless to say that 'God makes them so' is to be regarded as an explanation."[83] The second and third of these suppositions have been attacked by the first essay, and the first and fourth also fall in turn. His attack on the Cartesian conception of mind in the first essay demonstrates that Peirce sees these problems as interrelated and as avoided only through the avoidance of all four suppositions. Peirce considers each to be philosophically dubious and goes to great lengths to show that this is so.

It is within this context that Peirce offers his condemnation of the Cartesian conception of philosophical doubt: "We cannot begin with complete doubt . . . A person may, it is true in the course of his studies, find reason to doubt what he began by believing; but in that case he doubts because he has a positive reason for it, and not on account of the Cartesian maxim. Let us not pretend to doubt in philosophy what we do not doubt in our hearts."[84] No more can Descartes begin with the complete doubt that he claims and construct his philosophical position from there than can the skeptic begin with complete doubt and challenge all comers from there. To begin with complete doubt is to begin with self-deception. It is to leave unacknowledged the dubious conception of mind through which such doubt makes sense. If this conception of mind is not one with which we are naturally saddled, then neither is the doubt that comes with it. Our commerce with the world in our common lives gives us no positive reason to doubt the existence of that world; however, Peirce's assessment of the problems with the Cartesian conception of mind gives us positive reason to doubt that conception of mind. If we thought that our commerce with the world did lead to our doubting its existence, we would not be philosophizing; we would be institutionalized.[85]

In responding to the skeptical hypothesis by rejecting the naturalness of its picture of mind, Peirce's views in these early papers provide an effective rebuttal against the problems that arise from the radical hypothesis that Hume demonstrates. Chapter 4 will take up the more positive aspects of Peirce's conception of doubt and inquiry than we have space for here, but the consequences of such a view on the four-fold skeptical problem will be addressed below. First, in order for the overarching thesis of this project to hold—that Peirce and James are in many regards closer together philosophically than is often assumed—we must turn to James's work to see the ways in which this is the case. Obviously, my choice of dealing with the skeptical problem by pointing to Peirce's understanding of the continuity of thought has been a strategic one. Although it does bear considerably on the pragmatic response to radical skepticism, it also finds close affinities with the later works of William James.

David Lamberth has argued effectively that some of the basic conceptions of James's later radical empiricism find rudimentary form as early as *The Principles of Psychology*.[86] Although it is clear that James's use of the notion of the "stream" of experience in the *Principles* gives way eventually to his more highly developed metaphysics of pure experience in the *Essays in Radical Empiricism*, what is vital here is that we note the ways in which James's arguments for the continuity of thought relate to those expressed by Peirce and offer an effective response to the supposed naturalness of skepticism. In so doing, we will begin to see that the "practical" response to the skeptic from the perspective of our common life is not one that gives way to the asymmetries to which Hume points us.

In his later philosophy, James clearly recognizes the important connection between the rationalism that was his usual foil—whether in Cartesian, Kantian, Hegelian, or Roycean form—and earlier British empiricisms. The rationalist or "intellectualist" tradition with which James wants to contend prefers fixity and universality, but "in spite of Protagoras, Hume, and James Mill, rationalism has never been seriously questioned, for its sharpest critics have always had a tender place in their hearts for it, and have obeyed some of its mandates."[87] James proceeds from this claim to note the ways in which the intellectualist tradition has tackled the problem of motion by making it infinitely divisible into corpuscular parts such that it becomes "*decomposable ad infinitum* by our conception." The result is that we can grasp its many parts, but "of the steps by which that structure actually got composed we know nothing."[88] James clearly recognizes here the internal relationship between making concepts discrete entities and introducing skepticism. The world threatens to recede from us if we pursue the "intellectualist logic" that would "understand life by concepts . . . cutting it up into bits as if with scissors."[89] Neither the rationalist nor his empiricist or skeptical opponents seem to recognize their indebtedness to this way of thinking. James credits Henri Bergson for being radical enough to challenge the authority of this tradition in philosophy. With this dependency noted, it becomes possible to see James's conception of mind and its relationship to the world in their proper light.

James's response to the problems of radical skepticism is, perhaps unsurprisingly, indirect. Given the tangle of intellectualist logic that both the rationalist and the empiricist or skeptic use, any direct attack on their positions would need to be framed in terms with which their interlocutors could agree in order to be effective. Whether or not James consciously intends to respond to skepticism without granting the skeptic's premise, he manages to offer an alternative conception of our cognitive relationship to the world through which we might avoid the problems into which his opponents' conceptions have run.[90] Rather than subdivide the world into subject and object, mind and matter, thought and thing, James attempts to shift the conversation in two important ways. First, he dissolves the conception of the conscious mind as an inner space in which ideas are entertained and offers in its place a functional account of the mental. Second, he uses the highly flexible notion of "experience" as his fundamental category and includes under its aegis not simply our subjective responses to things, but both the things and their relations to each other and to us. Treating each of these in turn, we sketch not only the possible outlines of a Jamesian response to skepticism, but also the beginnings of a larger pragmatism.

James begins sketching his argument with the outright denial of the existence of consciousness as an entity and with it, it seems, a particular understanding of "thought." He links this denial explicitly to his adoption of pragmatism and his attempts to spell out its consequences in full. By the time of the writing of "Does Consciousness Exist?", James had, by his own account, "mistrusted 'consciousness' as an entity" for some twenty years and, more importantly, "suggested its non-existence" to his students for "seven or eight years" and "tried to give them its pragmatic equivalent in realities of experience."[91] James's denial of the existence of consciousness is intended as a denial of the dualism inherent in the Cartesian picture of the world, but its consequences reach considerably further. He explicitly claims that he is denying only "that the word stands for an entity," for some "aboriginal stuff or quality of being, contrasted with that of which material objects are made," but one need not be a dualist of the Cartesian sort for James's denial of consciousness as an entity to apply.

That Cartesian dualism between extended and unextended substances is not James's only target becomes clear when, in the first section of the essay, James turns his attention to Kant and neo-Kantians. He denies first the inherent dualism—even if not substance dualism—of the "object-plus-subject" formulation of the minimum unit of experience and then turns his attention to the possibility of an intuitive conception of consciousness. On the first head, what James is most interested to deny is the notion that consciousness as such, for all its "'epistemological' necessity," is impersonal and passive, "only a witness of happenings in time, in which it plays no part." On such a view, all the activities belong to the content of the experience while consciousness serves simply as its "logical correlative." The difficulty here is that rather than being an element of experience, consciousness becomes entirely removed from it, and we are left without "direct evidence of its being there."[92] What we think we experience when we think of ourselves as conscious is something that ever eludes our grasp. This leads directly, then, to the second head, where James attacks the possibility of an intuitive conception of consciousness.

When confronting the possibility of an intuitive conception of consciousness, James notes the duplicity of those who defend the notion of consciousness as an entity. While on the one hand suggesting that it might "be felt as a kind of impalpable inner flowing," the defenders of consciousness agree, on the other hand, that it is notoriously slippery and difficult to isolate. James picks particularly on G. E. Moore and Paul Natorp. Quoting Moore's claim that consciousness is distinguishable "if we know that there is something to look for" and Natorp's claim that the existence of consciousness "can be brought out by analysis," James makes explicit the dualistic implication that there is a separable entity of which we might be somehow aware.[93] There are two difficulties here. The first is that if the object-plus-subject were the minimum unit of experience, then becoming aware of consciousness as such would be impossible. However, James recognizes that this need not plague Moore or Natorp insofar as they are free to argue that one can distinguish what one cannot in fact separate, as one might when thinking of a blue pen as being both "blue" and a "pen." The second, and more important, criticism is that knowing "that there is something to look for" that "can be brought out by analysis" might be no more than an assumption on the parts of Moore and Natorp. Looking for two distinguishable factors in experience, we might find them only because they are what we are looking for.[94] By contrast, James argues that it is not by subtracting content from form that we come to understand what consciousness is, but by *adding* the entity of consciousness to the content that we arrive at the duplicity of experience.

James's functional account of the mental stands in contrast to the view offered by Moore and Natorp in two distinct ways: first, to call an experience "conscious" is to note that it plays a particular role within the larger context of "pure experience"; it is to note its functional relationships to other bits of experience. Second, to call his account of consciousness "functional" is to note that it is a particular kind of relationship within this larger context; it is to note that consciousness can be taken as both subjective and objective and that it is verifiable and concrete.

To say that a conscious experience is a particular functional relationship within the wider field of pure experience is to note two important things in James's account. First, taken in its broadest form, pure experience is entirely monistic; there is no dualism present at all. From this monistic field of experience, one might differentiate into various "bits" conjoined by a various relationships, but in its most basic form, all experience has the same metaphysical status. Within this field of pure experience, "knowing" identifies a particular cognitive relationship among "bits" of this experience. "Knower" and "known" share the same metaphysical status as bits of pure experience, and "knowing" expresses the relationship between these two bits. For James, then, to identify a relationship as "cognitive" is not to identify that relationship as having a special metaphysical or epistemological status; rather, it is simply to categorize it as one kind of *relation* between or among bits of pure experience.[95] Second, taken as a "functional" relationship, it is inherently unstable. A relationship between two bits of pure experiences that serves one function in a particular instance might serve another in others. The relationship of "knowing," which consciousness is intended to explain, is, for James, simply one such functional relationship. We might in other instances further identify conjunctive and disjunctive relations between bits of pure experience of different types that would serve other functions. Nonetheless, this instability does not undermine either the reality of the relationship or the function of the relationship within the field of pure experience. For the explanation of this, we can turn to the second point of divergence between Moore and Natorp on the one hand and James on the other.

Insofar as relationships are themselves bits of experience, "as real as anything else in the system," and that consciousness is one such relationship, the relationship of knowing, James argues that "knowing" is verifiable and "consciousness" is concrete.[96] To make sense of this dual claim one must take account of the intentional ambiguity in James's notion of "experience." For him, each bit of experience is a single "that" in its "first intention." Ignoring its manifold relations in this way, the experience can act as either object or mental state, depending upon the context in which it functions. "In its pure state, or when isolated, there is no self-splitting of it into consciousness and what the consciousness is 'of.'"[97] It is only the experience's functional relations with other bits of pure experience that allow us to view it as either "thought" or "thing"—or, in one of James's other favorite formulations, "thought" or "thought-of." The functional relations into which each bit enters resolve this fundamental ambiguity: "Its subjectivity and objectivity are functional attributes solely, realized only when the experience is 'taken,' *i.e.*, talked-of, twice, considered along with its two differing contexts respectively."[98] Because these functional relationships are as real as anything else in the system, they become concrete bits of experience in their own right. Thus, the relationship of knowing can become an object for verification along pragmatic lines, and the notion of consciousness can be a concrete object of investigation. Either these relationships obtain, in the sense of serving the functions intended by them, or they do not.[99]

James's battle against the existence of consciousness as a separable entity is thus set clearly within the larger milieu of his thesis of radical empiricism. As noted in Chapter 1, however, separating this thesis of radical empiricism from his pragmatism is no easy task. In exploring a few pieces of James's radical empiricism here, I have attempted to remain within the confines of those particular functional aspects of radical empiricism that James sees as both identifiable and pragmatically viable. Although the thesis of radical empiricism is metaphysical in the sense of positing the existence of the singular entity of pure experience as the basic stuff of the universe, the focus here has been on the question of consciousness and James's approach to it as a hypothesis. In the sense in which pragmatism itself is outlined in Chapter 4, this is to treat the notion of consciousness as a genuine hypothesis and ask what its appreciable effects would be were it to exist. James offers that so far as the Cartesian conception goes, it would have few. At the same time, James sees his overall project in these later essays as addressing the problems that arise through the early modern conceptions of "mind" and "idea" that give rise to radical skepticism. His approach with regard to skepticism and consciousness is to subject them, as hypotheses, to the pragmatic method itself and offer a negative assessment of their import and efficacy. In sketching an alternative in which the knowing relationship becomes a concrete relationship, James then offers a further account that would itself be subject to further pragmatic investigation. Thus, although James's radical empiricism and pragmatism are related, they remain separable, if complementary, ideas.

It should be noted here that the accounts of Peirce and James that I have offered thus far do not necessarily agree. On the one hand, Peirce points to the designation of "subjective" and "objective" elements in experience as being identifiable because of differences between the objects of experience rather than through the intuiting powers of the mind. Furthermore, his argument for the continuity of ideas with external objects seems to indicate the very kind of metaphysical realism—if not direct empiricism—against which I argued in Chapter 1. On the other hand, James points to the designation of subject and object as arising from the functional relationship between two bits of pure experience. He also argues for the concrete reality of these functional relations and, thereby, seems to be tilting in the direction of idealism if not metaphysical antirealism. Thus, it might seem that Peirce is arguing for a difference in kind while James is arguing for a difference in function and that both men are at least headed in different directions, if they are not on a collision course.

In order to avoid this perception, two reminders are in order. First, the point of this chapter was to show the depths to which Peirce and James went in their criticisms of the Cartesian conception of mind that gives rise to radical skepticism. Although both offer alternatives, these alternatives were not fully sketched here because the larger point is to show the sustained nature of the attack on Cartesianism made by Peirce and James. Nonetheless, we have seen a few common features of their views that will arise again when we consider their pragmatism more fully. Both Peirce and James deny—albeit in different manners—the notion of an inherent intuiting faculty of the mind through which our consideration of ideas as objects of investigation is made. Both also deny the notion that this intuiting faculty could be explained without reference to something intuited, some object of consideration or investigation that arises apart from the particular experience or investigation. Finally, Peirce and James see these moves as necessary for the avoidance of the Cartesian conception of mind and the multi-headed hydra of radical skepticism that comes with it. Insofar as our purpose here is the largely negative one of showing the distance between Peirce's and James's views of thought and consciousness and those that provide skepticism with its naturalness, the tension between their constructive views need not be addressed here, but it will arise again in the following chapter. There is a tension here worth noting, but it is not one that is ultimately destructive of the argument being made—at least, not yet.

Second, when it comes to the comparison of objects of investigation and their externality to the particular experience or investigation—that is, Peirce's apparent metaphysical realism and James's apparent metaphysical antirealism—I can but beg the reader's patience. What emerges in Chapter 4 is an argument for pragmatism's metaphysical neutrality, and much of the chapter is dedicated to making that argument from within the particular confines of pragmatic inquiry as defended there. Inquiry and its objects are clearly internally related for Peirce and James. What we have begun to address here is how this inquiry is to be conducted, what faculties might be involved in doing so, and what capacities we might have for success. By dealing with skepticism in the way that they have, I would argue that at least the first half of the couplet "mind-independence" ceases to have the sense it is intended to have in later discussions between metaphysical realism and metaphysical antirealism. This not only blunts the force of radical skepticism but also points us toward the examination of the second half of the couplet in the following chapter.

Pragmatism and Hume's Problems

In concluding this chapter, it should be clear how I think Peirce and James deal with the four problems affiliated with radical skepticism. The problem of the symmetry between any particular proposition one might ordinarily be considered to know and the skeptical hypothesis arises when these are viewed in isolation. "I have two hands" and "I do not know that I am not a brain in a vat" seem—without the marks of clarity and distinctness that Descartes thought we ought to find—to be symmetrical propositions. Skepticism's naturalness is apparent in being expressible in terms of platitudes we all accept. It seems a fairly simple thing to arrive at the skeptical hypothesis through the slightest philosophical reflection. In light of this naturalness, theoretical responses to radical skepticism suffer from the first problem of asymmetry. Their construction might either involve the denial of these platitudes or the philosophical construction of a far more complicated and less intuitive picture of our cognitive relationship to the world. If we choose not to engage the skeptic in argument, recognizing that radical skepticism cannot be toppled by philosophical theory, our response suffers from the second problem of asymmetry. Once having yielded the study to the skeptic, living our common lives can do little to dispel the instability of our knowledge claims. Claims to practical knowledge or hopes for practical responses to skepticism ring hollow even among the most ardent of their supporters. They are a mere "bluff" in the face of overwhelming doubt.

In responding to the problems of radical skepticism, the reading of Peirce and James offered has argued for a dual approach. First, they argue against the supposedly intuitive conception of a world neatly divisible into its objective and subjective elements, the latter being attributable to consciousness, and for a functional understanding of our interactions with the world. Second, they argue against the possibility of an isolable idea and for the continuity of thought. The first set of arguments undercuts the supposed naturalness of skepticism and, thereby, offers responses to both asymmetry problems. The second set of arguments addresses more directly the problem of symmetry. We can take each of these in turn.

By showing that the skeptic imports philosophical prejudices into the reflective process that gives us radical skepticism, Peirce and James each argue in their own way against the naturalness of skepticism. Peirce's direct assault on the Cartesian method is not inveighed simply to show Descartes' neglect of the more practical uses of reasoning but to show Cartesian doubt to assume a conception of mind that is neither necessary nor natural. Descartes assumes faculties of intuition and self-reflection for the mind that

Peirce argues we have no good reason to accept. Insofar as Descartes arrives at these conceptions by invoking a state of mind in which no one actually finds herself, the conceptions are less intuitive or natural than Descartes would like us to assume. James argues against the conception of consciousness at work in philosophy—whether of a Cartesian, Humean, or Kantian sort. On the one hand, James notes the ephemeral nature of consciousness on these earlier conceptions and reveals the theoretical assumptions underlying such conceptions; on the other, he argues for a concrete and verifiable conception of consciousness grounded in his radical empiricism. Although both Peirce's and James's understandings of our cognitive capacities deserve scrutiny, the important point here is how each recognized the *unnaturalness* of the conception of consciousness that underlies the skeptic's doubts. Once this is diagnosed, skepticism loses its easy foothold.

If skepticism operates with certain assumptions that are not as natural as they have been made to appear, then the first problem of asymmetry can be rather easily dissolved. Neither the radical skeptic nor his or her philosophical opponent begins with the more intuitive understanding of our cognitive relationship to the world. That is, the explanation of the skeptic's position in terms of "platitudes we all accept" is actually illusory. A close study of the background of the skeptic's doubts—rather than the bare hypothesis in which it is expressed—reveals these doubts to have theoretical underpinnings. Peirce's response to Descartes in the articles for *The Journal of Speculative Philosophy* ought to be seen in this light. His rejection of "certain faculties claimed for man" shows the philosophical apparatus to be just that, philosophical and not intuitive. James's contention that the conception of consciousness at work in other epistemologies is created "by addition" reveals the background to be theoretical as well. Although one might find epistemological responses to the skeptic's doubts unsatisfying, this will not be because the skeptic argues without theoretical assumptions. One might choose to share the skeptic's assumptions, like Descartes, and hope for a resolution to the skeptic's doubts, or one might choose to reject these assumptions. Insofar as the underpinnings are not natural but optional, the burden in responding to skepticism does not fall disproportionately upon the respondent. It is, at least, a fair fight.

If it is indeed a fair fight in the study, then the second problem of asymmetry—the asymmetry between deep philosophical doubt and the practical response of our common life—can also be dissolved. Although it is true that Peirce and James offer what might be seen as *practical* responses to the skeptic's doubts, these are set against a larger background of philosophical arguments from both. The second asymmetry problem, though, is dissolved when we come to recognize that the skeptic's doubts do not reveal a deep and natural instability in our claims to knowledge. Insofar as Peirce and James respond pragmatically to skepticism, emphasizing the importance of the practical, their pragmatism is no "bluff." Rather, it is an attempt to show the *actual* stability in our claims to knowledge against the *theoretical* instability offered by the skeptic. That we move rather readily between the actual and the theoretical reveals that there is likely greater continuity between the philosophical study and our common lives than the radical skeptic supposes there to be.

If thoughts cannot be isolated from one another and entertained in the space of the conscious mind—behind the veil of ideas—then the problem of symmetry can be dissolved as well. Peirce argues that thoughts are continuous with one another and cannot be clearly delineated. If we cannot consider a thought in isolation, then we must consider its relations to other thoughts and the route by which we arrived at it. There might be no distinct marks that show one proposition to be better founded than another, but there are chains of inferences that can be examined and understood. These connected thoughts can be understood not merely through their sources, but also through their leadings. By examining thoughts in this way, we can see the consequences, both conceptual and practical, of adopting one line of reasoning over another.[100] For James, all experience lies within the vast field of pure experience taken metaphysically. As such, thought is, by its very nature, continuous in a deeply metaphysical sense; each thought is a bit of experience, connected to other bits of experience by relationships that are themselves possible experiences. Although an argument that the continuity of thought can overturn the skeptical hypothesis has not been constructed here, the symmetry problem revealed by Hume rests upon the isolability of individual thoughts. Insofar as Peirce and James reject this notion, the burden lies on the skeptic to show that the symmetry problem could arise again.

Although Descartes' malicious demon has been replaced by an evil scientist, the problem that he introduced to philosophical discussion continues to plague it. This chapter has offered hints toward the more positive pragmatic response to the skeptical hypothesis, but the primary interest here has been to show the ways in which Peirce and James reject the theoretical underpinnings of the skeptical hypothesis itself. Thus, the project of the chapter has been largely negative. Such an approach might not satisfy the most ardent of skeptics or anti-skeptics. Although the student coming home for the holidays in our earlier example may have taken skepticism only seriously enough to try her mother's patience, philosophers continue to take such skepticism seriously while constructing philosophical systems. Even Richard Rorty, who so helpfully identifies the source of Cartesian skepticism, continues to take seriously the project of defeating the skeptic.[101] If our first-year philosophy student decides to take such skepticism seriously, she will at least have good company at the philosophical "kids' table." Nonetheless, the negative project that has been engaged here is an important one. If the four problems arising from Descartes' skeptical hypothesis can be diagnosed in the way that Williams suggests, then the debate with the skeptic can—at the very least—be recast. The more positive argument of this chapter has been that Peirce and James were engaged in such a recasting by rejecting the theoretical assumptions upon which radical skepticism is based. Peirce and James both took the challenge of skepticism quite seriously, but both recognized the importance of undermining the supposed intuitiveness of the larger conception of our cognitive relationship to the world as a response to the skeptic. The upshot of the chapter, then, can be put as a nested conditional: if Hume is right in showing the four problems of skepticism and if Rorty is right in showing their relationship to the Cartesian conception of mind and if Williams is right in showing the way to undermine the skeptic is to undermine the supposed naturalness of the hypothesis, then Peirce and James offer a response to skepticism that is adequate to the latter two conditions and thus dissolves the problems of the first.

Chapter 3

Thoughts, Things, and Theories

In *Philosophy and the Mirror of Nature*, Richard Rorty argues that the creation of the inner world of the mind leads both to skepticism and to Epistemology, Philosophy's own special field in which a theory of knowledge can be constructed. The Philosopher's duty is to provide the link between the inner world of mind and the outer world of sensation, thereby overcoming the skeptic: "The eventual demarcation of philosophy from science was made possible by the notion that philosophy's core was 'theory of knowledge,' a theory distinct from the sciences because it was their *foundation*."[1] Rorty contends that the creation of this "theory of knowledge" became the philosopher's quest *par excellence* such that philosophy became Epistemology, the singular search for the foundational theory that would defeat the skeptic. In order to become foundational, Epistemology had to be "independent of physiological discoveries and capable of producing necessary truths." Philosophy could not interfere in the province of the sciences but had to somehow be beyond it. It had to be "a *nonempirical* project" that supplemented the empirical projects of the natural sciences.[2]

Descartes' conception of mind as the inner theater behind the veil of ideas provided the first step. It gave this new discipline its object and method. Locke added to Descartes' project by attempting to make it scientific in accordance with the Newtonian model.[3] Locke's hope was to find out how the objects of the mind interacted, thus allowing for a normative "science of man" to complement Newtonian physics. The former would discover the laws of "inner space," and the latter the laws of "outer space."[4] However, this separation of the provinces of philosophy and science proves unsatisfactory. Hume was able to show that the Epistemologist is engaged in a paradoxical enterprise: having admitted the skeptic's doubt and its naturalness in order to mark out the inner world, the Philosopher is unable to quell this doubt.[5]

On Rorty's reading, Kant becomes the seminal figure in Philosophy that he is because of his novel invention for quieting the skeptic. Kant moved the "outer world" into the "inner world" through his "discovery" of "the constituting activity of the transcendental ego." If what we thought of as the outer world were also subject to the conceptual activities of the mind, then we could claim apodictic certainty "for the laws of what had previously been thought to be outer."[6] The "transcendental" of Kant's "transcendental idealism" is precisely this move: "The Copernican revolution was based on the notion that we can only know about objects a priori if we 'constitute' them, and Kant was never troubled by the question of how we could have apodictic knowledge of these 'constituting activities,' for Cartesian privileged access was supposed to take care of that."[7] Our knowledge is certain because it is knowledge of objects we have made, and only we can make the objects of which we have knowledge. Our intuitive faculties take care of the constituting, and we make judgments on the basis of objects so constituted. "Kant let us see ourselves as deciding... what nature was allowed to be like."[8] The "outer world" is brought into the "inner world," thus removing the gap that the skeptic exploits.

In order to keep his idealism from becoming absolute, Kant posits another gap between the knower and the known: that between the manifold (the noumenon) and the constituted appearances (the phenomena.)[9] This manifold is defined negatively in terms of the constituted; it is that which is absolutely incognizable through the forms of sensible intuition, which are the constituting faculties through which everything is known.[10] That is, Kant sets the bounds of sense through the forms of sensible intuition and then tells us what lies beyond them, the noumenon. In nothing less than a derisive tone, Kant goes on to tell us that although Epistemology stands on solid ground when dealing with the appearances that lie on this side of the bounds of sense, metaphysics supposes itself to offer "knowledge lying beyond experience."[11] Metaphysics is the project of describing what cannot in any way be experienced; its object is the noumenon, which is entirely independent of mind.

Having shown in Chapter 2 how the pragmatists avoid Epistemology conceived of as refutation of the skeptic by avoiding the concept of mind at play in such Epistemologies, it may seem that what we are left with is what J. E. Tiles has called "a world without withins."[12] Because the pragmatists reject the conception of the inner world at play in epistemology, this leaves open at least three possibilities regarding their positive stance on metaphysics. Peirce and James might claim that the world of objects has a structure that mirrors the mental or that it simply is mental. This would seem to align them quite readily with idealists of either the objective or the absolute type.[13] The pragmatists might claim that we do actually have knowledge of the objects that constitute our experience apart from the constitutive activities of the mind. This would seem to align them quite readily with the British empiricists who thought that the objects of sense were directly derivative from the objects in the world.[14] Similarly, the pragmatists could claim a causal link between the objects of our experience and the objects that lie beyond them. This would seem to align them with those contemporary philosophers who view mind as simply the determined causal product of material processes. Of this last group, Hilary Putnam notes that such philosophers view philosophy without Epistemology as the project of "commenting on and speculating about the progress of science, especially as it bears or seems to bear on the various traditional problems of philosophy." To their minds, "The best metaphysics is physics, or, more precisely . . . the best metaphysics is what the positivists called 'unified science,' science pictured as based on and unified by the application of the laws of fundamental physics."[15] Epistemology thus becomes cognitive science, the study of the ways in which neurological processes can be explained in terms of laws of biological interactions, which are reducible to the laws of physics. Given the pragmatists' general love of science and the scientific method, this last possibility would seem somewhat likely.

These characterizations of what is left to pragmatism given its stance on the concept of mind at play in Epistemology could only be accurate if the pragmatists somehow rejected that concept of mind but kept the notion of body or independence on the other side of the dichotomy. This chapter will explore that notion, looking at both its Kantian and its contemporary manifestations. We have already seen that for the pragmatists there is no independent, self-constituting "within." What remains to be shown is that there is also no "without," that which is entirely independent of any possible conceptions of it.

Kant and the Noumenon

There are two specific reasons for looking to Kant rather than Descartes for the conception of the world outside the mind that remains after the conception of mind is rejected. The first is methodological and the second is philosophical. First, I agree with Hilary Putnam, who writes at the beginning of his "Realism with a Human Face": "[A]lmost all the problems of philosophy attain the form in which they are of real interest only with the work of Kant."[16] Putnam's claim is rather straightforward: although it is far from true that all contemporary philosophers are Kantians, it remains the case that all of us carry significant philosophical baggage with Kant's name on the tag. The problems with which we are forced to deal on a regular basis have both the shape and weight that they do because of Kant's work.[17] It would be difficult to deny that Kant is a seminal figure looming over twentieth-century philosophy. Second, if we look at the way in which Kant sets up the division between noumenon and phenomena, it becomes obvious that the noumenon in one sense of Kant's conception of it could remain independently of his conception of mind. The noumenon is simply the manifold; it is what it is no matter what we may think of it. Thus, it is not tied to phenomena or to mind in any way. We could get rid of Kant's scheme with its constitutive activities of the mind and still be left with a noumenon. There is no logical problem here. We could get rid of Kant's mind but be left with his objects.

To begin the discussion of the noumenon in Kant, it is important to start with an account of what Kant means by "object." The assertion that Kant uses the term in at least two senses in the exposition of his position is commonplace in the literature. The first sense is the broadest: an object is the subject of a possible judgment.[18] In this first sense, the pure concepts of the understanding can be seen as objects. There is also a second, "weighty" sense of the term: an object is something that can be experienced. In this second sense, only that which can be represented—that is, only an appearance—can be an object because only those things which take on the forms of sensible intuition can be experienced.[19]

There is, however, a third sense in which Kant uses the term "object," and it is this sense that relates most directly to the project at hand. This third is the transcendental sense: the transcendental object is the thing-in-itself, independent of either any judgment about it or any sensible intuition of it.[20] This transcendental object has a dual function as both the correlate of the unity of appearances and the ground of appearances in general. This is only so because the transcendental object is nothing determinate. It is only a general "completely indeterminate thought of *something* in general."[21] However, this will prove problematic. Kant asserts both that we can have no knowledge of the transcendental object, the thing-in-itself, and then goes on to assert that it serves two positive functions and is "no arbitrary invention."[22] It must, therefore, be "out there" somewhere beyond the grasp of human intuition and knowledge, grounding it and serving as its correlate.[23] If we turn to a brief discussion of Kant's conception of the noumenon, this becomes clearer.

Negative and positive noumena

According to Kant, noumena (or transcendental objects) serve two distinct functions in human knowledge: first, the noumenon serves as a logical placeholder, negatively defined as the non-sensible; second, the noumena serve as objects of purely intellectual intuition, positively defined as that of which we have no knowledge because their existence lies beyond the conditions of our sensibility. In the end, the noumenon in the negative sense serves human knowledge as marking its outer limit, but noumena in the positive sense can only be asserted problematically and are, therefore, meaningless for the material extension of human knowledge. However, Kant still holds that this world must exist, that there are things-in-themselves that are what they are independently of any possible conception of them.[24]

The idea that the noumena serve a function in human *knowledge* is a bit misleading. If we review what Kant holds to be the conditions of human knowledge, this becomes obvious. Strictly defined, knowledge arises through the application of pure concepts of the understanding to objects. These pure concepts of the understanding, the categories, provide knowledge only through their application to the objects of sensible intuition. As Kant reminds us: "Without sensibility no object would be given to us, without understanding no object would be thought. Thoughts without content are empty, intuitions without concepts are blind."[25] Although it is possible to *think* a thing without sensible intuition, it is impossible to *know* that thing without sensible intuition. Although the categories do serve the function of providing the logical form for any data, the categories have only empirical employment in the creation of knowledge. This empirical employment of a concept is "its application *merely to appearances*; that is, to objects of possible experience."[26] Without this empirical employment the categories lack meaning and cannot be said to provide knowledge. Kant concludes: "We therefore demand that a bare concept be *made sensible*, that is, that an object corresponding to it be presented in intuition. Otherwise the concept would, as we say, be without *sense*, that is, without meaning."[27] In order for us to have any knowledge, both the concept and its object must be present. Thus, the general conditions for human knowledge are the synthetic unity of apperception and sensible intuition. Because the synthetic unity of apperception is given a priori and exists only in the understanding, its function is entirely formal; it is sensible intuition that provides the material condition of human knowledge. In this way sensible intuition marks the limits of human knowledge, and what is non-sensible must be said to lie outside its realm. This is simply to say that only Kant's "weighty" objects, appearances, can be known.

Kant understands the noumenon as whatever lies beyond the sensible: the noumenon is anything that is not available to our sensible intuition and not conditioned by its forms. He writes: "If by 'noumenon' we mean a thing so far as it is *not an object of our sensible intuition*, and so abstract from our mode of intuiting it, this is a noumenon in the negative sense of the term."[28] In this negative definition of the noumenon, two points come to the fore: first, that the noumenon itself cannot be an object of sensible intuition— that is, that the noumenon can *only be thought* if we abstract completely from our modes of intuition; second, that in order for the noumenon to mean anything positively, Kant must draw a distinction between sensible intuition and some other possible form of intuition.

As stated above, we can *know* only those things that are available to our sensible intuition, and all objects of our sensible intuition must be conditioned by the a priori forms of sensible intuition, space and time, or, at least, time. Remembering Kant's position on space and time developed in the "Transcendental Aesthetic," only objects of sensible intuition can be said to be spatial or temporal. Because the noumenon is non-sensible, we cannot apply the forms of our intuition to it. The pure form of our intuition grants temporality to the appearances in our experience but cannot grant temporality to objects that are non-sensible. We intuit these appearances in time and cannot intuit them otherwise. No object withdrawn from the condition of temporality can be a possible object of human knowledge, nor can any object be given to our sensible intuition without the condition of time. Therefore, the non-sensibility of the noumenon itself abstracts it from the forms of our sensible intuition, the only forms through which anything can be known.

Because the noumenon is non-sensible and thus not conditioned by time, the categories cannot apply to it: "For the categories have meaning only in relation to the unity of intuition in space and time; and even this unity they can determine, by means of general a priori connecting concepts, only because of the mere ideality of space and time."[29] As the arguments of the "Transcendental Aesthetic" applied above, those of the "Schemata" apply here. There can be no transcendental determinations of time in relation to the noumenon; therefore, the categories cannot apply directly to it. Of the application of the categories to the non-temporal, Kant writes: "In cases where this unity of time is not to be found, and therefore in the case of the noumenon, all employment, and indeed the whole meaning of the categories, entirely vanishes; for we have then no means of determining whether things in harmony with the categories are even possible."[30] Far from allowing us to intuit the noumenon non-sensibly, the categories cannot be thought to apply at all. The categories themselves have only an empirical employment in relation to objects of experience through the pure form of inner and outer sense, time. Withdrawn from this unity of time (as the noumenon is), the categories can offer no knowledge of what this noumenon may be.

Through these arguments regarding the inapplicability of both sensible intuition and the categories to the noumenon, the first point of the negative definition of the noumenon is made:

> The doctrine of sensibility is likewise the doctrine of the noumenon in the negative sense—that is, of things which the understanding must think without this reference to our mode of intuition, therefore, not merely as appearances but as things-in-themselves. At the same time, the understanding is well aware that in viewing things in this manner, as thus apart from our mode of intuition, it cannot make any use of the categories.[31]

Sensibility serves as the limiting principle of knowledge, and whatever lies beyond its bounds is noumenal and thus unknowable. Nothing to which neither sensible intuition nor the categories apply can be considered as playing a positive role in human knowledge. The thing-in-itself is wholly independent of the mental.

The second point made in this negative definition provides the bridge to what may be seen as the positive definition of the noumenon. Although Kant limits human knowledge to what is available to sensible intuition and the categories, the possibility that there may be a kind of intuition, which is not sensible, is left open. This form of intuition, which, he assures us, is wholly unavailable to human beings, Kant terms "intellectual intuition." Although we are not possessed of such a faculty, it is indeed possible for us to imagine what it would be. Intellectual intuition would be a mode of intuiting objects without the constraints of space and time and the categories; it would be akin to the ability of the understanding to *think* a thing aside from these conditions although the thing cannot be *known* in this way. Of this mode of intuition Kant writes: "That is to say, we have an understanding which *problematically* extends further [than sensible intuition], but we have no intuition . . . through which objects outside the field of sensibility can be given, and through which the understanding can be employed *assertorically* beyond that field."[32] We are possessed of a faculty to *think* things in this way, but we can in no way *know* them to be so. If it could be proven that we do possess a faculty of intellectual intuition, then we would have means of knowing the noumena and would be able to assert apodictically noumena in a positive sense, as things-in-themselves.

Positive noumena

Noumena in the positive sense follow directly from the limits established by the noumenon in the negative sense. The special form of intuition implied by the negative definition of the noumenon would have noumena in the positive sense as its object: "But if we understand by it an *object* of a *non-sensible intuition*, we thereby presuppose a special mode of intuition, namely, the intellectual, which is not that which we possess, and of which we cannot comprehend even the possibility. This would be 'noumenon' in the *positive* sense of the term."[33] This statement is puzzling at best. On the one hand, Kant seems to be positing exactly what Hegel, on Mounce's reading addressed in Chapter 1, claims he does—that there is some sort of thing, noumenon in the positive sense, that lies on the other side of the limits of human knowledge. On the other hand, Kant claims that we cannot comprehend even the possibility of such a thing. The key to making the kind of sense we need of this quotation is to note that the final clause of the first sentence must modify "a special mode of intuition, namely, the intellectual" and not "object of non-sensible intuition." That is, we can think of the possibility of an object of non-sensible intuition, but we cannot comprehend the possibility of a purely intellectual intuition because we can only comprehend possibilities through the application of the categories. Noumena in the positive sense can be thought but not cognized or known.

This is not to say that we cannot imagine the possibility of an intellectual intuition or that we may not be able to consider such a thing. We cannot *comprehend* the possibility of an intellectual intuition or the objects that such an intuition would intuit because our knowledge—and, thereby, our comprehension—is limited to the possibilities available to us through sensible intuition. That Kant does not mean that intellectual intuition cannot even be imagined is obvious from the fact that he does indeed discuss the possibility of such an intuition and the possibility of knowing things-in-themselves through it. Like the negative definition of the noumenon, the positive definition of noumena brings two points to the fore: first, that noumena can indeed be thought; second, that noumena would be the objects of intellectual intuition if such an intuition could be proven to exist.

The fact that we can imagine noumena in the positive sense helps to explain why we often think, like the transcendental realist, that the understanding can provide knowledge of things as they are in themselves.[34] Because the pure concepts of the understanding can be thought without the conditions of space and time, they can be thought without determinate objects. However, they are only forms that admit of no empirical knowledge when considered in this way: "[I]f . . . I leave aside all intuition, the form of thought still remains—that is the mode of determining an object for the manifold of possible intuition."[35] The understanding provides forms of thought and, therefore, extends to things in general, undetermined by the forms of sensible intuition. As stated above, it is possible to *think* of a noumenal object in this way, but it would be false to believe that this means that these pure concepts can be *applied* to this noumenal object. Kant claims: "The categories accordingly extend further than sensible intuition, since they think objects in general without regard to the special mode (the sensibility) in which they may be given. But they do not thereby determine a greater sphere of objects."[36] Objects can only be determined through the forms of sensible intuition; thus, the application of the categories is only possible through sensible intuition. If we were capable of another form of intuition that could intuit objects apart from the conditions of sensible intuition, then a transcendental employment of the understanding would be possible, and our thoughts of noumena would be knowledge of noumena in the positive sense. As it is, our thoughts of noumena in the positive sense often serve only to delude us into believing that we can extend our knowledge beyond its empirical reach to a transcendental knowledge of things-in-themselves. Kant's definition of noumena in the positive sense helps to explain our delusions of knowledge of it. It is only a thought and, thus, only a possibility.

Anything that is given to sensible intuition is an appearance, and every appearance is conditioned by space and time. To think a thing in the understanding, apart from the forms of sensible intuition, is to consider that thing not as an appearance, but as it is in itself. Although the following quote from the "Transcendental Doctrine of Judgment" does not employ either the term "intellectual intuition" or the words "things-in-themselves," the possibility of the existence of intellectual intuition and things-in-themselves is obvious in it:

> For if the senses represent to us something merely *as it appears*, this something must also in itself be a thing, and an object of non-sensible intuition, that is, of the understanding. In other words, a [kind of] knowledge must be possible, in which there is no sensibility, and which alone has reality that is absolutely objective. Through it objects will be represented *as they are*, whereas in the empirical employment of our understanding things will be known only *as they appear*.[37]

From such an employment of the understanding we can consider noumena apart from the conditions of space and time, as things-in-themselves. In this way the doctrine of things-in-themselves can be said to be the doctrine of noumena in the positive sense. Although this positive sense of noumena lies outside the possibilities of human knowledge, it cannot be said that noumena as things-in-themselves are an impossibility. The fact that we can consider such things provides grounds for the possibility of their existence, although it cannot establish it apodictically.

In order to truly know things-in-themselves we would have to possess the faculty of intellectual intuition, but this faculty cannot be proven to exist. Therefore, in our thinking we assume such a thing in order to assume the existence of things-in-themselves and have a concept of noumena as objects that ground what Karl-Otto Apel has called "the objective validity of science."[38]

> However, in order that a noumenon may signify a true object, distinguishable from all phenomena, it is not enough that I *free* my thought from all conditions of sensible intuition; I must likewise have grounds for *assuming* another kind of intuition, apart from the sensible, in which such an object can be given or else my thought, while indeed without contradictions, is nonetheless empty.[39]

The difficulty in positing the existence of such an intuition expressed in the first edition is given more concrete form when Kant more clearly expresses a definition of noumena in the positive sense. The noumena can be defined positively only because of the possibility of the purely intellectual intuition that Kant's negative definition of the noumenon implies.

In the end, the concept of noumenon/noumena functions in human knowledge both negatively and positively, and a tension exists between these negative and positive functions. Negatively, the noumenon marks the limits of sensible intuition and what can be known. Positively, noumena are things-in-themselves, objects known by intellectual intuition unconditioned by space and time. Negatively, the noumenon cannot be known because it is not an object of experience and thus not temporally determined. Positively, the noumena can be considered as unconditioned by space and time but determined as objects for purely intellectual concepts. Put simply, the noumenon in the negative sense is a recognition of the limits of what can be known by us; the noumena in the positive sense are a recognition of the possibility for other forms of intuition and, thereby, knowledge. Kant concludes his discussion of the noumenon as follows:

> When, therefore, we say that the senses represent objects as they appear, and the understanding objects as they are, the latter statement is to be taken, not in the transcendental, but merely in the empirical meaning of the terms, namely as meaning that the objects must be represented as objects of experience,[40] that is, as appearances in thoroughgoing interconnection with one another, and not as they may be apart from their

relation to possible experience (and consequently to any senses), as objects of the pure understanding.[41] Such objects of pure understanding will always remain unknown to us; we can never even know whether such a transcendental or exceptional knowledge is possible under any condition . . . *Understanding and sensibility,* with us, can determine objects *only when they are employed in conjunction.* When we separate them, we have intuitions without concepts, or concepts without intuitions—in both cases, representations which we are not in a position to apply to any determinate object.[42]

When we employ the understanding and sensible intuitions separately, all we can achieve are blind thoughts and empty intuitions. The negative definition of the noumenon relates the noumenon to sensible intuition and through sensible intuition to the understanding. As such, the negative definition serves a role in human knowledge as the prescription of its limits. The positive role of the noumena is as a purely intellectual concept—a pure concept of the understanding. As such, it is a possibility—but not a source or object—of human knowledge.

The entirety of the above account is given from the standpoint of human knowledge, and what I have tried to show therein is that neither the noumenon nor the noumena (transcendental objects) can function as objects for human knowledge. The thing-in-itself—the real, mind-independent object—is entirely unknowable for human beings because our intuition or perception of an object is merely the perception of an appearance, which may or may not be caused by a thing-in-itself.[43] The objects with which we deal as human beings are simply things as they appear to us through the forms of sensible intuition and the categories. These appearances are, therefore, mind-dependent. We are without a faculty that would allow us to see the connection, if one exists, between the thing-in-itself and the thing-as-it-appears, the mind-independent (transcendental) and mind-dependent (weighty) object. However, Kant does leave open the possibility for a pure intellectual intuition that has as its object the thing-in-itself. This purely objective view of reality from the standpoint of pure intellectual intuition is the world as it really is, apart from human minds. It is, in other words, the fixed totality of mind-independent objects, what the world would be apart from any possible conception of it.

This discussion brings to the fore three distinct ways in which these mind-independent objects are "independent" from human minds. The first two ways are causal, and the final way is cognitive. First, mind-independent objects do not depend upon the existence of minds or perceptions by minds in order to exist. The noumenon could continue to exist as noumenon if there were no human minds. Kant constructs his very doctrine of mind-independent objects in order to counter an idealism that would make existence dependent upon any human-like intuition. His refutation of Berkeley's idealism is a refutation of this very notion.[44]

Second, minds themselves do not depend upon particularities of mind-independent objects for their existences. Although Kant is quite clear in the refutation that "consciousness of my own existence proves the existence of objects in space outside me," he is equally clear that minds, considered as the synthetic unity of apperception, are dependent only upon appearances and the forms of sensible intuition.[45] To postulate more would be to postulate a transcendental causal connection between appearances and things-in-themselves, which is disallowed by Kant's claim that causation is simply the connection of appearances in succession. Transcendental causal connections cannot be postulated because the very notion of "cause" is bound up with the forms of outer and inner sense, space and time.[46] To put these two points together is quite simply to suggest that causation is itself a mind-dependent notion in that it operates through the forms of inner and outer sense. It is therefore impossible to speak either of causation among transcendental objects or causation between transcendental objects and appearances. That is, mind-independent objects are not simply causally independent of minds but independent of the very notion of causation.

This leads directly to the third way in which mind-independent objects are "independent" of human minds. If the forms of inner and outer sense and the categories do not apply to these objects, then the objects themselves are cognitively external to any and every human mind. That is, because the very forms and categories through which we intuit and understand objects cannot apply to things-in-themselves, our very cognitive powers cannot extend to these mind-independent objects. These mind-independent objects are quite simply incognizable. Neither the forms of sensible intuition nor the categories can be applied here.[47] Any and all human understanding is cognitively external to these objects in that it cannot transcend its own forms in order to apply to these objects.

The epistemological impact of Kant's doctrine should be quite clear. If, as Kant argues, mind-independent objects are causally and cognitively independent of minds, then it seems that access to them has been summarily denied. With such independence in place, the chasm between appearance and reality cannot be bridged by our sensible intuition. We have knowledge of appearances; we have none of transcendental objects, things-in-themselves.

Attempts at epistemic contact with mind-independent objects are futile. Knowledge of the world of mind-independent objects is ruled out in principle.[48]

Contemporary Kantians

The above conception of the thing-in-itself has worked its way into contemporary philosophical discussion in a number of important ways. The description of the historical transition from Descartes to Locke to Hume to Kant given at the beginning of this chapter tells part of the story. However, it is only when the conception of mind discussed there is coupled with the conception of the thing-in-itself given in the previous section and is then summarily dismissed that we get the notion of the thing-in-itself with which contemporary philosophy functions. In fact, it is, as Rorty notes, a result of the contemporary philosopher's inability to recognize the contingency of the "transcendental turn" that leaves us with the notion of the thing-in-itself and new substitutes for "mind" that would make it either continuous or coextensive with the real, things-in-themselves.[49]

Post-Kantian realism

This Kantian current in contemporary philosophy has been picked up by the ardent metaphysical realist Michael Devitt. In *Realism and Truth*, Devitt claims: "External objects exist objectively (in my sense . . .) only as things-in-themselves."[50] He then goes on to comment that Kant's view is that "the object is external to the mind—'out there'—but is partly constituted by us."[51] Devitt's own view is that the reality that counts as objective is that reality which is what it is entirely independent of any possible conception of it. That is, we can have no conception of the world that would alter what the world actually is. Devitt complains that Kant's use of the thing-in-itself is an epistemological device: Kant assumes we have knowledge, and then builds a metaphysic to support this assumption. At best, Kant is a "weak realist" in that he assumes that there must be something out there, but because he assumes that the objects of our knowledge are partially constituted by us, he creates a gap between the known world and things-in-themselves. Devitt writes: "Only things-in-themselves, which are forever beyond our ken, exist absolutely."[52] Appearances, on the other hand, exist only contingently because we are partially responsible for their construction. This, claims Devitt, puts the "epistemological cart" before the "metaphysical horse."[53]

We are guilty of assuming knowledge and constructing a world to ground it if we think as Kant did. However, Devitt's complaint is against Kant's method, not against his conception of the thing-in-itself. Devitt gladly accepts this notion.

In order to set Kant's account aright, Devitt thinks that we must put the metaphysical horse back in front of the epistemological cart by positing first that there is a world that is what it is independently of us and our concepts, and then by asking how we can have knowledge of this world. Devitt finds the possibility for such an investigation through the positing of two characteristics necessary to his Realism: "For the realist, the material or physical world he believes in must exist not only objectively, but non-mentally . . . [T]he world exists *independently of the mental.*"54 Although Kant's own conception of the mind allowed for the existence of the objective world through the noumenon, the objective world was defined through its relationship to this mental world. For Devitt, on the other hand, in order for us to have knowledge of something that can actually count as an objective world, that world must be definable independently of any conception of mind. Devitt then attributes to Kant the notion that this independent world must consist of "a structured set of entities," which would be "simply a Kantian noumenal world of things-in-themselves." Devitt wants to go yet further than this to posit that these things-in-themselves must somehow yield "common-sense physical or material entities" that have the same kind of existence as Kant's noumena.55 Only in this way can the metaphysical horse get back in front of the epistemological cart. We have to first decide what counts as a world, and then we can worry about claims to knowledge. This allows us to consider different ways of carving up that world, different "conceptual schemes," as simply different means to the same end—the description of the world of mind-independent objects.56 To give us some idea of what such a world looks like, Devitt posits that it is the world that our current best science says exists.57

Ridding ourselves of realism

It is the very world that Devitt wants to posit that Richard Rorty considers "well lost." A world that exists independently of the mental leads back to the Kantian notion of noumena in the positive sense, in that it is the preconceptual "given" element in experience. Whether or not noumenal objects are differentiated in the way in which Devitt requires or simply undifferentiated "stuff," Rorty claims that the very notion of a world that is given and then conceived of differently under "different conceptual schemes . . . must be the notion of something *completely* unspecified and unspecifiable—the thing-in-itself, in fact."[58] However, Rorty recognizes that this, once again, brings Epistemology into our metaphysics. Devitt, on Rorty's account, fails to admit that there cannot be the concept of the world that he would want to use unless there were some epistemic concepts smuggled in, even if these are used only negatively. Rorty's charge is that Devitt is right to think that the account of "different conceptual schemes" requires the notion of some world that is being "carved up" by our concepts but wrong to think that this speaks for the truth of his realism. Because such a view continues to presuppose a gap between the world and the knower, it thus continues to be plagued by skeptical problems.[59]

The way Rorty sees around this issue is to simply give up any such conception of "the world" because of its ties to Epistemology: "[T]he notion of 'the world' that is correlative with the notion of 'conceptual framework' is simply the Kantian notion of a thing-in-itself . . . If you start out with Kant's epistemology, in short, you will wind up with Kant's transcendental metaphysics."[60] Thus, to lose "the world" is to lose that conception of a thing-in-itself inherited from Kant which would have us carving up some given that exists independently of us or of our conceptions of it. Rorty finds such a notion impossible to sustain and therefore concludes that no such world can be posited. In the end, for Rorty: "[T]he specter of alternative conceptual frameworks shrinks to the possibility that there might be a number of equally good ways to modify slightly our present set of beliefs in the interest of greater predictive power, charm, or what have you."[61] If "the world" is indeed "well lost," then we are left with simply any number of "noncompeting trivialities" that supply us with our means to belief attainment and knowledge.[62]

"The world"—which Kant would make inconceivable, Devitt would find necessary to preserve, and Rorty would see as well lost—is a concept with a distinct heritage. Devitt and Rorty are both conscious of the fact that Kant made coherent the notion that there needed to be something outside our knowledge that both extended beyond it and provided its ground. This world, with its absolutely objective existence, is the world as it is entirely apart from our current actual conceptions of it or our future possible conceptions of it. It is that to which our knowledge and beliefs are accountable. The difference between Devitt and Rorty is over whether or not this world can be said to exist in the specified sense. Devitt thinks so; Rorty thinks not.

Kant offers us a world entirely independent of us, our concepts, and our knowledge. This world is the world of noumena in the positive sense, transcendental objects, things-in-themselves. Such a world is defined as that which is necessarily beyond our ken, that which is absolutely incognizable. Because the sensible forms of intuition and the categories limit our cognitive powers, any and all knowledge that we have must be achieved through these means. Although we are capable of thinking a thing apart from these forms, and thus of imagining some other form of intuition, we are incapable of knowing a thing in this way and are not possessed of such a form of intuition. There is a real, objective world beyond the world that we experience, and there is an unbridgeable gap between the world that we experience and this objective world. In contemporary philosophy, the debate is framed precisely in these terms. Although Devitt claims that such a way of putting this conception of the world of things-in-themselves puts epistemology before metaphysics, he readily admits that this conception, differently defined, serves the same role in his realism. It is the objective world that exists independently of the mental. This world is comprised of the objects that our current best science tells us are there. Rorty denies that such a world could exist in the way specified by this reading of Kant and Devitt. From this, he concludes that it is necessary for us to give up the very conception of a world and any notion of contact with it.

In "Freedom, Cruelty, and Truth: Rorty versus Orwell," James Conant brings the lesson of the Kantian notion of things-in-themselves—noumena in the positive sense—into contemporary focus by noting the ways in which realists like Devitt use this concept. According to Conant, the realist to whom Rorty is opposed takes the following stance:

> [W]e should not mistake the limitations of our knowledge, imposed on us by our finite cognitive capacities, for limitations that are inherent in the nature of reality as such. The idea that our experience is *of* the world (that the appearances are *appearances* and not mere illusions)—that is that there is something which our descriptions are *about*—presupposes the further idea that there is a way which is *the way the world is in itself* . . . It is only by postulating the existence of such a noumenal reality that we render coherent the supposition that all our apparent knowledge of reality is indeed *knowledge* of a genuinely mind-independent external reality.[63]

The present debates within epistemology and metaphysics continue to use the conception of what it means for the world to be independent of human knowledge as worked out by Kant. In order for our knowledge to be knowledge of something, that "something" has to be what and how it is entirely independently of both our present ideas of it and our possible conceptions of it. For Kant, this required the further supposition that the noumenal not be ruled by the limitations of time and space, the forms of inner and outer sense. Although few involved in the present debates continue to argue this, they do continue to presuppose that the limitations to our knowledge require that there be something that is independent of our abilities to know it, something that lies beyond the bounds of cognition. To think otherwise would be to think, with the idealist, that the boundaries of cognition mark the boundaries of the universe.

Conant notes that such a view of what the world is in itself entails a further notion regarding our means of accessing that world and our means of judging our descriptions of that world:

> In so far as our aim is to achieve knowledge of things as they really are, a description of reality formulated solely in terms of concepts [that are not peculiarly ours] represents a *metaphysically privileged mode of description*. Such concepts furnish us with the means to achieve a non-perspectival, transparent mode of access to how things really are in themselves. The resulting descriptions are descriptions of objective reality.[64]

It is only through the separation of the concepts that come from our "partial parochial perspectives on reality" from the concepts that "every properly conducted inquiry into the ultimate nature of reality . . . is eventually fated to converge upon" that we are able to arrive at accurate descriptions of the way that the world actually is.[65] Those descriptions would then constitute real knowledge of the world. Thus, on the contemporary scene, there remains a radical separation between the world as it is known by us, in and through our partial and parochial perspectives, and the world as it is in itself, entirely divorced from those perspectives. It is this latter world that is the real objective world to which our concepts must attach themselves if we are to make properly formulated claims to knowledge.

Conant makes explicit what Devitt and Rorty simply imply: there is a tenuous relationship between the notion of the thing-in-itself and the conditions of human knowledge. We have seen that this conception of the thing-in-itself is operant in both Devitt's and Rorty's works. Although Rorty denies that there can be things-in-themselves in the specified sense, Devitt is quite happy to assert that only such things-in-themselves have real, objective existence, and that our very best science requires that there be a bridge—even if it is currently hidden—from our partial, parochial perspectives to that reality. The question before us now is where the pragmatists stood on this matter.

Pragmatism-in-Itself

Peirce and James were quite aware of the place of Kant in the history of philosophy and the need to deal with his system, but they acknowledged their debts in different ways.[66] Peirce was deeply affected by reading Kant early in his philosophical career: "In the early sixties I was a passionate devotee of Kant, at least as regarded the Transcendental Analytic in the *Critic of Pure Reason* [sic]. I believed more implicitly in the two tables of the Functions of Judgment and the Categories than if they had been brought down from Sinai."[67] Even William James credits Kant for having the insight that "experience merely as such doesn't come ticketed and labeled . . . Kant speaks of it as being in its first intention . . . a mere motley which we have to unify by our wits."[68] They recognized Kant's importance and, to some extent, their own philosophical dependence on his work.

Richard Rorty is critical of Peirce's relationship to Kant, claiming that Peirce "remained the most Kantian of thinkers."[69] However, Rorty offers accolades to James (and Dewey) for "breaking with the Kantian tradition altogether."[70] Such a reading of early American pragmatism's relationship to Kant's philosophy fails to recognize that Peirce himself was very concerned with breaking with the Kantian tradition and saw himself as harkening back to the scholastic realism of Duns Scotus rather than to the transcendental idealism of Kant. However, because this reading of Peirce's relationship to Kant is rather widespread, it is necessary to begin by dispelling the notion that reading Peirce as a Kantian offers a tenable reading of his work.[71] Such historical considerations aside, Rorty's assessment of James's philosophical relationship to Kant is correct so far as it goes. The pragmatists, including Peirce, did see themselves as breaking radically with the tradition in which Kant is perhaps the principle figure. We can focus this rather broad claim by first looking at how Peirce viewed the Kantian notion of things-in-themselves, and then at how James saw the rejection of that notion as tied to pragmatism's break with the philosophical tradition in which such a notion is thought intelligible.

However appreciative the pragmatists may seem to be of Kant, they were also highly critical of his work, and it is these criticisms that are of interest to us here. Specifically, the early American pragmatists contend that the Kantian notion of the thing-in-itself cannot be made fully intelligible. It is a concept that cannot be given a sense. In this way, the pragmatists differ from Devitt and other realists who contend that the world of things-in-themselves is the real objective world and that knowledge of this world is real objective knowledge. However, the pragmatists also hold that this conclusion need not—indeed, cannot—lead to any further conclusions regarding human knowledge. In this way, the pragmatists differ from Rorty, who argues that because the concept cannot be made fully intelligible, there can be no objective knowledge and that we are, therefore, left with nothing but our partial and parochial understandings. In order to make clear these differences, this section will proceed first by showing that the pragmatists were critical of the sensibility of the thing-in-itself. The way that I want to focus this rather broad claim is by showing how Peirce and James viewed the Kantian notion of things-in-themselves and the logic used to support it. It will then be argued that the pragmatic method, and the logic that arises from it, marks a significant break with this tradition. This latter point will be made by relating these criticisms of Kant back to the hallway that is pragmatism-in-itself.

The problem of Peirce and Kant

That Peirce's relationship to Kant borders on the problematic is easy enough to see. In his first essay in the *Journal of Speculative Philosophy*, Peirce claims that his theory of space and time need not conflict with that of Kant or with his general agreement with Kant's two principles from the 'Transcendental Aesthetic': "First, that universal and necessary propositions are not given in experience. Second, that universal and necessary facts are conditioned by experience in general."[72] Here, Peirce aligns his aim with that of Kant: to find the link between the universal, necessary "facts" and human experience. Even in his later work, he recognizes a significant debt to Kant: "The present writer was himself a pure Kantist until he was forced by successive steps into Pragmaticism. The Kantist has only to abjure from the bottom of his heart the proposition that a thing-in-itself can, however indirectly, be conceived; and then correct the details of Kant's account accordingly, and he will find himself to have become a Critical Common-sensist."[73] Karl-Otto Apel, among others, takes this latter quote to be the true espousal of Peirce's "pragmaticism" and to help mark the distance between Peirce and the later pragmatists.[74]

That Peirce continues to use Kant's terminology in the exposition of his own position further complicates matters. Thus, when Peirce writes, "We have *direct experience of things in themselves*,"[75] the term "things in themselves" has been supposed to have a Kantian ring. However, to read this statement as an espousal of Peirce's Kantianism is itself impossible, given that the thing-in-itself is that which lies beyond the bounds of possible experience. Peirce's own conception of the thing-in-itself is made clear by what immediately follows: "Nothing can be more completely false than that we can experience only our own ideas. That is indeed without exaggeration the very epitome of *all* falsity. Our knowledge of things in themselves is entirely *relative*, it is true; but all experience and all knowledge is knowledge of that which is, independently of being represented."[76] It is in fact *because* we have experience of the things-in-themselves that Peirce finds the term useful in explicating his position. This experience and the knowledge produced through it is "entirely relative" in relation to further determinate experiences and knowledge; but if the thing-in-itself were not experienced, then we could not make sense of this "relative." That is, this knowledge is relative precisely in relation to other experiences of the thing-in-itself, which may in fact be different and may therefore produce different "knowledge." Peirce thus alters the very meaning of the term and creates a decidedly un-Kantian position out of a supposedly Kantian notion.

When Peirce's own statements seem to conform at least partially to Kant's, the problem of Peirce's supposed Kantianism is exaggerated. Take for example the following claim: "[T]hat to which the representation should conform, is itself something in the nature of a representation or sign—something noumenal, intelligible, conceivable, and utterly unlike a thing-in-itself."[77] Here, the confusion is created by the use of "noumenal" and "thing-in-itself" as contraries. Indeed, from the perspective of the first main section of this chapter, it is impossible to make sense of this claim at all. However, unless Peirce is being consciously contradictory, it must be clear that in this passage he means something other than what Kant meant by "noumenal." My contention here is that "noumenal" is to be read in the same way as "real": that which is "not affected by any cognitions, whether about it or not, of the man to whom it is external."[78] This is simply to suggest that being independent of the particular representation is both the necessary and sufficient condition for the thing's being noumenal. This need not carry with it the Kantian notion that to be noumenal is to be either entirely unknowable (noumenon in the negative sense) or the object of an intellectual intuition (noumenon in the positive sense.) Thus, when Peirce claims that "something noumenal" is "utterly unlike a thing in itself," the former term must be given this Peircean sense whereas the latter must be thought of in a more strictly Kantian sense.

Further complications arise when we turn to Peirce's treatment of Berkeley's idealism and we see Peirce offering what may appear at first blush to be a very Kantian position. With regard to Berkeley's supposition that to be an object is to be experienced, Peirce writes: "That an object's independence of our thought about it is constituted by its connection with experience in general [Berkeley] has never conceived."[79] Here, an object is defined as something that belongs to experience in general, which would seem to be an acceptance of Kant's "weighty" sense of object—something it is possible to experience. Furthermore, if read in isolation, this statement could be viewed as a formulation of Kant's conception of the transcendental object as the ground of experience in general. However, Peirce makes clear that his connection to Kant is minimal. For Kant the "weighty" sense of object only applies to a determinate object, to a particular appearance, to which the forms of inner and outer sense must apply. This means that a "weighty" object is a particular determination occurring in a particular intuition for Kant. An object must have been intuited in order to be a "weighty" object. For Peirce, an object is anything related to experience in general, any thing that has been or could be experienced. Thus, the basic condition for being an object is simply to be or to have been cognizable.

To further mark the distance between Peirce and Kant on this point, it is important to emphasize that Peirce's claim is that to be an object is to be dependent upon experience *in general*. This must necessarily include all future determinations of experience, which forces Peirce to admit that the set of objects is itself indeterminate apart from any particular standpoint in time. However, this does not imply that the set of objects, like Kant's noumenon, is nothing determinate. Kant's claim is that the noumenon is nothing determinate because the form of inner sense, time, cannot apply to it. Thus, for Kant, there are no noumenal objects although there is a noumenon. Peirce's suggestion, on the other hand, is that the set of objects would itself be indeterminate if we were to extrapolate over experience (and thus time) in general; however, this need not entail that there are no objects apart from particular experiences. That is, because time applies to experience in general in the same way in which it does to a particular experience, and because determinations of objects occur only within these particular experiences, the set of objects must be said to be indeterminate with regard to experience in general. When the time comes, the objects will be determinate.[80]

Although it will be made significantly clearer by what follows, the argument here has simply been that neither Peirce's own conception of his relationship to Kant nor his continued use of Kantian terminology offer sufficient reasons for thinking him to remain "the most Kantian of thinkers." In fact, a careful reading of these passages (and others) in the larger context of Peirce's philosophy provides good reason for thinking entirely the opposite: Peirce was hardly Kantian in his thought. Peirce's recognition that he was, at one time, "a pure Kantist" is of greater historical than philosophical importance. In fact, it is only through a decidedly non-Kantian reading of Peirce's allusions to Kant that we can make sense of these allusions. Peirce's adoption of Kantian terminology must be read as an adaptation of that terminology that gives new meanings to the terms, and these new meanings have little resemblance to those given to the terms by Kant. Once this is recognized, the continuity between Peirce and James can more easily be seen.

If we are to make sense of the positive claim that the early American pragmatists broke significantly with the philosophical tradition that runs through Kant, then it will be necessary to show that this break does not simply entail the falsification of various Kantian proposals. Several post-Kantian philosophers have disagreed with Kant without truly breaking from the Kantian tradition writ large. As the discussion of Rorty and Devitt and the comments of Conant above show, one need hardly identify explicitly as a Kantian in order to continue to owe Kant a severe philosophical debt. However, the pragmatists' reaction to Kant is notably different from those sketched above. Rather than denying or affirming the existence of the thing-in-itself or our access to it, the pragmatists call into question the very sensibility of the notion. That is, the pragmatists question whether any sense can be made of the thing-in-itself such that its existence, or our access to it, could be either affirmed or denied.

Peirce's argument against Kant's conception of the thing-in-itself begins with a brief analysis of an ordinary concept. He remarks, "An external object is anything that is not affected by any cognitions, whether about it or not, of the man to whom it is external."[81] This is simply the recognition that we cannot make objects what we want them to be by thinking of them in a particular way. Thinking about it or not thinking about it can have no effect upon its existence as an external object. Peirce goes on to suggest that such a conception quickly gives way to philosophical confusion: "Exaggerate this, in the usual philosophical fashion, and you have the conception of what is not affected by any cognitions at all. Take the converse of this definition and you have the notion of what does not affect cognition, and in this indirect manner you get a hypostatically abstract notion of what the *Ding an sich* would be."[82] When the initial notion of the external object is exaggerated, we arrive at the notion of thing-in-itself as that which neither is affected by nor affects human cognition. The thing-in-itself is that which is absolutely incognizable; it is entirely independent of both particular cognitions and all possible cognition.

Recognizing both that Kant's conception of the thing-in-itself is an exaggeration of an ordinary concept and that the thing-in-itself is supposed to be both unaffected by and ineffective toward human cognition makes clear the problem with the concept itself. For the pragmatist, the reality of any object is dependent upon the possibility, however remote, of its being known. To know is to have some concept of, and to be conceivable is to be knowable. To posit that which cannot be cognized in any way is to posit nonsense. Peirce rightly recognizes the difficulty with the notion of the thing-in-itself that is created by its complete cognitive independence.

The sixth of Peirce's "Questions Concerning Certain Incapacities Claimed for Man" provides the means for making this point. All that we can know we know by means of conceptions, and these conceptions must all come through judgments. Thus far, Peirce agrees with Kant. However, in recognizing that "all our conceptions are obtained by abstractions and combinations of cognitions first occurring in judgments of experience," we are also led to recognize that there are certain terms—which seem to carry conceptions with them—that cannot be linked to possible experience.[83] If, upon examination, we find that no experience can—either directly or indirectly—give rise to the conception supposedly entailed by the term, then we are left to conclude that the term itself cannot be made sense of: "Accordingly, there can be no conception of the absolutely incognizable, since nothing of that sort occurs in experience. But the meaning of a term is the conception which it conveys. Hence, a term can have no such meaning."[84] To posit that there is something that is entirely incognizable and to posit at the same time that it is still *some thing* is to posit the self-contradictory. It is to predicate of that which can have no predicates by definition. This is simply a logical point that foreshadows Peirce's pragmatic account of inquiry according to which meaning is determined by practical consequences.

Peirce is not defending the naïve position that only those conceptions that have direct links to particular perceptual experiences can be given meaning. Rather, his suggestion is that if no link to the very experience of cognition in general can be made, then no link between the term and the conception can be made: "Over against any cognition, there is an unknown but knowable reality; but over against all possible cognition, there is only the self-contradictory."[85] The error in positing the absolutely incognizable is to confuse the conditions for particular cognitions with the conditions for all possible cognition. What is *absolutely* incognizable is that which is *absolutely* independent of experience in general—all possible experience. What this might be is inconceivable.

In "Some Consequences of Four Incapacities," Peirce reiterates the conclusion of this argument: "The absolutely incognizable is absolutely inconceivable."[86] We are entirely without the means to conceive of that to which no conception can be attached; we cannot conceive of what we could never know. To conceive of something is to attach a concept to it, and to attach a concept to it is to know something about it. Thus, Kant's conclusion that the noumenon is in some sense real but is at the same time incognizable must be rejected because to do so is to attach a concept to that to which, by definition, no concepts can be attached. Peirce concludes, "[W]hatever is meant by any term as 'the real' is cognizable in some degree."[87] This is simply a logical point for Peirce: we cannot make sense of what it would be for something to be real and yet be unknowable because our very conception of what it is to be real is tied up with our experience and knowledge. Thus, the predicate "real" cannot be attached to that which lies beyond experience and knowledge. In the "Logic of 1873," Peirce puts the point this way:

> What idea can be attached to that of which there is no idea? For if there be an idea of such a reality, it is the object of that idea of which we are speaking, and which is not independent of thought. It is quite clear that it is quite beyond the power of the mind to have an idea of something entirely independent of thought—it would have to extract itself from itself for that purpose; and since there is no such idea there is no meaning in the expression.[88]

The thing-in-itself, defined as it is by Kant, is a term without a conception by definition and the attachment of a conception to the term creates a contradiction within the term itself. Thus, no sense can be made of the term, and any claims made regarding the thing-in-itself cannot be given a sense. We cannot extract our thought from itself to find a metaphysically privileged mode of description of a world that is entirely independent of our thoughts about it. Peirce's argument is that neither such a mode of description nor such a conception of the world can be made sense of.

The consequences of this argument are easily summarized. If no concept can attach to the term "thing-in-itself," then the term cannot be given a sense. If it cannot be given a sense, then claims made using it cannot be either true or false. The very incognizability of the thing-in-itself undercuts the possibility of using it sensibly. With this in mind Peirce writes: "The *Ding an sich*, however, can neither be indicated nor found. Consequently, no proposition can refer to it, and nothing true or false can be predicated of it. Therefore, all references to it must be thrown out as meaningless surplussage [sic]."[89] Again, Peirce rejects propositions that contain the term "thing-in-itself" not because these propositions made sense and turned out to be false, but because sense could never be made of the term and, therefore, of propositions containing it. Thus, neither the acceptance nor the denial of propositions regarding the thing-in-itself—mind-independent reality—can have substantive philosophical consequences. To recognize this is to follow Peirce's directive to abjure from our hearts the proposition that "the thing in itself can, however indirectly, be conceived" and break significantly with philosophies that would not.[90]

There are two points to be made in summary that reveal the outcome of this argument not to be the proposal of a theory to replace Kant's. First, it is important to note that Peirce's objection to the sensibility of the Kantian thing-in-itself is not purely conceptual. His argument is not that the Kantian notion conflicts with our conceptual apparatus. Because our conceptual apparatus must be tied to our experience, when concepts which are thought to belong within that apparatus fail to find content in lived experience, then those concepts cannot be given a sense and must be discarded. Second, Peirce's use of "thought in general" ought not to be equated with Kant's use of the "transcendental apperception" nor should its relationship to our own particular thoughts be equated with that between Kant's "transcendental unity of apperception" and our particular thoughts.[91] Whereas Kant's transcendental concepts precede cognition and serve as its ground, Peirce's general concepts arise out of the particular cognitions of particular cognitive beings living in community with one another, their world, their ancestors, and their descendents. Kant's concepts are constitutive; Peirce's concepts are regulative.[92] Kant's transcendentals are fixed across time; Peirce's generals are indeterminate across time and fixed only in time. In the end, although it is rather abstract, Peirce's argument is rooted in his pragmatism in that it is the relationships between concepts and experience—or the lack thereof—that are determinative in his philosophical disagreement with Kant.

James, Kant, and intellectualism

As in the previous chapter, it is this continuity between our experiences and our concepts that provides the bridge between Peirce and James. The works of William James may at first seem an odd place to look for a sustained treatment of Kant. While Peirce and Dewey can at least lay claim to some formal training in philosophy and to some rigor of thought, James seems *prima facie* to be both ill-equipped and unmotivated for a sustained critique of Kant's system.[93] Thus, it is hardly surprising that a head-to-head confrontation such as that between Kant and Peirce cannot be sustained here. Even a cursory knowledge of each philosopher's work reveals that Kant's writing has the logical rigor of the professional philosopher addressing others in the field that James's often seems to lack almost entirely. The latter's lectures and articles are largely addressed to a popular but learned audience and only rarely to the philosophical professional.[94] Thomas Carlson notes that these differences in style seem to belie greater philosophical differences: "Kant was a lover of unity and systematicity, and exalted the absolute and necessary features of our experience; James had little patience with philosophical systems, thought there was much less unity to the world than often imagined, and denied there were any utterly indefeasible elements in our experience."[95] Kant loved the necessary and universal; James constantly pointed to the particular and relative. On such a reading, philosophical differences and differences of temperament seem to go hand in hand, making comparison of the two philosophers, or even conversation between them, a near impossibility.

James's own disparaging comments regarding Kant's importance to philosophy in general serve only to reinforce such a picture. In an address to the Philosophical Union at the University of California in 1898, James claimed: "Kant bequeaths to us not one single conception which is both indispensable to philosophy and which philosophy either did not possess before him, or was not destined . . . to acquire after him."[96] Not only does James find Kant's system superfluous to the history of philosophy, but he also sees the study of Kant as an impediment to philosophical progress. In an oft-quoted remark, James writes: "The true line of philosophic progress lies, in short . . . not so much *through* Kant as *round* him . . . Philosophy can perfectly well outflank him."[97] Were James to heed his own advice, it seems he would do better to avoid Kant than to address him. Given that James's rhetorical skills seem less well-served by constructing arguments from premises to conclusion than by putting forward his own position with a flourish, it seems he should heed this advice. However, I want to argue here that James offers a philosophical critique of Kant. In the end, James's bald claim that philosophy ought to "outflank" Kant has its roots in *philosophy* and not in *temperament.*

James's philosophical critique of Kant and Kant's notion of the thing-in-itself occurs within a larger discussion of the problems with "intellectualist logic," "the current notion that logic is an adequate measure of what can or cannot be."[98] Only what can be quantified and manipulated in logic is allowed to exist in the world itself. James's complaint against such logic is that "it makes experience less instead of more intelligible."[99] As an example of the ways in which such logic obscures what is clear in our experiences of the world, James cites Zeno's paradox and the concept of change operant therein.

James begins by noting that philosophy has borrowed its concept of change from mathematicians, much to its own detriment. According to this mathematical conception, "The stages into which you analyze a change are *states*, the change itself goes on between them. It lies along their intervals . . . and thus eludes conceptual explanation altogether."[100] Change itself is abandoned, and fixed states become the object of study. When such a notion is imported into philosophy, it begets a "ruling tradition" in which "fixity is a nobler and worthier thing than change."[101] This preference for "fixity" necessitates certain doctrines in both metaphysics and epistemology: "Reality must be one and unalterable. Concepts, being themselves fixities, agree best with this fixed nature of truth, so that for any knowledge of ours to be quite true it must be knowledge by universal concepts rather than by particular experiences, for these are notoriously mutable and corruptible."[102] Reality, truth, and knowledge each must be fixed and unchanging if the world is to be a noble place. The noblest philosophical concepts are those that are universal and necessary. Only these could yield knowledge.

James then immediately takes aim at Kant and "the transcendentalist philosophers" who have come after him, summarizing the position of Kant's *Critique of Pure Reason*: "What that critique professed to establish was this, that concepts do not apprehend reality, but only such appearances as our senses feed out to them. They give immutable intellectual forms to these appearances, it is true, but the reality *an sich* from which in ultimate resort the sense-appearances have to come remains forever unintelligible to our intellect."[103] The concepts with which the intellect operates in Kant's system are fixed and immutable, and they operate only on appearances. Thus, James is right to claim that "reality *an sich*" remains forever beyond our grasp. Theoretical reasoning allows us to posit that this reality, this thing, must exist, but the limits to our own powers of reasoning prevent us from knowing that it is there. We can think it, but it cannot be known.

James draws out the consequences of a doctrine according to which something lies beyond the limits of our conceptual powers and thus beyond the limits of our knowledge: "Not only . . . the relation of various empirical data to their 'conditions,' but the very notion that empirical things should be related to one another at all . . . has seemed . . . full of paradox and contradiction."[104] These paradoxes are created by the supposed need for fixity, and Kant sought the solution to the paradox of relation between empirical things and their conditions "outside of and *before* our experience, in the *dinge an sich*."[105] Because the unity and immutability of the world lies beyond our ken, the *dinge an sich* are simply posits of theoretical reason that

Kant and his successors both propose must be there. It goes against the intellectualist logic to claim knowledge of it. However, to then suggest that this unknowable something resolves the paradox created by the philosopher's faith in fixity is not to resolve the paradox at all: it is simply to suggest a way in which, if correct, it might be resolved that remains beyond our reach. This, James claims, is no solution at all because it creates a contradiction at the very heart of "intellectualist logic"; we can know only because of that which is impossible to know. The logic that was to clarify our relationship to the world has served only to obscure it.

Lest we think James simply to be reiterating the criticisms of the "pluralistic empiricists" and to be siding with them against Kant, it is important to note that John Stewart Mill, David Hume, and John Locke are not spared this critique. In fact, James sends a very Kantian criticism their way, claiming that these empiricists have used the very same "intellectualist logic," premised on the nobility of fixity and its own adequacy as the measure of the world, to argue that "finite experience" is all there is. Such philosophers accept the fixity of the concepts that are used to carve up our experience but simply reject the possibility that there is a ground or absolute that is their cause or consequence. The paradox created by the impossibility of relating this finite experience to its "conditions" remains, but attempts to resolve this paradox are thought impossible. James concludes, "The empiricists use their logic against the absolute, but refuse to use it against finite experience."[106] The logic that would carve experience up into discrete but unrelated states is used as fully by the pluralistic empiricists as by the transcendentalist philosophers. The empiricists too operate on the assumption that there must be some fixity that underwrites the flux of experience.[107]

James's criticisms of the "intellectualist logic" would fall a bit flat and seem largely unrelated to the point at hand if not conjoined with his larger project in the essay under discussion. The example of change, which is used to show the inconsistencies between the intellectualist logic and our experiences in general and the paradoxes created thereby, is used in the larger context of denying "that mere conceptual logic can tell us what is impossible or possible in the world of being or fact."[108] James's larger critique is of the procedure used to substantiate what are, in the end, attempts to ground the ordinary world of fact through some abstract philosophical argument. Such arguments are both made and founded on the supposition that theoretical reason can extend knowledge while being divorced from the world of everyday experience. Logic, James claims, gives "primarily the relations between concepts as such, and the relations between natural facts only secondarily or so far as the facts have been already identified with concepts and defined by them."[109] Although such a conception of logic is correct so far as it goes and establishes "a vast and definite sphere of influence where its sovereignty is indisputable," James argues that there is significantly more to experience than what can be given by such a fixed notion of the way in which things are known.[110] Motion, change, and other such relations are "activities," and intellectualist logic is ill suited for understanding them.

The inconsistencies between our experiences and the conclusions of intellectualist logic have led the intellectualist philosophers to believe that it is only when such logic is divorced from the vagaries of these experiences that it can yield its proper results. This, in turn, results in the separation of the theoretical realm in which such logic operates from the practical realm in which we have experiences and the privileging of the former over the latter. It is this move of which James is most critical, and his reasons are clear: "We live forward, we understand backward, said a Danish writer; and to understand life by concepts is to arrest its movement, cutting it up into bits as if with scissors, and immobilizing these in our logical herbarium where, comparing them as dried specimens, we can ascertain which of them statically includes or excludes which other."[111] The conceptual method, supposing concepts to be fixed, only allows us to compare the fixed with the fixed. If we then make the mistake of thinking that this comparison of the fixed with the fixed gives us the world itself, we draw a conclusion that runs contrary to our very experiences of motion, change, and other activities. James argues, however, that we can avoid this mistake entirely if we recognize the importance of our "interests of practice" to "our interests of theory."

If we pause here and rehearse James's argument, it would seem to beget the following conclusion: because our concepts extend only so far and no further and we can only know the fixed by its means, the world, which our experience reveals to be inherently in flux, is either entirely unknowable in itself or known to be unavailable to conceptual logic but knowable by some other means. This, however, would seem to align James with Kant with the notable exception that James holds that we do have a faculty (practical reason or "experience") that serves the same function as Kant's intellectual intuition. He would then be choosing between the horns of the intellectualist dilemma, between the transcendental and empirical philosophies. However, James does not suppose that this thoroughgoing critique of pure, intellectualist reason can yield such conclusions. In fact, the sentence immediately preceding the above quote provides the key to understanding how James avoids such conclusions: "[T]he conceptual method is a transformation which the flux of life undergoes at our hands in the interests of practice primarily, and only subordinately in the interests of theory."[112] Our theoretical interests are tied to our practical interests and theoretical reason is used best when linked to these practical ends. James makes this clear: "What we do in fact is to *harness up* reality in our conceptual systems in order to drive it the better. This process is practical because all the termini to which we drive are *particular* termini, even when they are facts of the mental order."[113] James's suggestion is that theoretical reason cannot yield the general conclusions that it would because its generality is in fact only feigned. It is a generality in service of the particular ends of our practical lives. Our lived human interests drive even the most purely theoretical endeavors, such as metaphysics, which in turn undercuts the supposed authority and superiority of metaphysical claims.

Unfortunately for James, even when his proviso regarding the importance of practical interests to theoretical projects is admitted, the argument as it stands is still incomplete at best and inconsistent at worst for two reasons. First, James has conceded to the intellectualist philosophers that concepts are fixed and immutable and capable only of relationships among themselves. Thus, they remain, as the intellectualist has argued all along, radically disconnected from the world itself. In fact, he says later in the same essay: "[T]hese concepts are not *parts* of reality . . . but *suppositions* rather . . . and you can no more dip up the substance of reality with them than you can dip up water with a net, however finely meshed."[114] This is clearly the intellectualist position as well. What then of the concepts to which James draws our attention with his example of motion and change, which is supposed to undercut such a notion of the conceptual method? Certainly, motion, change, and relation are concepts as well as activities, but James seems to be arguing that these arise more directly from the "flux" than those used by the intellectualist and are therefore less "conceptual." However, it is not as if we get about in our practical lives without any concepts whatsoever.[115] Second, James seems to have conceded to the intellectualist philosophers a division between pure, theoretical reason and practical reason. The former operates with concepts; the latter with life as lived in the flux. This, conjoined with the above objection, would lead us to believe that James is asserting that the world is still divided between the conceptual and the sensible; it is simply the case that the latter trumps the former for James.

That James recognizes these objections, obvious though they are, is often difficult to see within the essay in which the argument occurs. However, he later acknowledges that these difficulties seem insurmountable:

> As long as one continues *talking*, intellectualism remains in undisturbed possession of the field . . . [A]n *intellectual* answer to the intellectualist's difficulties will never come, and . . . the real way out of them, far from

consisting in the discovery of such an answer, consists in simply closing one's ears to the question . . . No words of mine will probably convert you, for words can be the names only of concepts.[116]

It seems we can avoid the intellectualist's difficulties only by ceasing to talk or by ceasing to hear. This would be akin to the "bluff pragmatist's" response to skepticism—to avoid it by ignoring it—if James continued to privilege the intellectualist logic and its method according to which pure concepts serve the interests of theoretical knowledge alone. Thus, a direct defense of James's argument would seem impossible. In fact, James seems to recognize that it is attempts at a direct defense of the argument that lead to the objections raised above.

James has, however, a much larger project in mind, the clue to which is given here: to *show* how the "concepts we talk with are made for purposes of *practice* and not for purposes of insight."[117] Far from drawing a clear distinction between theoretical and practical concerns and theoretical and practical reason, James claims that the theoretical is a broader and more remote version of the practical. It is because we have practical need of the theoretical that it develops in the first place; in turn, when its results fail to support our practical ends, these results must be re-evaluated. Once the concessions made to the intellectualist philosopher are rescinded, James's argument may be allowed to stand. The following chapter will take up this defense of James's argument against intellectualist logic, which ought not to be confused with formal or conceptual logic, by showing its ties to his larger views of rationality and inquiry. In the meantime, it should be sufficient to note that there is a distinction in James between the use of concepts (conceptual or formal logic or, sometimes, Aristotlean "logic of identity") and intellectualist logic. David Lamberth notes that "intellectualist logic" refers to a combination of three distinct notions. Intellectualist logic (or, occasionally, "the conceptual method") holds to the "idealist principle that things are (really) as they appear," that concepts have priority over precepts, and that standard logic offers appropriate rules of deduction and inference.[118] Noting this will lead directly to the heart—or hallway—of pragmatism, which will be taken up in the next chapter.

Peirce, James, and Logic

Having surveyed Peirce's argument against the sense of Kant's notion of the thing-in-itself and James's argument against the intellectualist's conceptual method, it is now possible to move to defenses of these arguments. However, before doing so one more objection must be countered. Even if we were convinced that Peirce's argument does not need defense from a Kantian counter-attack, it would still seem that Peirce's argument is vulnerable to James's attack on the conceptual method. Peirce's argument trades largely in concepts and, in fact, hinges on whether or not the concepts "incognizable" and "inconceivable" are in conflict. It seems that it is a battle between Peirce's theory of concepts and their use in cognition and Kant's theory of concepts and their use in cognition that is being waged; that is, it is a *conceptual* conflict. The obvious method for a conceptual argument would seem itself to be conceptual. If this were the case, then James's objections to intellectualism and the conceptual method would seem to be as effective against Peirce as they are against Kant. Thus, if we can overcome the objections to James's argument raised above, Peirce's argument would fall with Kant's method. At the same time, a direct defense of Peirce's argument against James's attack would require the undermining of that attack, rendering it as useless against Kant as against Peirce. Obviously, such choices regarding which pragmatist to defend against the other ought to be avoided within a project attempting to find the ties that bind Peirce and James. That they are opposed to Kant hardly makes them historically or philosophically remarkable.

James's admission that engaging in philosophical argument seems to cede too much ground to the intellectualist would seem to raise further difficulties for the project at hand. Talk, or philosophical argument, is doomed to use concepts, and attempts to undermine concepts cannot help but fail because they use what they would undermine. The problem here is similar to that with a definitive refutation of skepticism: once the naturalness of the skeptic's doubt is admitted, the attempt to defeat with theory what arises naturally cannot help but fail. In the present case, once the necessity of the conceptual method and intellectualist logic for our "knowledge *about* things" is admitted, attempts to argue against the conceptual method and intellectualist logic are forced to use it in arguments about things—including concepts and methods.[119] Thus, arguments against it are doomed by circularity.

Unlike the case of skepticism, which can be avoided by showing the philosopher's conception of doubt to be tied to a particular theoretic picture and not to our natural cognitive situation, we cannot simply *avoid* the use of concepts in general. The use of concepts is natural. Without it, communication and understanding would be impossible. Nonetheless, like the case of skepticism, recognizing the special and decidedly unnatural context of intellectualist logic (as opposed to the use of concepts) allows us to sidestep the particular use to which it is supposed to be put and thereby provides a means for avoiding the conflict that arises between intellectualist logic and conceptual logic. It need not be shown that the pragmatists do not use concepts or logic in their own arguments, or that the pragmatists reject the theoretical use of reason. Rather, what must be shown is that the pragmatic method provides a description of the formation and function of concepts and, thereby, a description of the relationship between the theoretical and practical use of concepts that differs greatly from the descriptions of the role of concepts in intellectualist logic as given by James above. In the end, intellectualist logic can be shown to be just as much a distortion of our actual cognitive situation as is the philosopher's conception of doubt. Understanding that the pragmatists were offering an alternative to this logic and this method is vital to recognizing both their distance from the philosophical tradition that runs through Kant and the ways in which they avoid that tradition's conceptions of the world and knowledge of it.

This recognition that intellectualist logic is necessary only within its particular philosophical context provides the means to an indirect defense of Peirce and James simultaneously. Although James's argument certainly allows for the reading that results in the objections raised above, such a reading assumes James's attack to be more direct than it is, and his statements regarding the relationship between the theoretical and the practical provide the key to seeing this. Similarly, recognizing that the pragmatic method, and not intellectualist logic, is at work in Peirce's argument provides both the key to understanding that argument and the key to dissolving the apparent conflict between Peirce and James. Thus, the pragmatic method and each pragmatist's embrace of it is the means to dissolving the appearance of conflict between them. Although this provides an *indirect* defense of the arguments in the preceding section, it is a *direct* view at pragmatism itself as a method and as an implicit critique of the very notion of pure reason.

If we review the two legacies of Kant toward which Conant points us above, the ways in which the early American pragmatists differ from the tradition that runs through Kant will be clear. First, Conant notes that part of Kant's legacy is the notion that a noumenal reality is a necessary condition of knowledge about mind-independent reality. There must be a world that is what it is in itself, apart from its effects on us and our effects on it. Second, Conant remarks that access to this world is granted through concepts that are not peculiarly ours, that do not belong to the "partial, parochial perspectives" with which we normally operate. Early American pragmatism's distance from the Kantian tradition is marked by its distance from these two features of the Kantian legacy. First, the sense of the notion that there could be a world that lies *entirely* outside experience in general is denied. Any concept is conceived through its possible effects; a concept without such effects is no concept at all. Second, because the effects that make conception possible occur within our experience, only our "partial, parochial" perspectives could provide us with tools for knowledge. Knowledge, including knowledge of the objective world, if it is to be had, is to be had through the pursuit of inquiry in particular contexts and with particular aims. There is no other kind of knowledge. Thus, the practical world in which we live ought not to be even called "practical" as if to distinguish it from the theoretical; likewise, the practical use of reason that we use to find our way about in that world also ought not to be modified for the same reason. We live and reason in commerce with the world; we cannot conceive of what it would be like to do otherwise. Without a context, there is no sense. Only thought that is at work within the context of inquiry—thought that is *effective*—is really thought at all. Recognizing this allows us to begin to see the outlines of pragmatism as a method of inquiry, which the next chapter will address directly.

Chapter 4

Inquiry, Metaphysics, and Rationality

This project has, thus far, relied on an implicit distinction that is worth making explicit here through an example borrowed from Lars Hertzberg. Consider the following two claims: "Caesar crossed the Rubicon," and "Caesar is a prime number." In the former instance, the meaning of the words and the sense of the sentence seem obvious. However, this is only of psychological significance; we have simply managed to pick out determinate meanings for each of the words in the claim such that the claim as a whole makes sense.[1] This need not point us in the direction of making larger philosophical claims regarding what can and what cannot make sense. In the latter instance, "Caesar is a prime number," it seems we have uttered nonsense; however, it is entirely possible to provide a context in which the latter claim makes sense. In "The Sense Is Where You Find It," Hertzberg offers the following way of doing so:

> Imagine the following conversation between two judges at a dog show:
>
> A: What are the prime contenders in this class?
> B: Well, Caesar is a prime number.
> A: Which one is that?
> B: It's number 53.
> A: Yes, you're right, of course, 53 really is a prime number.[2]

Although Hertzberg admits that the example is "a bit strained," it allows us to see both that "Caesar is a prime number" can be given a sense and that "53 is a prime number" can be given a sense that is independent of its use in mathematics. The larger point to be made here is that utterances, which appear prima facie to have a particular sense or to have no sense at all, may have a different sense than originally thought, or may have a sense when thought to have had none. Nonsense is as context-dependent as sense.

The rhetorical strategy of the last two chapters has been to show that Peirce and James found the particular conceptions to which those chapters were addressed to be philosophically problematic within the contexts from which they were supposed to derive their senses. Although Peirce and James have both been read often enough as standing outside the early modern European philosophical tradition or as offering practical objections to philosophical doctrines within that tradition, I have tried to show that their objections are philosophical in nature, revealing difficulties internal to the use of the concepts of mind and the thing-in-itself, respectively. To this point, the project has been largely critical and only minimally constructive.

Part of the difficulty in the task in which I have engaged thus far is that isolating Peirce's and James's pragmatism from their other philosophical ideas is considerably more difficult than simply leaving a room and entering a hall, if I may push James's metaphor from *Pragmatism*. The work of the last two chapters has been primarily to demonstrate that Peirce and James were not only happy to do without philosophical concepts that are quite deeply imbedded in contemporary epistemological and metaphysical discussions, but also worked to show that the concepts could not have the senses they appeared to have, whether it be the naturalness of skepticism or the mind-independence of the thing-in-itself. Claims or utterances containing these terms were not false but nonsensical.

The importance of distinguishing between rejecting that a claim makes sense—that it has a sense—and rejecting the claim as false is vital to the work ahead. In order to make the latter determination, that a claim is false, one would have first to have made the former determination, that the claim has a sense, that it can be true or false. For example, when Peirce claims that the concept of the thing-in-itself cannot be given a meaning, his claim entails that further sentences, propositions, or beliefs in which it operates cannot be either true or false if we continue to take that term as, in Kant's sense, the "incognizable." To claim that there is a world of mind-independent objects (in the sense in which "mind-independent objects" is equivalent to "things-in-themselves") is not to make a false claim, it is to make a claim that is incapable of being either true or false. However, this is not to reject that the concept or claim can be given a sense *tout court*. Such proclamations would run against the pragmatic grain. Rather, it is to claim that, given the context within which we are operating, the claim cannot be given an appropriate sense. When that context is as large as Peirce's "experience in general," it may seem that he is claiming that no sense could ever be made of the concept or of claims containing it. However, his continued use of the term suggests that it may be salvageable *in some other sense*. The problem is not with the term itself but with its Kantian and later metaphysical realist sense.

To suggest, then, that the work here has been critical rather than constructive is to imply a care that might not seem readily evident. It is tempting to think of the pragmatists' project as a refutation of the tradition that runs from Descartes to Kant from which specific conclusions are intended to follow. However, in the attempt thus far to disentangle Peirce and James's pragmatism from other philosophical positions, I have tried not to draw such specific conclusions. Showing "'Twas brillig" to be false would lead to the conclusion "'Twas not brillig"; showing "'Twas brillig" to be nonsense leads to no particular conclusion.

Returning to Rorty

Given what was said in previous chapters regarding metaphysical realism's acceptance of at least two notions in which early American pragmatism fails to find any sense, my take on metaphysically realist readings of pragmatism should be obvious: the pragmatism of Peirce and James cannot be accurately classified as either metaphysically realist or Realist with regard to truth because such pragmatism rejects the sensibility of both the supposition that there is a world that is mind-independent in the specified sense and the notion that our knowledge of that world is a matter of linking up mind-dependent concepts with a mind-independent world. Truth cannot involve "some sort of correspondence" if "correspondence" is construed as a privileged species of this "linking up."[3] Thus far, I would agree with Richard Rorty in thinking that the early American pragmatists were neither metaphysical realists nor Realists with regard to truth. Even conflating forms of realism, as Rorty often does, I would agree with his arguments against understanding the pragmatism of James in this way but would include Peirce as well.[4]

What needs to be made clear, though, is that Rorty's own position is plagued by the very controversies he scorns; he assumes the conceptions he would deride specifically for the purpose of falsifying them. That is, Rorty assumes that what is meant by "world" is, necessarily, tied up with both the Kantian notion of the thing-in-itself and Realist notions of truth such that we would be better served by ridding ourselves of these notions in favor of his own proposals—that the world is simply those planks in the boat which are not currently being moved about and that truth is simply a matter of justification to larger and larger possible audiences.[5] Thus, in Rortian parlance, the world and truth are both "well lost," but we have found something else to take their respective places.

The contrast to be made between a Rortian neo-pragmatism that is antirealist and Nonrealist and that with which I am arguing the early American pragmatists operated, turns precisely on this point. Whereas the early American pragmatists were happy to show that the terms in question could not mean what those uttering them wanted them to mean, given the contexts in which they were being used, and *then* went on to show how these terms could mean something else in the context of their pragmatism, Rorty's formulation of an antirealist/Nonrealist pragmatism is parasitic on each of *those* terms having precisely *that* sense. For example, in "The World Well Lost" Richard Rorty writes, "If you start out with Kant's epistemology . . . you will wind up with Kant's transcendental metaphysics."[6] Because Rorty refuses to allow epistemology to be anything other than the very Kantian conception of it that leads to a transcendental metaphysics, his own position is still very much in the grip of these Kantian notions. As James Conant notes: "[Rorty] invariably ends up affirming a thesis that has the same logical form as a thesis which the Realist affirms, but with one difference: a negation operator has been introduced into the content-clause of the thesis."[7] Rorty's affirmations depend for their sense on what he would reject. The early American pragmatists would agree with Rorty's assessment of the symbiotic relationship between the Kantian thing-in-itself and Realist conceptions of truth but would disagree with his assessment that ridding ourselves of such ideas rids us of the world or of truth.

In marking the contrast between my reading of pragmatism and realist or antirealist readings of pragmatism, I am in agreement with those who view pragmatism as being metaphysically neutral. Although both Peirce and James did develop important metaphysical pictures, glimpses of which we have seen in earlier chapters, pragmatism is not itself a metaphysical view. It need not commit one to realism, idealism, or antirealism. James's formulation from the Lowell Lectures makes clear that pragmatism is simply its method and in a wider sense this method plus a view of truth.[8] However, pragmatism's metaphysical neutrality need not imply epistemological neutrality. Separating the metaphysical and epistemological issues in the way that Kirkham suggests leaves plenty of room for argument on this second head.

In this chapter, I want to begin the constructive project alluded to in earlier chapters. What will emerge is both a fuller view of the metaphysical neutrality of pragmatism as well as an argument for a kind of epistemological neutrality. This is not to suggest that pragmatism is contentless; rather, it is to argue that attempts to settle the issues of pragmatism's realism or antirealism and Realism or Nonrealism cannot help but flounder. By examining three intimately related themes in the pragmatism of Peirce and James—inquiry, metaphysics, and rationality—the more constructive picture of what might be termed a "thick pragmatism" will emerge, one with appropriate resources for addressing the issues in philosophy of religion with which the conclusion of this book is concerned.

Peirce on Objects and the Limits of Inquiry

What makes pragmatists pragmatists is a concern with the practical. Although this appears tautological, it is often difficult to see just how far the early American pragmatists were willing to reformulate philosophy in light of this concern. John Dewey notes that pragmatism forces one to rethink a host of traditional philosophical and epistemological concepts: "[T]he point that the critics of pragmatism have missed with a surprising unanimity, is that in giving a reinterpretation of the nature and function of knowledge, pragmatism gives necessarily a thoroughgoing reinterpretation of all the cognitive machinery—sensations, ideas, concepts, etc."[9] The early American pragmatists viewed thought itself as being concerned with the practical and developed a logic that recognized this. Peirce's original formulation of the pragmatic maxim was intended as a maxim of logic.[10] Thought is a means for directing our efforts because belief is simply the formation of a habit of action. Peirce claims that the connection between thought and purposive action was so close as to have given pragmatism its moniker: "Now quite the most striking feature of the new theory was its recognition of an inseparable connection between rational cognition and rational purpose; and that consideration it was which determined the preference for the name *pragmatism*."[11] Rational inquiry is conducted to develop rational purposes, which in turn become the aims of rational action. The continuity of thought, purpose, and action lies at the very heart of pragmatism and points us toward a fuller understanding of the relationship between the theoretical and the practical in pragmatism.

Peirce's early formulation of the pragmatic principle in the *Popular Science Monthly* articles of 1877 and 1878 begin with an account that might seem at first blush to run athwart my claim that pragmatism is metaphysically neutral. In "The Fixation of Belief," Peirce advocates for the method of science by stating explicitly the basic presupposition about the world into which science enquires: "There are real things, whose characters are entirely independent of our thoughts about them."[12] However, this claim need not be construed upon metaphysically realist lines. Nothing would bar Berkeley, for example, from admitting to the same construal of "real things," whose characters would be independent of *our* thoughts about them while being dependent upon *God's* ideas about them. When Peirce situates his account of the real in the larger context of "experience in general" (whether this is identified with God's experience or not), it might seem as if something along these lines is the case. However, Peirce offers this particular account within the larger argument for the method of science as superior to others for the fixation of belief. The quotation regarding the character of objects is but the first clause of a sentence that continues: "[T]hose realities affect our senses according to regular laws, and, though our sensations are as different as our relations to the objects, yet, by taking advantage of the laws of perception, we can ascertain by reasoning how things really are, and any man, if he have sufficient experience and reason enough about it, will be led to the one true conclusion."[13] The claim about the independent characters of objects, then, is made within the context of explicating the procedures of scientific inquiry, which is the means by which we come to understand the regular laws of perception.

Definition and pragmatic elucidation

As Christopher Hookway claims, Peirce's early formulation of the relationships among truth, inquiry, and reality makes use of the notions of reality and truth and does not offer definitions of either of them. The success of scientific inquiry is not explained by its abilities to connect thoughts with independent objects but rather by science's success at identifying and formulating the laws that govern our interactions with objects, at leading us to the truth about these real things.[14] This is simply to note that the relatively strong claim regarding the independent characters of real things is a claim about inquiry and that its sense can only be derived from within this context. It is a claim about those things about which scientific inquiry purports to be; the account of objects is internal to the account of inquiry.

Peirce's brief mention of objects and inquiry, then, in "The Fixation of Belief," seems to offer something of a paradox. Realities are those things whose characters are independent of our thoughts about them; our inquiries into them determine their characterization as objects. One means for resolving this paradox would be to assert that the characterization of objects given in the article is a necessary presupposition of scientific inquiry. On such an account, scientific inquiry requires that its objects of investigation maintain their characters independently of empirical inquiry into their natures and behaviors.[15] The mind-independence of the objects is settled, at least provisionally, prior to engaging in scientific inquiry, and the successful and unsuccessful formulations of scientific laws are explicable by the mind-independent characters of the objects. Such a reading of Peirce's formulation here runs into two specific problems. The first is that it hews very close to making of Peirce a proto-positivist and reading a kind of verificationism into his account of inquiry. The second is that it fails internally to take account of his fuller application of pragmatic inquiry in subsequent writings.

When Peirce enters into the discussion in "The Fixation of Belief," his concern is not simply to offer an account of belief and doubt and the role of inquiry in resolving the latter to return to the former. The larger illustration in which Peirce is engaged in the six papers that comprise the series is an attempt to identify the scope of logical and empirical investigations more generally, and to separate those investigations that could be conducted according to sound logical principles and those that could not. One sees this, for example, in his claim that "common-sense, or thought as it first emerges above the level of the narrowly practical, is deeply imbued with that bad logical quality to which the epithet *metaphysical* is commonly applied; and nothing can clear it up but a severe course of logic."[16] The implication is not only that our common-sense beliefs are unlikely to withstand investigation, but also that improperly conducted investigations might lead us to metaphysical speculation, the conclusions of which seem unlikely to withstand logical scrutiny. Part of the project, as A. J. Ayer noted, is to limit the kinds of hypotheses that might be suitable prospects for inquiry and, thereby, belief.[17]

Peirce offers his account of the objects into which scientific investigation inquires within this larger frame and hopes to offer a method by which we might come to relatively stable beliefs. Just before the passage regarding the objects of science quoted above, he writes: "To satisfy our doubts, therefore, it is necessary that a method should be found by which our beliefs may be caused by nothing human, but by some external permanency—by something upon which our thinking has no effect."[18] Science recommends itself as a method because it proceeds upon the "fundamental hypothesis" that there are such objects. The project to which scientific investigation directs itself, then, is to the formulation of the laws according to which these external permanencies relate to our experiences of them. In the subsequent paper in the series, in which Peirce offers the pragmatic maxim, he notes that one of its purposes is to clarify our ideas such that they are not susceptible to deceptions of the metaphysical sort.[19] Peirce follows this admonition by claiming the impossibility of having "an idea in our minds which relates to anything but conceived sensible effects of things."[20] By apparently ruling out metaphysics and tying meaningful belief to sensation, Peirce seems to be espousing the positivist line.

Although one could read Peirce in this way, it seems highly uncharitable to do so for two reasons. First, it creates a larger paradox across the six papers that comprise the series *Illustrations of the Logic of Science*; second, and more seriously, it ignores the ways in which Peirce later expands his account of the pragmatist principle in order to accommodate the wider range of hypotheses with which he is concerned. These objections to the verificationist reading of Peirce can be taken up in turn.

The fifth of Peirce's six papers for *Popular Science Monthly* in 1877 and 1878 explores two hypotheses apparently ruled out for significance by the verificationist reading of the pragmatic principle at work in inquiry. Peirce here considers the possibility of theism and the possibility of the uniformity of nature and finds both to be lacking in evidence according to the pragmatic principle.[21] Nonetheless, he does not find the speculative hypotheses through which these possibilities would be investigated to be without meaning: "If we could find out any general characteristic of the universe, any mannerism in the ways of Nature, any law everywhere applicable and universally valid, such a discovery would be of such singular assistance to us in all our future reasoning that it would deserve a place almost at the head of the principles of logic."[22] Such metaphysical speculation might be difficult to follow through—it might be difficult to specify the particular practical consequences that would follow from the hypothesis being true—but the hypothesis itself is not ruled out *tout court*. Peirce mixes theistic with non-theistic considerations in evaluating metaphysical speculations as part of the illustrations of the logic of science. Although he concludes that the mixture of metaphysical and religious hypotheses has been unfortunate for both fields, he claims that this view would not prevent him "from joining in that common joy at the revelation of enlightened principles of religion which we celebrate at Easter and Christmas." Peirce suggests that it is not the character of the world as something either created or designed by a personable and perfect being, but rather "that aspiration toward the perfect that constitutes the essence of religion."[23] As long as religion recognizes its visions of perfection as aspirations or aims, then it need not run athwart the aims of the logic of science.

If we reject an understanding of the objects of scientific inquiry as being entirely empirical objects but remain somewhat sympathetic to metaphysical and religious hypotheses, then it is tempting to understand and explicate these hypotheses as being non-cognitive or emotive, as expressions regarding the speaker's state of mind Ayer, for example, construes religious claims along these lines—though he is less sympathetic than Peirce seems to be above.[24] In doing so, though, the question becomes one of empirical investigation yet again. We are faced with ascertaining whether or not the speaker's state of mind is as reported. This would be a fact for psychological investigation, insofar as psychology could be construed as an empirical science. The second possibility left open by this sort of proto-positivism would be to construe the hypotheses of metaphysics and religion as being mathematical or logical. Clearly, the former is ruled out, but the latter need not be *prima facie* implausible. One might wish, for example, to think of Anselm's ontological argument as being a formal argument in this particular sense. In such a case, the hypotheses of metaphysics and religion would be meaningful, but they would be mere tautologies; they would not assert anything.[25] But if such claims are tautological, then they are true *a priori*, and attempts to construct *a priori* metaphysics are subject to some of Peirce's harshest attacks. Both metaphysical and religious hypotheses, then, need be construed in different ways if we can inquire into them.

In later years, when Peirce turns more specifically to metaphysical and theistic questions, he argues that both can be investigated in such a way that they would be subject to the pragmatic method, and would thereby be meaningfully answered. By 1898, Peirce is arguing that metaphysics be construed upon the lines of an "observational science" and thus be rescued from its "backward state."[26] That metaphysical hypotheses can be so considered is a result of their being about the world in much the same way in which scientific hypotheses regarding objects not directly observable are about the world. The difficulty in isolating the observable phenomena with which metaphysics deals "is that it rests upon the kinds of phenomena with which every man's experience is so saturated that he usually pays no particular attention to them."[27] The generality of metaphysics, not its lack of connection to experience or inquiry, explains its difficulty. Although there are bad metaphysical views, this is not because they are metaphysical; rather, it is because they are attempts to construct views that accord with "the personal interests of some person or collection of persons."[28] Here, Peirce's foil is again the *a priori* metaphysics that he assails in "The Fixation of Belief," a metaphysics the method of which is "to adopt whatever belief we are inclined to."[29] Even though his later investigations of both metaphysical and theistic issues according to his account of inquiry might be judged to fall short of their marks, the pragmatic principle cannot be taken as eliminating such considerations or investigations because of an implicit verificationism.[30] This suggests that Peirce's first formulation of the maxim in terms of consideration of *sensible* effects requires some further modification in order not to limit unduly the process of inquiry.

Thus far, the investigation of the objects for scientific inquiry rejects the view that we can safely construe Peirce's understanding of mind-independent objects as being those verifiable by strictly empirical inquiry. What is implicit in such a view is that there is a distinction in Peirce's thought between the methods of the physical sciences and the method of scientific inquiry.[31] Although the former provide a model of sorts for the latter in that they operate by formulating hypotheses and evaluating these according to evidence, they are simply a familiar example of the pragmatic method, the method of scientific inquiry. Furthermore, the view of objects explicated thus far rejects the view that metaphysical and religious hypotheses are merely formal in the way that mathematical or logical hypotheses are. The question that presents itself, then, is whether or not there is a way for construing "objects whose characters are entirely independent of our thoughts about them" that does not fall prey to the problems with reading verificationism into Peirce's account of inquiry, and which allows for metaphysical and religious hypotheses to continue to be subject to the method of scientific inquiry. The way forward, here, is to look carefully at the way in which Peirce treats mathematical and logical hypotheses.

When Peirce turns his attention to hypotheses of this sort, he argues that they are just as subject to the principle of pragmatism as are claims about the physical world. That is, mathematical and logical hypotheses, in order to be meaningful, must be construed in terms of their consequences. These consequences, however, need not be construed empirically, though they are construed experientially. These experiences will be of a different type than our sensory experiences, and our hypotheses about them will contain non-empirical (e.g., mathematical), content. Experiments can be carried out on such content, but they are experiments in which "operations upon diagrams, whether external or imaginary, take the place of the experiments upon real things that one performs in chemical and physical research."[32] Cheryl Misak points out that Peirce is relying at this point upon a distinction between two kinds of experience, "ideal" or "inner" and "real" or "outer." The mathematician's operations upon diagrams are observations of the ideal relationships among mathematical objects, but the observations are, nonetheless, experiences "in a very peculiar sense."[33] Despite the fact that such experiences are ideal or inner, they are no less experiences. Misak argues that for Peirce the distinction "is not hard and fast" and is explicable by the fact that "the inner world exerts comparatively slight compulsion upon us, whereas the outer world is full of irresistible compulsions."[34] Insofar as mathematical and logical hypotheses are about this ideal world, this suggests that the practical consequences in terms of which mathematical and logical hypotheses are to be evaluated are different from the kinds of consequences in terms of which hypotheses in the physical sciences are to be evaluated.[35] That is, we ought to continue to expect consequences, but we ought not to expect only empirical or sensory consequences.

It is a bit difficult at this point to know exactly how to construe Peirce's claim that the scientific hypothesis requires realities whose characters are entirely independent of what we might think of them once we have loosened the requirement that the practical effects of such realities be sensible, having suggested above that separating "scientific inquiry" and the "scientific hypothesis" from the "empirical sciences" requires that we do so. This becomes particularly problematic in light of Peirce's claim that the inner and outer worlds are distinguished by the compulsion of their experiences and not by any strict demarcation of realms. We seem, in moving away from verificationism, to have moved very close to idealism, though not the kind of idealism espoused by G. W. F. Hegel and rejected by Peirce.[36] It would be an idealism roughly characterized by two hypotheses: first, that the laws that govern scientific inquiry and the laws that govern experience must in some way coincide; second, that the objectivity of our investigations can be maintained by the independent character of these laws from *our* thoughts. The difficulty with such a view is that it lends itself all too easily to a reading in which the convergence of final opinion is guaranteed by something external to the process of inquiry itself. If the pragmatic method is to have the wide application to scientific inquiry that Peirce wants, then the process of inquiry must lead to convergence on its own; it must be capable of self-correction.[37]

The way ahead is by returning to Hookway's distinction alluded to above between the definition of a concept and its use. Peirce's project in offering the pragmatic maxim is not to offer a definition of the terms contained within it, nor is his project in the six papers from 1877 to 1878 to offer definitions that will help limn the boundaries of scientific inquiry. Rather, his project is to offer, as the title of the series indicated, illustrations. That is, Peirce is concerned with applications and not with definitions. In later writings, he laments that his original title for the *Popular Science Monthly* series, "Illustrations of the Logic of Science," was omitted.[38] Misak makes explicit the important distinction "between providing a definition of a term and the less formal business of spelling out the implications of hypotheses containing the term, i.e., of providing a pragmatic elucidation of the term."[39] The former project can be an important one, but it might not have the sort of pragmatic significance that Peirce requires in order for it to be elucidative. A definition could be helpful in pragmatic elucidation, but its significance as a definition would be granted by the pragmatic elucidation and not by its formal sufficiency.[40] We have already seen some of the ways in which such a project might head, and I want to turn now to a more direct address of this project of pragmatic elucidation.

A few requirements of the pragmatic elucidation of the concepts at work in the pragmatic maxim are worth making explicit here from what has come above. The first is that identifying the objects of scientific inquiry with the objects of the empirical sciences—with the objects of sensible experience—is too limiting. What is required is a more inclusive understanding of the realities into which science inquires. The second is that we cannot, to use Peirce's phrase, "block the path of inquiry" by ruling out classes of hypotheses that could be investigated.[41] What is required is a more inclusive understanding of the hypotheses open to pragmatic elucidation. The third is that we can distinguish between empirical and formal hypotheses in terms of their content and still subject both to the pragmatic maxim. What is required is a conception of experience that is flexible enough to accommodate this without being so loose as to allow that any difference in any interpreter's experiences count as practically significant. We can turn now to consideration of the pragmatic maxim as a maxim for scientific inquiry with these requirements in hand.

In "The Fixation of Belief," Peirce considers four different methods through which clarity of thought can be achieved and opinion be settled.[42] After noting that the method of tenacity, the method of authority, and the *a priori* method each have their merits, Peirce recommends: "A man should consider well of them; and then he should consider that, after all, he wishes his opinions to coincide with the fact, and that there is no reason why the results of those three first methods should do so."[43] If we are to keep in mind the requirements of our conception of inquiry outlined above, we ought to also remember here that the same could be said of the verificationist understanding insofar as such a reading is too restrictive of the hypotheses to be investigated. We should consider well of it but wonder if it offers access to the full world of fact in which we are interested. Peirce then argues that the method of experimental science recommends itself in logic (the clarification of thought) and in practice (the use of thought).

The pragmatic maxim that comes in Peirce's following essay is but a more general statement of this method. Having argued above that the reading according to which the "practical effects" of our conceptions are to be construed as sensible effects is overly limiting and that a wider understanding of experiential effects is needed, we can turn now to the maxim: "[T]he rule for attaining the third grade of clearness of apprehension is as follows: Consider what effects, which might conceivably have practical bearings, we conceive the object of our conception to have. Then, our conception of these effects is the whole of our conception of the object."[44] Our conception of the possibility for practical effects by the object provides us with our conception of the object. For Peirce, we attain clarity of thought about an object when we have exhausted the examination of its possible effects. This is the principle of pragmatic elucidation, but it is not a principle for finding definitions.

Peirce's target here in laying out the maxim is, again, Descartes, but he holds the philosophical tradition since Descartes equally responsible for the failure to notice the importance of pragmatic elucidation, having "ever since copied his words." Descartes deserves credit for having noticed the importance of the first two levels of clearness of apprehension—observation and definition—but Peirce encourages us to find "something better adapted to modern uses."[45] Misak argues that recognizing the distinct (though related) levels of clarity provides us with the appropriate context for understanding the limits of the pragmatic maxim. What is required of the investigator is a "threefold competence" according to which full understanding can only be achieved when the investigator can: "(1) pick out what objects the term refers to . . . (2) give a definition of the term . . . (3) know what to expect if hypotheses containing the term are true; that is, know the consequences of hypotheses containing the term."[46] Insofar as we seek this third grade of clearness—which Peirce thinks his great contribution to philosophy to have noted—in our thoughts about objects, we are compelled to investigate the practical consequences that our conceptions might have. This pragmatic elucidation, then, is the purpose for engaging inquiry insofar as inquiry aims at the settlement of doubt.

Seeking this third grade of clearness is not merely an intellectual exercise carried out by those of a scientific bent. Peirce argues that the third grade of clearness is the most important. Just before offering the characterization of the real as "the object represented" in the opinion "fated to be ultimately agreed to by all who investigate," Peirce gives an example to show that apparent differences in the first two levels of clearness can be overcome by reference to the third. If nine different scientists set out to investigate the velocity of light through nine different methods of observation, Peirce holds that they would, "as each perfects his methods and processes," be led "to one and the same conclusion." As the investigators clarify their procedures and their conceptions of the practical consequences of their concepts, they will approach agreement with one another inasmuch as they are investigating the same property, the velocity of light. If one scientist measures the velocity in one way and another scientist measures it in another but the two conceptions turn out to have identical experimental and theoretical ramifications as the investigation is pursued, then the pragmatic maxim allows us to clarify their apparent differences in both denotation and connotation. That is, defining the velocity as x or defining it as y—whether or not these are taken to be synonymous—makes no non-terminological difference for any hypotheses containing the term.[47] Although a complete account of Peirce's grades of clearness requires engagement with his theory of signs, it is sufficient for our purposes to note that all three grades can be necessary while the importance of the third is maintained. That is, the three are closely interrelated, but only the third provides us with a means for clarifying what Peirce argues are real differences, differences that have practical consequences.

If we return, then, to where this section began, an important aspect of the independent characters of the object of inquiry becomes clear. In the velocity of light example, that the nine scientists are investigating the same property becomes clear in the examination of various hypotheses according to their practical effects. The property is the same property insofar as it has the same practical effects, and this is discovered in the process of scientific inquiry. As doubts are settled and beliefs are tested, the various independent inquiries begin to converge on the one property. Whatever the differences in observation and definition, the third grade of clearness allows for a convergence in effects. In offering the pragmatic maxim, Peirce is neither offering a means by which the objects of inquiry might be observed, which would belong to the first grade of competence, nor offering a definition for the objects of inquiry, which would belong to the second grade of competence. Rather, Peirce is offering a pragmatic elucidation of the function of the term "object" within the larger process of inquiry. That is, the independence of the characters of objects is neither a presupposition of, nor an external limit to, inquiry; it is an elucidation of the role that the term "object" plays when we inquire into its character.

Locating Peirce's account of inquiry within the context of the grades of clearness makes possible an account of pragmatism that is metaphysically neutral. Chapter 3 argued that the metaphysical project is construed as an account of the things that *actually* make up the *real* world (as opposed to *mere* appearances). In that sense, it is engaged in providing the second level of clearness. Metaphysics attempts to develop definitions of the terms that tell us what really exists, necessarily and universally. Peirce is engaged in providing the third level of clearness, of telling us how the things that make up the world impinge upon our inquiries into them and have effects upon our experiences. Although there are instances in which the definitional project produces accounts that are pragmatically viable, by 1905, Peirce is clearly arguing that by stopping with the definitional project, metaphysical accounts produce "meaningless gibberish—one word being defined by other words, and they by still others, without any real conception ever being reached."[48] The definitional project and the pragmatic project need not conflict, but they should not be confused.

When Peirce turns his attention to questions about objects and the limits of inquiry, he draws a distinct line, which seems to have gone largely unnoticed, between the definitional project and the pragmatic project.[49] Just after the example of the investigation into the velocity of light, he offers his controversial conception of the relationship between truth and reality, between inquiry's goal and its objects: "The opinion which is fated to be ultimately agreed to by all who investigate is what we mean by the truth, and the object represented in this opinion is the real. That is the way I would explain reality."[50] "Defining" and "explaining" might be co-terminus projects as they prove to be in the velocity of light example. There, we saw that through the process of explaining, providing pragmatic elucidation in terms of consequences, the inquiry eventually converges upon a definition—despite having started with different definitions. However, "defining" and "explaining" are not synonymous projects. Pragmatic elucidation alone engages in the latter.

Peirce picks up this thread, though less clearly than one might have hoped, in the paragraph immediately following: "But it may be said that this view is directly opposed to the abstract definition which we have given of reality, inasmuch as it makes the characters of the real depend on what is ultimately thought about them."[51] Peirce appears to respond with a definition according to which the object of final opinion is simply the real itself, as long as we recognize that our individual inquiries and thoughts are distinct from the long process of inquiry pursued sufficiently far to settle into beliefs that would not be subject to further surprises and, thereby, to doubts. "[O]n the one hand, reality is independent, not necessarily of thought in general, but only of what you or I or any finite number of men may think about it; and . . . on the other hand, though the object of the final opinion depends on what that opinion is, yet what that opinion is does not depend on what you or I or any man thinks."[52] If the distinction between definition and explanation is properly maintained, then this can be read as a pragmatic elucidation of reality, a working out of the function that reality plays in scientific inquiry. Reality is known by the effects it has on inquiry, by the compulsion it has on that pursuit—whether this compulsion is internally or externally experienced. This is an explanation, then, and not a definition; thinking of reality in this way explains reality's function. The internal relationship between real objects and scientific inquiry in general is maintained, while the reality of the characters of the objects themselves remains independent of inquiry because such independence is required by the inquiry. That is, the characters of the objects function independently of the individual inquiries into their characters. We recognize this when we are surprised that a well-conducted inquiry does not yield the result predicted by the hypothesis, when belief becomes unsettled.

Truth and the Peircean biconditional

At this point, Peirce introduces the notion of truth within the context of explaining the function and progress of inquiry. A hypothesis is true if and only if it would be believed at the end of inquiry, if no other experiences would unsettle it. Misak argues that this biconditional, "'*H* is true if and only if it would be believed at the end of a prolonged inquiry' . . . may epitomize Peirce's account of truth." Nonetheless, given Peirce's project of pragmatic elucidation, it cannot be taken as a definition of truth, nor can the two sides of the biconditional be understood as having the same status. Misak refers to the first, "*if H* is true, *then* if inquiry relevant to *H* were pursued as far as it could fruitfully go, *H* would be believed," as the "T-I conditional," the pragmatic elucidation of "*H* is true."[53] In this explanatory project, Peirce shows the expectation we would have of *H* if *H* were true—namely, that inquirers would be led to settled belief in *H*, which would not be dislodged by further experience or investigation. This leads to the second conditional, which Misak dubs the "I-T conditional": "*If*, if inquiry relevant to *H* were to be pursued as far as it could fruitfully go, then *H* would be believed, *then H* is true."[54] In this explanatory project, Peirce shows the expectation we would have of inquiry into the truth of *H* if the inquiry were pursued to its end—namely, that such inquiry would yield beliefs in hypotheses that were true. We can take up each of these in turn.

The T-I conditional tells us what to expect of true hypotheses. It offers the pragmatic consequences of a true hypothesis expressed in terms of the results of inquiry into the hypothesis itself. The result is settled belief. Because this is an *expectation* we have of inquiry into a true hypothesis, we recognize that it might go unfulfilled, as our other expectations often do. The T-I conditional, then, is not put forward as a guarantee that our process of inquiry *will* lead to truth; it is not something we can assert. Rather, it is a "regulative assumption of inquiry" on the part of the inquirer.[55] When a genuine hypothesis is put forward, we expect that there could be a final resolution of it, whether our particular inquiry into it offers that resolution or not. If we did not have this expectation, we would not bother to inquire. The pragmatic project is both less ambitious and less formal than that usually engaged by a "theory of truth." The regulative assumption is one that fails to *define* truth, showing instead that it is "essentially typically" the case with regard to true hypotheses that they "figure in the final opinion."[56] This might not be the case with all true hypotheses, but it is the case for all true hypotheses into which genuine inquiry can be pursued.

The I-T conditional tells us what to expect of inquiries into genuine hypotheses that are pursued as far as they can fruitfully go. The I-T conditional, then, requires some elucidation of the notion of a "genuine hypothesis." A genuine hypothesis for Peirce must meet two conditions: it must arise as a result of the unsettling of a belief and it must specify a means to return to a state of belief. Because beliefs are simply habits for action, they become unsettled when our expectations regarding our actions are not met. This creates a "surprise," which is the only cause of genuine doubt for Peirce.[57] When doubts arise, we attempt to settle them through inquiry in order to return to a state of belief, a state in which actions will have the desired or expected experiential results. The specified means for returning to a state of belief, then, must be a set of expectations or predictions that can be fulfilled by further experiences. Genuine hypotheses and genuine beliefs must be sensitive to experience, capable of both being dislodged by experience and being reinforced by it.[58] Because the I-T conditional is expressed as a subjunctive conditional and Peirce holds that subjunctive conditionals (and not merely indicative conditionals) are capable of being true, he is able to assert that the I-T conditional is true. That is, the pragmatic elucidation tells us what would be the case for inquiry if inquiry were pursued as far as it could fruitfully go; inquiry would alight upon hypotheses that would not be dislodged, which is all we mean by calling an hypothesis "true." Any other conception of "true" is not pragmatically significant.

Given the restrictions placed upon the process of scientific inquiry itself, that it must take place within the context of experience and must specify the expectations we are to have should the hypothesis be true in order to be a *genuine* or *scientific* inquiry (in the broad sense), the important upshot of the pragmatic elucidation of the T-I conditional and the I-T conditional is that the former is only a regulative assumption and the latter is only an assertion in these genuine inquiries. That is, the T-I conditional is only a regulative hope insofar as the genuine inquirer thinks that the hypothesis can have the specified effects and that the surprise that led to the doubt the inquiry is intended to settle can be resolved into belief again. There might be other inquiries in which we could engage that would not be subject to this regulative assumption, but these hypotheses would not be capable of meeting the standard of the third grade of clearness.[59] Likewise, the I-T conditional can only be asserted insofar as the hypothesis under investigation is genuine and is one that would settle doubts through genuine inquiry. There might be other hypotheses that would be true, but these hypotheses would not be pragmatically significant.[60]

The upshot of this lengthy excursion through Peirce is fairly straightforward. The bounds of the pragmatic maxim mark the bounds for genuine hypotheses—hypotheses that are pragmatically significant. Only such hypotheses are worthy of inquiry or belief or the designation "true." All genuine hypotheses need to be expressible in terms of experiential consequences—whether inner or outer—and scientific inquiry (in the broad sense) alone is capable of settling belief in such hypotheses. Categories of hypotheses are not ruled out *tout court*, but they might be ruled out as objects for pragmatic elucidation if they are not expressible in terms of experiential expectations or predictions. This last consideration means that pragmatism is metaphysically neutral, if we think of the project of metaphysics as being the definitional project. If what metaphysics does is to tell us what objects are like apart from their roles in inquiry, then pragmatism need not take a stand one way or the other regarding the existence of objects independently from inquiry other than to note that their characters are independent of our specific inquiries, insofar as our inquiries often lead to surprises regarding their characters.[61] Furthermore, we should not make the mistake of thinking that this explanation of the real as the object represented in the final opinion would only apply to the objects of sense. As we saw above, Peirce holds that objects diagrammatically represented (e.g., mathematical objects), are real objects insofar as they too could be represented in the final opinion produced by sufficiently prolonged inquiry.[62] The status, then, of pragmatism's claims about real objects are not of the status desired for metaphysical claims about the real. There is neither an affirmation nor a denial of metaphysical realism in the contemporary sense entailed by the pragmatic maxim and the pragmatic account of inquiry.

When it comes to questions of truth, a kind of neutrality holds as well. Although a number of commentators could be singled out here, it is worth noting in brief that Richard Kirkham labels Peirce a Nonrealist with regard to truth because he believes Peirce to be engaged in what he calls "the essence project," the attempt to provide an essentialist definition of truth. Clearly, this is not the case. The pragmatic elucidation of truth that comes from considering the T-I and I-T conditionals separately reveals that Peirce's primary interest is in showing the consequences for genuine or scientific inquiry in holding a hypothesis to be true. *Defining* truth as a formal equivalence with another predicate—for example, correspondence—is of little difference to the expected or predicted experiences offered by the hypothesis. Peirce often accuses such theories of being "transcendental" in that they wish to identify the aspects of truth that outrun scientific inquiry. However, insofar as the pragmatic elucidation of truth requires that truth would be the result if inquiry were carried sufficiently far, what the transcendentalist identifies must be compatible with the pragmatic elucidation or its result or be pragmatically meaningless. If it is the last, then it falls to the same criticisms as bad metaphysics. Although definition retains its importance, "Peirce regards the most important thing to be said about truth to be a specification of what we can expect of a true hypothesis," as Misak puts it.[63] In spelling out his pragmatism, Peirce is after only the third grade of clearness. If this assists in showing equivalencies among some definitions or eliminating others in the second grade of clearness, then so much the better.[64] However, these definitions need to gain their sense within the context of genuine inquiry. To the extent that they do not, they are as spurious as bad metaphysics.

James and the Balance of Inquiry

Although there are other points at which they diverge as well, one common place to locate the distinction between Peirce and James is with regard to their respective positive metaphysics—Peirce choosing to offer his scientific and agapic conception of the world and James choosing to offer his pluralist panpsychic conception of the world. Nonetheless, I have claimed for the purposes of this chapter to agree, in general, with Hookway's assessment of the metaphysical neutrality of pragmatism, and have also chosen to argue for a kind of epistemological neutrality, at least as regards the definition of truth. Although this is a difficult argument to make with regard to Peirce, the way has been paved by Hookway and Misak, whose excellent analyses of Peirce provide substantial resources for the former, if not the latter. Making the parallel argument with regard to James is slightly more difficult for two reasons. First, commentaries on James often note his "popular style"—a thing James himself often resented—which makes a systematic analysis of

James difficult to perform and consistency hard to find. Second, and perhaps as a result of the first, James's pragmatism is often taken—as it was by Peirce—as having a much wider scope than Peirce's original maxim of logic and, thereby, as entailing a broader epistemological, if not a metaphysical, view.[65] Both of these problems can be addressed here by paying closer heed to the ways in which James views his own pragmatism and its relationship to his larger philosophical project. On the first head, James's pragmatism, despite other inconsistencies and stylistic problems, hews much closer to Peirce's understanding of pragmatism as a maxim of logic than has been supposed. On the second head, James's narrower understanding of pragmatism allows for a more fruitful consideration of its application to various ideas, including truth.

James, rationality, and method

Chapter 3 argued that James's criticisms of Kant come within the confines of his criticisms of the "intellectualist" or "conceptualist" method within philosophy. In many ways, such a view dovetails nicely with Peirce's distinctions among the three grades of clearness above. The intellectualist or conceptualist takes the end of his or her investigations to be the second grade of clearness, while Peirce and James see the end of inquiry to be the third, the pragmatic elucidation of the concept. One notable distinction between Peirce and James is that James seems to deny the importance of the first two grades of clearness, if not the necessity of them. James can, without much difficulty, be defended against charges that he denies the legitimacy and necessity of the first grade of clearness, the observational. He dealt with many such charges from critics of his later philosophy.[66] It is slightly more difficult to defend James against charges that he denies the legitimacy and necessity of the second grade of clearness, the definitional. He often seems to conflate pragmatic elucidation with definition; however, in his post-1903 works, James does distinguish more carefully between the second and third grades.

We can begin the exploration of James's understanding of the process of inquiry and the distinctions among the grades of clearness in much the same place as we began the discussion of Peirce—namely, in his views of, and responses to, other metaphysical projects. James's disparaging views of absolute idealism are well covered, but what is of interest here is the context in which these views occur. Upon his invitation to deliver the Hibbert Lectures at Manchester College, Oxford, which he gave in May 1908, James chose to address "The Present Situation in Philosophy." The series, eventually published as *A Pluralistic Universe*, thus sets itself a meta-philosophical task, and James is happy to use a broad scope, if not a popular style, in offering the lectures.[67] David Lamberth argues that James launches a two-pronged attack against the absolute of idealism in the lectures: "First . . . he argues that the absolute is not logically coercive (or necessary), but rather is merely an hypothesis . . . Second, he launches a frontal assault, arguing that his contenders' understanding of the unity of the absolute and the world is internally incoherent."[68] After offering a typology for thinking about philosophy in the first lecture and attacking monistic idealism in the second, James turns his attention to philosophic method in the third and carries this concern through the remaining lectures. Although it has been some ten years at this point since James first resurrected Peirce's pragmatic method, the series provides good context for thinking about James's own understanding of the scope and limitations of the pragmatic method.

In Lecture III, James takes the first tack in addressing Hegel's method with a particular eye to the consequences of the absolute. Before applying his own pragmatic test to the hypothesis of the absolute, though, James offers credit to Hegel for the dialectic method. In offering it, Hegel, on James's account, recognized the perpetual flux of the universe and the need for a philosophic method that could account for the "dogging of everything by its negative, its fate, its undoing." The dialectic, taken this way, is "not only harmless, but accurate."[69] It captures the spirit of James's pluralism by emphasizing the importance of the environment and relations for the existence and constitution of each individual thing. The difficulty for Hegel comes on two heads. First, James faults Hegel for having taken the dialectic to be capable of encapsulation entirely within the mind through the consideration of concepts. In so doing, Hegel "clung fast to the old rationalist contempt for the immediately given world of sense and all its squalid particulars" and substituted "logic," which he supposed coercively necessary for his system to be "a product of eternal reason."[70] Because Hegel takes on the rationalist preference for the whole to the parts while clinging to the dialectic, the dialectic itself must be resolved by that which contains its own negation, "the only whole by which *all* contradictions are reconciled . . . the all-inclusive reason."[71] Thus, whatever Hegel's pretentions for having captured, or at least recognized, the inevitable flux in which we live, he asks that this flux resolve itself in something which is not subject to such flux—the absolute.

This resolution of the many by the one leads to the second head on which James faults Hegel. Hegel derives from the flux some necessary principle according to which any progress, "in the Hegelian universe, has, in short, to proceed by the apodictic words *must be* rather than by those inferior hypothetic words *may be*, which are all that empiricists can use."[72] Consideration, then, of the pragmatic method can be approached through consideration of the dialectic and its product, the absolute. In so doing, we can take the approach suggested in the prior subsection and ask whether or not the absolute has consequences that stand the test of pragmatic elucidation, which would be to consider James's first prong, and we can take the approach suggested in the prior section and ask whether or not the absolute—like spurious metaphysics—has specifiable consequences at all, in which case it would not rise to the level of a genuine hypothesis.

Interestingly, when James approaches idealism, he does not first take on what may be the more prominent target, the religious and moral advantages that the absolute is supposed to provide. He dismisses the religious advantages in one succinct paragraph by noting that the absolute could not be "more different . . . than the God, say, of David or of Isaiah." Instead, he focuses his attack on the rationality of the hypothesis of the absolute, remarking that "making the world appear more rational" would have the consequence of making the hypothesis of the absolute "be accepted as more probably true than an hypothesis that makes the world appear irrational."[73] In considering the absolute as an hypothesis, then, James intends to subject it to the test of the pragmatic method, asking that it fulfill the conditions set out for a genuine hypothesis—namely, that it have specifiable consequences.

In the particular case of the rationality of the world in which we live, James argues for a more expansive understanding of rationality than the one with which the idealism of his day operated. It is not mere intellectual sense we want to make of the world; "rationality has at least four dimensions, intellectual, aesthetic, moral and practical." None of these four has a necessary priority over the others. Understanding rationality in this way makes difficult finding "a world rational to the maximal degree *in all these respects simultaneously.*" Various philosophies manage to corner one form of rationality well enough but always at the expense of another. Even the practical realm of rationality is not spared this criticism, being "irrational to moral and artistic temperaments."[74] Although James does not argue directly for it here, he alludes to the conclusion that perfect rationality in all four respects simultaneously might be unattainable.

Keeping these contextual and cautionary remarks in mind, James turns his attention more directly to the claim that the absolute makes the universe more rational. The key criterion for judgment is "balance" among the four dimensions because "whatever demand for rationality we find satisfied by a philosophic hypothesis, we are liable to find some other demand for rationality unsatisfied."[75] James judges the rationality of the absolute, then, by examining it with regard to the four dimensions, assessing its "credits" and "debits" in the four columns of the ledger. Although the concept has its aesthetic, intellectual, and moral merits, it is less meritorious practically. Nonetheless, James credits the absolute for offering "the assurance that however disturbed the surface may be, at bottom all is well with the cosmos—central peace abiding at the heart of endless agitation."[76] The appeal of such peace is not merely emotional but rational as well; the world becomes a system subject to laws and reasons that transcend it, not subject to the change and striving that characterize the finite world. Insofar as we grasp these laws and reasons, we transcend our partial and parochial perspectives and grasp the eternal, participating in the perfecting of the universe. James credits the absolute: "This admirable faculty of transcending, whilst inwardly preserving, every contrariety, is the absolute's characteristic form of rationality."[77] The absolute makes its strongest appeal in allowing us to make sense of the world and our place within it by relating our every effort and aim to those that exist in static eternity. "We are but syllables in the mouth of the Lord," James writes.[78]

Counting against the absolute when treated as a hypothesis is the weighty problem of evil, which inveighs against any conception of the absolute according to which what occurs in the finite world is somehow required for the infinite perfecting of the absolute itself. "Its perfection is represented as the source of things, and yet the first effect of that perfection is the tremendous imperfection of all finite experience,"[79] claims James. As either a source or a consequence of the finite world, the absolute is plagued by both the sheer existence of imperfections and their number. However, such a failing in the concept of the absolute is not religious. Having included morality among the dimensions of rationality, James notes that there are problems with the consequence of the rationality of the world that flow from the existence of imperfections: "In whatever sense the word 'rationality' may be taken, it is vain to contend that the impression made on our finite minds by such a way of representing things is altogether rational."[80] Even in the case in which one might hope that some balance among the four dimensions of rationality could be achieved despite the impossibility of perfect rationality, the absolute suffers from a balance deficit.

If the importance of the rationality of the world offered by the absolute is cashed out in terms of truth, the deficit runs even deeper. "Truth" and "error" can be substituted for "perfection" and "imperfection," and the consequences of the argument above extend to truth. If truth is viewed as coherence, it seems necessary that error be explicable in terms of truth. Citing the prominent British idealist, Harold Joachim, James notes that even Joachim admits to insoluble problems with the conception, despite remaining convinced of its correctness. James puts the rhetorical question to Joachim, whom he then quotes: "If truth be the universal *fons et origo*, how does error slip in? 'The coherence-theory of truth,' [Joachim] concludes, 'may thus be said to suffer shipwreck at the very entrance of the harbour.'"[81] The conception of the absolute seems to require not rational argument but faith in its truth despite *prima facie* irrationality. The consequence for which we hope is one that might be ideally satisfied, but it is not one that will be satisfied here and now.

Although explicitly pursuing the first tack here in treating the absolute as a hypothesis, because the argument concerns the rationality of the absolute, James's assessment of it here has consequences for the question of the logical coherence of the notion as well. In a paragraph so brief it can be quoted in full, James claims: "The trouble is that we are able to see so little into the positive detail of [the absolute], and that if once admitted not be coercively proven by the intellectualist arguments, it remains only a hypothetic possibility."[82] Once one removes the logical coercion of the absolute—once one admits that denying its existence is not self-contradictory—and treats it as a hypothesis, it proves more opaque with regard to its measurable consequences than genuine hypotheses ought to be.

We can turn, then, to the question of whether or not the absolute can be counted as a genuine hypothesis. To take this task upon ourselves is to frame the question along the lines suggested by Lamberth's second prong of James's attack—namely, the logical coherence of the notion of the absolute. Making this turn actually allows us to see the ways in which James does distinguish, albeit somewhat unclearly, between the second and third grades of clearness noted by Peirce. What is somewhat more difficult in James is to separate his disparaging remarks regarding the "vicious intellectualism" of rationalist logic and his own only slightly less disparaging discussion of the definitional project. Nonetheless, such a separation can be made and will offer a clearer view of James's perspective on, and use of, the pragmatic method.

In treating Rudolf Hermann Lotze's "monistic idealism" in the second Hibbert Lecture, James makes the distinction between definition and vicious intellectualism, but only implicitly. His interest in the lecture is to argue against a particular *reductio ad absurdum* that is intended to make the absolute a necessary posit of reason. Considering two objects, *a* and *b*, the question is whether these objects are separate and independent, in which case their interaction would seem to require some third fact, an "influence," through which *a* acts on *b* and likely a fourth through which *b* is influenced by *a*. Taking it this way would mean that it is *a*'s influence that interacts with *b*'s being influenced and so on *ad infinitum*. Thus, no two objects would ever interact with each other and would be "mutually impenetrable" or "mutually irrelevant." Worse yet, *a*'s influence must, once it has detached itself from *a*, find *b*'s "being influenced by *a*" instead of finding *c*'s or *d*'s or *n*'s. The *reductio*, then, is supposed to show the necessity of *b*'s nature being "somehow fitted to *a*'s nature in advance." James paraphrases Lotze's solution: "The multiple independent things supposed cannot be real in that shape, but all of them, if reciprocal action is to be possible between them, must be regarded as parts of a single real being, M."[83] By taking such an approach, Lotze is able to argue that *a* and *b* are not independent but *interdependent* and must be so if they are going to exert mutual influence.[84]

James's counterargument strikes on two heads. First, he argues that the solution offered by Lotze is "pretty" but "purely verbal." Changing the word does little to explain their actual interaction. All Lotze has done is to suggest the necessity of re-categorizing our thinking about how objects relate to one another. On James's pluralistic account, two objects can be interdependent without need for there to be some all-encompassing "absolute" to which they are related. He can thus accommodate the relations among objects without being pushed to monism. The second head on which James attacks Lotze is over his construal of what definitions actually tell us about objects. Here, what is required is the distinction between definition and elucidation that is used above. In switching from the discussion of the many, which are independent and mutually exclusive, to the one, which is interdependent and mutually inclusive, James claims that all Lotze has done is to offer us "verbal permission" to say that *a* and *b* could be interdependent and thus change. What Lotze has failed to do is to offer us any insight into "the actual process by which real things that are one can and do change at all." Lotze's difficulty is that he has taken the abstract concept of "independence" to be the entirety of our conception of *a* and *b*. It is an abstract name applied to *a* and *b*, which in their characters might include any number of other properties. James condemns such an approach: "To construe any one of their abstract names as *making their total nature impossible* is a misuse of the function of naming." Lotze has abstracted from the objects one characteristic, named it, and declared that its existence makes the very existence of *a* and *b* impossible (not just inexplicable) without the absolute. However, doing so, on James's reading, Lotze has taken "independence" to be the fact *simpliciter* rather than a fact *secundum quid*. That is, Lotze has reduced a particular expression of the thing to the thing itself rather than having seen it as but one *definite respect* according to which we might come to understand *a* or *b*.[85] Lotze has offered definitions but failed to offer elucidations, having stopped his project in the same place in which spurious metaphysics, according to Peirce, so often does.

Having mistaken the definitional project to be the entire project for understanding objects and their relations leads, very quickly, to vicious intellectualism. In fact, it helps us understand what James intends when he accuses Lotze of it: "The treating of a name as excluding from the fact named what the name's definition fails positively to include, is what I call 'vicious intellectualism.'"[86] Vicious intellectualism stops at the project of definition and fails to look for concrete interactions or effects. This turns quickly into the "intellectualist logic," according to which the concepts upon which logic operates are taken to be the only possible real objects. Lamberth notes that despite James's inconsistency in terminology, his attack is not on what we might call "standard logic" or "conceptual logic," the basic rules according to which logical operations are performed with concepts. Rather, what James has in mind here is "a more complex referent" that arises from the conjunction of two distinct positions with standard logic: "This more complex referent includes certain premises of idealism, most notably the idealist principle that things are (really) as they appear, and the rationalist's preference for concepts over percepts (or sensation)." This combination means that the only real things are the conceptual things because it is only those concepts that turn out to be present to the mind. Lamberth remarks: "Given this preference for the conceptual order as indicative of appearances (the rationalist thesis), and the notion that things are as they appear (the idealist thesis), 'vicious intellectualism' thus follows from standard logic."[87] What is required in order to undo these errors of vicious intellectualism is a means for disentangling the priority of the conceptual order from standard logic, which, when combined with the idealist thesis, dictates reality.

In taking on this project, James's accusation of "vicious intellectualism" needs to be seen as the first step in the argument against the logical coherence of idealism. It is not that the concepts themselves are problematic; rather, it is the notion that operations of standard logic on these concepts might dictate their instantiation, their reality. James makes this direct attack on idealism in Lecture V. The issue for idealism is that it takes as a premise that the percept is real as it appears to the mind. For Hegel, who did not accept the priority of the conceptual or standard logic, this is relatively unproblematic.[88] For then-contemporary idealism, this proves to be the downfall.

Idealism, on James's account, cannot account for the relationship between the many and the one in the way it proposes. On the one hand, the idealist accepts Berkeley's conception that with regard to mental existence, "its *esse* is *sentiri* or *experiri*"; on the other, the idealist holds that the "higher and the lower in the universe are entitatively identical."[89] When we have some experience of a grouping of things—for example, tiles on a floor—the idealist suggests that this is one experience. At the same time, the experience itself might be of an indeterminate number of things, having taken no time in the experience to account for the definite number of tiles. Thus, the many—the determinate number of tiles—are taken together as one, despite the one being indeterminate with regard to the exact number of tiles. Because the one and the many are presumed identical in such instances, the number of tiles is both indeterminate and determinate at the same time. The one fact of the experience of the tiles taken together, which must—according to Berkeley's principle—be simply as it is experienced, is indeterminate and thus contradicts the many that we recognize must be present to give rise to the one and can be made determinately many simply by counting. However, because the "forms of appearance are so different, the all and the eaches cannot be identical" without violating the principle from Berkeley.[90] In clinging, then, to both intellectualist logic and idealism, idealism proves incoherent.[91]

What is important to us here is to note that this line of argument against idealism does not, as the argument against idealism's supposed rational advantages, take place at the level of pragmatic elucidation. Rather, James takes on idealism here on its own terms at the definitional level. In so doing, James at least implicitly distinguishes between definitional clarity (the second grade) and pragmatic elucidation (the third grade). James's disparaging remarks regarding Lotze's "purely verbal" solution aside, the definitional project proves important in that it can provide clarity. Not only does James's own argument against idealism make use of the definitions to indicate idealism's incoherence, but he also makes several suggestions regarding idealism that trade in these very definitions. In a rather remarkable passage, given the impression of James as a less than systematic thinker, he argues that the idealists could be rescued in two fashions: "They ought either to refute the notion that as mental states appear, so they are; or, still keeping that notion, they ought to admit a distinct agent of unification to do the work of the all-knower, just as our respective souls or selves in popular philosophy do the work of partial knowers."[92] James's clear suggestion here is that the incoherence in idealism could be overcome at the definitional level by relinquishing either the rationalist or the idealist premise. The other option for the idealist is to relinquish the "logic of identity" and embrace the pluralism that James himself proposes, admitting that the "all-form" and the "each-form" are not identical, and that a plurality of knowers exists. James's more positive argument for his pluralism hinges, then, on its being clearer and less contradictory at the definitional level than monistic idealism (as well as being capable of pragmatic elucidation as a genuine hypothesis).

Having made this recommendation, it seems that we are left with what James calls "the actual trilemma that confronts every one of us." We can give up our empiricism and embrace the soul proposed by scholasticism, give up on intellectualist logic, or "face the fact that life is logically irrational."[93] He cannot, in his post-Kantian and post-Humean temper, embrace the soul, which leaves him with a mere dilemma. He must choose between the last two options—maintaining intellectualist logic and holding the world to be fundamentally irrational or relinquishing intellectualist logic and holding the world to be somehow rational nonetheless. Given the arguments detailed above regarding idealism's embrace of an intellectualism that quickly becomes vicious, it should be clear which of these James chooses. James does relinquish intellectualist logic or "the logic of identity" when he embraces his four-fold conception of rationality. It is not that he relinquishes logical consistency; it is that he rejects the rationalist thesis regarding the priority of the conceptual order and, with it, the right of standard logic (at the definitional level of working solely with concepts and not their effects) to determine reality. Perfect rationality in the intellectualist sense cannot be maintained; what we are left to strive for is balance. This balance is best achieved, then, through the application of the pragmatic method.

My suggestion here is that we ought to see these arguments against idealism in much the same light as Peirce's arguments against spurious metaphysics were viewed above. They provide a background for making the distinctions necessary between genuine hypotheses and spurious ones, between those capable of pragmatic elucidation and those capable only of offering verbal or definitional solutions. Again, for Peirce and James, the difficulty for both spurious metaphysics and absolute idealism is two-fold. On the one hand, the pragmatic consequences they are supposed to provide prove not to follow from them when considered as hypotheses. On the other hand, by stopping with the definitional project rather than continuing to the project of pragmatic elucidation and, for James on idealism at least, proving logically problematic at the level of definition, they succumb to "vicious intellectualism" and fail to rise to the level of a genuine hypothesis that would be capable of pragmatic elucidation.[94]

This lengthy discussion of James's arguments against idealism is intended to lay the groundwork for the metaphysical neutrality of his pragmatism. James is not unsympathetic to the project of metaphysics, as his own radical empiricism shows. James is, however, unsympathetic to the metaphysics that succumbs to vicious intellectualism. As David Lamberth has argued, James has sympathies with idealism that run deep because of idealism's commitment to a pantheistic and "intimate" world-view.[95] Because of the common perception that James is, on the one hand, unsystematic in his thinking and thus ill-equipped for the kind of distinctions Peirce employs in his arguments for the logical priority of pragmatism and, on the other hand, anti-metaphysical at best or simply confused regarding the role and importance of metaphysics, I have gone to some length here to provide the context for James's embrace of pragmatism and the pragmatic method. We can turn now to that direct address.

James's pragmatic turn

James does not see pragmatism as entailing a metaphysical view. He does see certain metaphysical views as being better suited to pragmatism—e.g., his own radical empiricism—he even goes so far on occasion as to suggest that radical empiricism entails a commitment to pragmatism.[96] Nonetheless, in the introduction to *Pragmatism*, James claims, quite directly, that one could remain a pragmatist while rejecting radical empiricism.[97] I would argue that it might be the case that radical empiricism, as a metaphysical thesis, is likely to entail a commitment to pragmatism, as an epistemological thesis, but that the reverse would not hold. Again, making such claims requires that we keep two relatively narrow points in mind: first, that metaphysics, as usually engaged, operates with definitions rather than elucidations; second, that pragmatism works broadly as a logical method that applies across domains.

In James's case, pragmatism recommends itself as a means for achieving balance across the four dimensions of rationality that he outlines in the Hibbert Lectures. The pragmatic method, in its earliest statement from 1898, echoes Peirce's quite closely: "To attain perfect clearness in our thoughts of an object, then, we need only consider what effects of a conceivably practical kind the object may involve—what sensations we are to expect from it, and what reactions we are to prepare." James even sets this claim within the context used by Peirce in the articles of 1878, noting that the pragmatic method is a method for the settlement of doubt and the return to a state of belief. He admits that he might have expressed it "more broadly than Mr. Peirce expresses it," and turns rather quickly to use the term "truth" to expand his explanation. Much like Peirce, though, James is using the term here rather than offering a definition of it. "The ultimate test for us of what a truth means is indeed the conduct it dictates or inspires . . . [T]he effective meaning of any philosophic proposition can always be brought down to some particular consequence, in our future practical experience, whether active or passive."[98] In this early statement of the pragmatic maxim, which resuscitated the method that had lain dormant for twenty years, James offers a two-fold understanding of the application of the maxim, one that is both descriptive and prescriptive. On the one hand, we are to find the conduct dictated or inspired, what we will do on the basis of the predicted consequence of the maxim. On the other hand, we are to hypothesize regarding the consequences that would follow in our practical experience were the proposition to prove meaningful.[99]

Although there are a number of places and ways to approach James's pragmatism, that James distinguishes explicitly between definitional clarity and pragmatic elucidation becomes clearest when he approaches the discussion of truth, which is where he thinks the advantage of pragmatism shows itself most explicitly. Having used the designation "pragmatism" when explicating his view of truth in the Lowell Lectures of 1906 and 1907, he regrets the term's association with the practical, suggesting that it had been "an unfortunate choice" because of "its suggestions of action."[100] Given what was said above about the four dimensions of rationality that James identifies, we might see his disclaimer here as being an admission of the over-emphasis placed on but one dimension of rationality in the discussions and rejoinders of those lectures. Disjointed and somewhat disconnected though they are, the essays and papers from the last five years of James's life do provide us with two distinct advantages when discussing the descriptive and prescriptive ways in which James understands the pragmatic maxim. First, James offers a fairly mature examination and defense of the pragmatic maxim from the perspective of his conception of truth, which had, since the lectures that became *Pragmatism* were published, been assailed on a number of fronts. Second, despite his occasional lapses of clarity, James does offer a fuller exploration of the application of the maxim to issues of epistemology in these later essays than elsewhere. Because of the presumed distance between Peirce and James over the latter's conception of truth and the coverage given above to the relationship between real objects and the process of pragmatic inquiry, it seems appropriate here to take up these epistemological issues in James.

Perhaps James's greatest failing in *Pragmatism* was to clarify his relationship to either then-contemporary-realism or then-contemporary idealism when it came to the question of truth.[101] This is not especially surprising, but it is not because of James's lack of systematic coherence or ability. Rather, in offering a new conception of truth through the application of the pragmatic maxim, James is engaged in a project different from that of his opponents on either side. James's early critics accused him primarily of subjectivism, taking psychological satisfaction to the individual to be the mark of truth. Certainly, James does himself no favors in this regard, even when responding to his critics. In the response to the "first misunderstanding," James claims that pragmatism has "contented itself with the word 'truth's' *definition*." When clarifying this claim, though, James states pragmatism's primary question: "What kind of things would true judgments be *in case* they existed?" Defending himself against the psychological reading of his detractors, James claims that this question "belongs obviously to a purely speculative field of inquiry." However, he does not mean by this that the question of truth is entirely definitional although it is "a logical question."[102] Given what was said above about the way in which James views logic, some clarification is needed here.

When James claims that pragmatism's treatment of truth is "logical" or "theoretical," he means that it trades in conceptual logic rather than in an empirical investigation. His interest is not in investigating some empirical state of psychological "satisfaction" but rather in offering conceptual clarity with regard to the notion of truth. This conceptual logic is not to be confused with intellectualist logic, with its three compounding theses, but it ought to be seen in the same broad way in which Peirce's conception of logic was seen above. Pragmatism's conception of truth, then, works on the "refined theoretic question," which must be answered before "secondary corollaries of a practical sort follow."[103] In applying the pragmatic maxim to the question of truth, James intends to settle the intellectual (though not intellectualist) question before turning to the practical or sensible effects of pragmatism's response. This is not to settle with a mere definition of truth but to note that concepts can be just as effective in the intellectual dimension of rationality as empirical realities can be in its practical dimension.

In order to make this claim while maintaining his defense against subjectivism or worse, solipsism, James employs a notion of "reality" that is surprisingly redolent of Peirce. According to the view James puts forward here, "previous realities," including ideas, are "independent variables" when it comes to questions of truth. Despite their independence in one sense, they remain responsive to the process of inquiry, and ideas become "complemental factors of reality," objects of and for pragmatic elucidation.[104] Ideas are thus both the products of, and the objects for, pragmatic inquiry. What pragmatism attempts is to formulate a means by which we ought to be able to see this complementing activity. In the case of both the empirical realities and the mental realities with which inquiry deals, the process of investigation is the same. The object of inquiry is an independent variable in an investigation but not independent of all investigation. When James turns his attention most explicitly to the question of the relationship between verification and truth, this becomes clearer.

In responding to the sixth misunderstanding of pragmatism, that it conflates verification with definition, James argues that pragmatism means to explain not only the former but also the latter. The difficulty for the objector to pragmatism is that the pragmatic project inverts the order in which the question of verification and the question of definition are to be answered. Given that for James or Peirce a definition can only be understood fully through the process of pragmatic inquiry, this is hardly surprising. A difference in definition is only meaningful if it makes a difference in the result of inquiry. James accuses the anti-pragmatist of thinking the abstract question of definition to be more important than the concrete question of verification; in this sense, the anti-pragmatist is the paradigmatic intellectualist whom James criticizes for ascribing to the abstractions "a higher grade of reality." The pragmatist has "no objection to abstractions" and "relies on them as much as anyone" but refuses to give such abstractions priority, finding them empty compared to the rich facts of experience but nonetheless useful *because of* their emptiness.[105] The objection is not to abstract concepts but to an intellectualism that views them as the primary order of experience and reality.

The focus on the process of inquiry offered by pragmatism not only provides concrete reasons for believing that an idea is true, but also provides a pragmatic elucidation of truth-relations. Whereas the anti-pragmatist tears the "hows and whats asunder," the pragmatist "tells us what [truth] is incidentally to telling us how it is arrived at." Under the question of "how," James includes not only the understanding of how a particular individual might come to believe something to be true, but also the understanding of how some idea might be true. For James, these two notions are not identical, but they are complementary: "The reasons why I find it satisfactory to believe that any idea is true, the *how* of my arriving at that belief, may be among the very reasons why the idea *is* true in reality." The discoverable, concrete relations that make an idea true are the very discoverable, concrete relations that provide the best reasons for belief, those revealed in inquiry pursued sufficiently far. In offering this view, the pragmatist demonstrates the "links of experience sequent upon an idea" that "form and for the pragmatist indeed *are* the *concrete* relation of truth."[106] Although any number of other ideas that are not so easily demonstrable might be true in some abstract sense, it is the concrete ideas under investigation that pragmatism helps us evaluate. In so doing, the truth relation itself becomes concrete, and "truth" as an abstract concept does as well.

James follows this response with a more detailed engagement of the relationship between pragmatism's practical and theoretic interests and defends pragmatism against the charge that it simply assumes the former to trump the latter. On the account just given, the concrete relation that is truth has both a practical consequence and a theoretical status. The concrete relation works both between ideas and experiential objects and, insofar as they can be taken as objects for investigation, between ideas and other ideas. In this way, the concrete relation takes precedence "in the order of logic as well as in that of being."[107] James's interest is not so much in elucidating the *practical* but in the *particular* nature of the consequences. He offers that "ideas *are* practically useful in the narrow sense" and thus can be open to pragmatic elucidation. Furthermore, James holds that true ideas' practical utility in the narrow sense shows us why the question of truth became of concern in the first place.[108] Nonetheless, he accuses the anti-pragmatist of making the mistake of reading "practical" in only this narrow sense, as being opposed to the theoretical; the anti-pragmatist fails to account for looser uses of the term, which allow it to mean "untrue in strict practice" but "true virtually, *certain to be true.*"[109] This suggests not so much that James has in mind a practical outcome but a concrete one, which might be conceptual or theoretical but nonetheless practical in this broader sense of being opposed to "abstract, general, and inert." This is not to suggest that the abstract thoughts are untenable, but only that they are to be worked out in terms of particular consequences, although their operations are "the purely logical ones of analysis, deduction, comparison, etc."[110] The pragmatist is anti-intellectualist, but the pragmatist is not opposed to either the use of abstract concepts or the use of conceptual logic in the explication and elucidation of truth. The theoretical can be a subject for pragmatic elucidation as much as the practical can be.

The discussion of these later remarks on truth thus far has been engaged to show the ways in which James uses the pragmatic elucidation of the conception of truth to clarify the relationship between the pragmatic project and the realities (including true ideas) that it investigates. Although the convoluted nature of James's discussion of the relationship between truths and "absolute truth" in his response to the charge of relativism makes it a difficult place to look for further clarification of the independent nature of the objects of investigation, these remarks are surprisingly instructive when read in that context. In "Abstractionism and Relativismus," James takes on the charge that his conception of truth fails to offer any reason to think that more is involved in truth than what we currently believe. Responding to "Professors Rickert and Münsterberg," who complained that pragmatists "reproduce that protagorean doctrine that the individual man is 'the measure of all things'" because of their attempts to "make truth grow . . . out of human opinion," James accepts the charge of relativism and then offers a pragmatic elucidation of the concept in relation to which the charge was framed. These two "cleverist brandishers" of the accusation of relativism object on two fronts to James's pragmatic conception of truth. First, they charge James with inconsistency or incoherence, thinking his own conception of truth to be absolute while being debarred by pragmatist principles from claiming an absolute truth. Second, they charge James with being incapable of explaining the convergence of opinion that is supposed to result from properly conducted inquiry because of the lack of an absolute truth toward which inquiry is heading.[111]

On the first head, James frames his response to the rationalist objection by claiming both that the pragmatist and the absolutist are not as far apart on truth as the absolutist thinks, and that the pragmatist uses the notion of absolute truth as "an ideal standard" that helps explain her fallibilism. Both James and the rationalist believe firmly in their own accounts of truth, but their disagreement centers on whether or not this belief amounts to an assertion. James suggests that the only challenge to absolute truth on the part of the relativist is to "the pretence on anyone's part to have found for certain what the shape of that truth is."[112] Most rationalists, he notes, are "sometimes skeptical enough to admit the abstract possibility of their own present opinions being corrigible and revisable," which would seem to offer an admission that the rationalist has no greater access to absolute truth than the relativist.[113] Even Rickert admits that absolute truth is a regulative notion of "what we *ought* to believe" and refuses to claim any special possession of it.[114] Insofar as pragmatists maintain fallibilism, admitting their corrigibility, they hold that this fallibility can best be explained in terms of the testing and correction that take place within genuine inquiry. When it comes to the pragmatic conception of truth, this too is to be gauged through its responsiveness to correction and its eventual settlement of belief. James claims: "[T]he more fully men discuss and test my account, the more they will agree that it *fits*, and the less will they desire a change." Both the fit and the correction involve the regulative use "of the notion of absolute truth," which "no relativist who ever walked the earth has denied."[115] In taking on the charge of relativism, then, James formulates a conception of absolute truth that focuses on its role in genuine inquiry and notes the ways in which pragmatism and absolutism share at least this notion of absolute truth as a regulative ideal. In this manner, pragmatism not only allows for a conception of absolute truth but also offers a pragmatic elucidation of the role such a notion plays in our thinking.

On the second head, James returns to the arguments against vicious intellectualism that animated parts of the Hibbert Lectures, preferring here the label "vicious abstractionism." The pragmatist defines absolute truth as "an ideal set of formulations towards which all opinions may in the long run of experience be expected to converge."[116] Although James is less careful later about keeping the subjunctive mood in place, he is careful when offering this definition to mention that it is a postulate for inquiry, that absolute truth is a proper object for investigation. When the anti-pragmatist attacks this notion of absolute truth, the argument focuses on the use of the word "opinion" and its connotations of independence from the thinking of others and the conditions of the world toward which it is meant to be directed. Opinions are thus "insulated and unmotivated abstractions" held by individuals and insensitive to outside evidence.[117] Unlike the abstractionist's, James's view of opinions attempts to put them in their concrete context, "surrounded by their grounds and the influences they obey and exert, and along with the whole environment of social communication of which they are a part and out of which they take their rise." Opinions do not form in the individual mind but in this larger context that requires reference to experience, which "the pragmatic definition postulates *is* the independent something which the anti-pragmatist accuses him of ignoring."[118] The social and experiential context in which opinions grow and take shape helps explain *how* convergence takes place, but the independence of the long run of experience in general from the particular opinions of individuals helps explain toward *what* opinions are converging. It is this end that pragmatism postulates as absolute truth. But it is not an absolute truth that lies outside of and beyond investigation; rather, it is an absolute truth that functions within that investigation. That particular ideas and opinions become stable is a result of the investigation into their veracity; it is not because of their relations to something called "absolute truth."[119] The function of absolute truth within the investigation is that of a regulative hope that helps motivate inquiry, but it provides no guarantees. Neither are we guaranteed to arrive at such truth through properly pursued investigation, nor is the propriety of our investigation guaranteed by such truth.

Although it would be a bit strained at this point to argue that James would go so far as to endorse Peirce's T-I conditional, it should be clear that there are important parallels between the regulative nature of absolute truth in James's pragmatism and the regulative nature of the T-I conditional in genuine inquiry. In James's functional account of absolute truth, he notes that the conception of absolute truth is what motivates inquiry. It is our desire for true beliefs—which would be stable and not dislodged by further experience—that motivates our investigation. Beliefs that are absolutely true would be those that were most stable and most incorrigible. As Lamberth puts it: "Truth absolute . . . is a necessary conceptual commitment, expressive of our phenomenological awareness of our philosophical desire for systematic and thorough knowledge and thus instructive of habit."[120] However, to claim that "truth absolute" is such a regulative commitment for James is also to claim that the process of pragmatic inquiry provides a means for finding stable and systematic knowledge.

One can no more decouple truth and pragmatic inquiry for James than one can for Peirce. The pragmatic elucidation of the concept offers conceptual clarity—Peirce's third grade of clearness—regarding truth by noting the effects upon beliefs of calling them "true." James's account of truth in its absolute, regulative form separates its function from its definition and shows that James does distinguish, though less explicitly than Peirce, between definition and elucidation. In 1907, James distinguishes more clearly among the three grades, which he identifies as the "which," the "what," and the "that." Without consciously doing so, he echoes Peirce's observational, definitional, and elucidatory aspects of understanding: "The 'which' means a possibility of pointing or of otherwise singling out the special object; the 'what' means choice on our part of an essential aspect to conceive it by . . . and the 'that' means our assumption of the attitude of belief, the reality-recognizing attitude." Insofar as belief is tied to the pragmatic method of inquiry, it seems clear that James sees this later exposition as distinguishing the project of pragmatic elucidation from the project of definition. He claims explicitly, though, that the "which", the "what", and the "that" are "points determinable only by the pragmatic method."[121] When read in the context of this section, my contention is that James does not mean here that the pragmatic method simply subsumes all three aspects of understanding. Rather, James's broader contention is that the pragmatic method allows one to engage all three aspects of understanding and avoid the vicious intellectualism that comes from failing to refer to the functional possibilities of concepts.

Much like Peirce, despite having high esteem for the pragmatic method and holding it to offer a grade of clarity beyond the others, James continues to distinguish among the three grades of clearness. Perhaps more than Peirce, though, James argues that the definition and the pragmatic meaning are intimately related. While his critics have offered definitions, James has offered an application, an understanding of "what the word 'true' means when applied to a statement."[122] Without reference to the function of the predicate, its conceivable effects within the context of investigation and belief-formation, the meaning of the word "true" remains vague and inert, much like Lotze's "merely verbal" solution to the problem of relations among objects. With regard to statements and beliefs, James challenges his opponents to "*define what you mean* by calling them true without referring to their functional possibilities." Only through reference to these possibilities can a complete conception of the object of investigation—here a true claim—be had, and these functional possibilities for a true belief give the "whole *logical content*" to the truth relation.[123] The reference to logic here is not incidental. James maintains that the pragmatic maxim is logical in much the same broad sense in which Peirce originally formulates it. On the one hand, it provides a means for logical consistency without vicious intellectualism; on the other hand, it offers the broader scope of pragmatic elucidation under which formal and empirical investigations can be conducted.

Maintaining the broadly logical character of the pragmatic maxim and the distinction between definition and elucidation offers James's pragmatism the same metaphysical neutrality that underlies Peirce's. Although both James and Peirce offer metaphysical views, these views ought not to be seen as necessary entailments of their pragmatism. Both Peirce's agapism and James's radical empiricism would need to be subjected to pragmatic elucidation (much like James's treatment of idealism as an hypothesis) before such a judgment could be made. Even so, it seems we should stick with the metaphor of the hallway and allow innumerable metaphysical chambers to open off it. Although James's pragmatism does not require a particular metaphysical commitment in the sense just sketched, it does involve new conceptions of particular epistemological notions. Rationality is conceived through a broader lens as a four-fold endeavor; conceptual logic is decoupled from intellectualism; and truth—including absolute truth—is conceptually clarified through the application of the pragmatic maxim.

A Narrow and Neutral Pragmatism

All thought occurs within an experiential context. From that context we acquire the "irritation" that starts us on the road to inquiry, and the thoughts used in the process of inquiry are directed back toward that context. It is in this way that we see what is meant by the pragmatic maxim itself. The maxim, although logical, is a maxim regarding the connection of thought to a context of investigation. We attain complete clarity (Peirce's third grade) when we have ascertained all possible effects of a particular object with regard to all possible investigatory contexts. This is not to suggest that our thought requires such clarity in its everyday employment; rather, it is to suggest that *complete* clarity arises through continued application of thought within varied but concrete investigations. Peirce's complaint against Kant and James's complaint against the conceptual method, are in fact both complaints regarding the divorce of thoughts from contexts of inquiry. Peirce complains that the incognizable is that which can neither be effected nor have an effect. It is, therefore, without context and, as Peirce remarks, without meaning.[124] Likewise, James argues that Kant attempts to ground our experience "outside of and *before* our experience in the *dinge an sich*."[125] In each case, we are asked to think of that which cannot have any experiential effects, even construing experience as broadly as Peirce and James do. Without such effects, we have no clear idea of what the concept could possibly mean. Without a context, there is no sense. Only thought that is at work within a context—thought that is *effective*—is really thought at all.

Although I cannot hope to have fulfilled the demands of a "thoroughgoing reinterpretation of all the cognitive machinery" here, this chapter has attempted to show the ways in which Peirce and James start this reinterpretation through the application of the pragmatic maxim, which remains simply a maxim of logic, albeit a slightly broader logic than that of their opponents. For both philosophers, pragmatism reins in metaphysical extravagances by requiring that any hypothesis be subject to pragmatic elucidation in order to be significant. This limits the range of genuine hypotheses and narrows the field of pragmatic inquiry. At the same time, because pragmatism would subject all genuine hypotheses to elucidation by means of their conceivable effects, its application is exceptionally broad. For Peirce, at least, if not for James, even mathematical hypotheses are subject to elucidation through the application of the pragmatic method. Although James does not make the application to mathematics, because he subjects the particular formal notion of truth to the test of the pragmatic method, one is led to think that he would not be unsympathetic to Peirce's application. Furthermore, insofar as ideas for James can become the objects of inquiry, such formal notions as mathematical ideas would likely be subject to the same form of examination as all our other ideas.

The claims made here have attempted both to draw Peirce and James together with regard to pragmatism and to avoid specific discussion of their many differences. My purpose in doing so has clearly not been to offer a detailed historical examination of both philosophers' works. Rather, my purpose here has been to show that careful attention to their account of inquiry—from Peirce's early formulations to James's much later writings—provides a fuller understanding of what pragmatism means and shows two thinkers with far more in common than their critiques of the Cartesian conception of mind and the Kantian thing-in-itself. In offering this view of pragmatism as a maxim of logic, several of its important features have become clear. Pragmatism holds that truth is a regulative norm for properly pursued inquiry; that complete clarity can only come as a result of pragmatic elucidation; that concepts acquire their meanings—though not their definitions—only through this pragmatic elucidation; that genuine metaphysical inquiry can be engaged; and that the theoretical and practical are closely related and complementary, though not interchangeable, aspects of rationality. In offering this view, it might be argued that I have chosen to take up pragmatism in something other than what Robert Brandom has called its "broad and interesting sense"—implying, I suppose, that narrow, neutral pragmatism is boring. The conclusion will offer some indications of why I think this not to be the case.

Conclusion

Philosophy Without Priestcraft

An underlying current from the Introduction and Chapter 1 is worth bringing back to the surface here. What several recent philosophers have found most interesting and compelling in early American pragmatism are those resources that can be brought to bear in the contemporary discussions regarding realisms and their counterparts. Although applicability is hardly a vice, making it the criterion in this case has caused, I have argued, certain peculiar distortions of Peirce's and James's own views. Both Rescher and Mounce, for example, think that the most compelling reason to return to the classical pragmatism of Peirce is its avoidance of the relativism and subjectivism that supposedly plague Rorty's position. Both see the dual embrace of a kind of metaphysical realism and Realism with regard to truth as the proper context within which to view pragmatism; and both argue that these realisms get around the difficulties with which Rorty's and Dewey's pragmatisms are saddled. Rorty, on the other hand, suggests that pragmatism points us beyond the dualisms inherent in both metaphysical realism and Realism with regard to truth. The recommendation that we return to pragmatism is the recommendation that we give up on trying to get what we cannot have—"the world" and "truth"—in the hope that philosophical insights can be made more relevant to democratic politics. Rorty's turn from talk of truth to talk of justification is but one instance of this.

There is a certain attraction to both these proposals. We should avoid extreme relativism and subjectivism. Likewise, we should avoid irrelevance. However, these are hardly compelling reasons to take up *pragmatism*. There are certainly several other philosophical traditions that have tried to overcome relativism and subjectivism and to be relevant. In fact, if we follow the lines of Mounce's and Rescher's arguments, it would seem that we should be inclined to take up pragmatism only insofar as it does intersect with metaphysical realism and Realism with regard to truth. How else ought we to take their respective dismissals of Dewey and James? Likewise, if we follow Rorty's argument, we should be inclined to take up pragmatism only insofar as it shows the irrelevance of the realist senses of "the world" and "truth" and offers itself to the establishment of liberal democratic politics based on solidarity and justification. Thus, in each case, pragmatism recommends itself for reasons that lie outside pragmatism itself; or, to use the metaphor offered in the Introduction, pragmatism is to be embraced simply because it is the corridor off which these rooms lie. If we happen to enter one of these rooms from an outside door, so much the worse for pragmatism.

There are more compelling reasons than these for returning to the pragmatism of Peirce and James, and these reasons lie within the corridor itself. If we keep in mind that the original formulation of pragmatism was made in order to help us "attain clarity of thought", or "Peirce's" third grade of clearness, this will be obvious; pragmatism recommends itself because it helps us to see clearly what may otherwise be obscured. Through the application of the pragmatic method, we can see where there are real differences that make a difference and where the differences are merely apparent. Quite simply, if it makes a difference in practical consequences, then it is a real difference; if not, then it is not. What we have seen by touching on Rorty's work is that his differences with the tradition are often more apparent than real.

Because my focus throughout has been on pragmatism as a method of inquiry with its internally related conceptions of truth, rationality, reality, and belief formation, my intent in this conclusion is to offer some anticipatory remarks regarding work to be done in the pragmatic philosophy of religion. I do not intend to offer a thorough rehashing of the traditional issues in the philosophy of religion—arguments for and against God's existence, questions of religious truth, problems of theodicies, and so on—but I do want to look briefly at the question of whether religious belief can be subjected to the kind of pragmatic investigation that Peirce and James require. The question before us is not whether or not religious beliefs are true, but rather what it might mean for them to be true in the manner suggested by pragmatism.

John Clayton remarks that one philosophizing in the vein in which Clayton does "might be inclined to linger rather a long time over the question *What would it be for such-and-such claim to be true?* and also over the question *What would count as reasons for holding such-and-such claim to be true?* before asking whether such-and-such claim *is* true."[1] Sage advice; but the editors' note throws down a gauntlet, citing Clayton's marginalia at this point: "Not committed to holding that correspondence theory of truth is adequate in rel[igious] contexts: pragmatic theory may be more appropriate. Not everyone will be happy with this. Not even all pragmatists, some of whom deny that prag[matism] offers a 'theory' of truth."[2] Given what was said in prior chapters, I would agree with those Clayton mentions who deny that pragmatism offers a "theory of truth" in the contemporary sense. Likewise, it is difficult to see pragmatism as offering a definition of truth. Nonetheless, his remarks do point us in the direction of being able to offer a pragmatic elucidation of the status of religious beliefs. In so doing, pragmatism's metaphysical neutrality will be important to keep in mind. Pragmatism is not committed, as Clayton notes, to a correspondence theory of truth, or to any other for that matter. Pragmatic elucidation is not that project.

Epistemology and Religion

The problems with the philosophical tradition against which Rorty wants to rebel are similar to the problems with the religious tradition against which Nietzsche wanted us to rebel. In a response to Michael Williams, Rorty cites appreciatively the Nietzschean point brought out in Heidegger that the philosophical tradition is simply an account of humanism, "a series of attempts to put more and more power into the hands of human beings."[3] As religion began to recede from the horizon at the end of the medieval era, philosophy and science stepped in to fill the void that remained. Religion, philosophy, and science are, on Rorty's account, united in thinking that there is some power beyond ourselves to which we are answerable. Rorty puts the questions with which these areas of culture deal in the following way: "The scientific question is 'how do things work?' The religious question is 'what should we be afraid of?' and the philosophical question 'Is there something non-human out there with which we need to get in touch?' All three are questions about the whereabouts of power, and they obviously interlock."[4] Different responses to these questions would shift the loci of scientific, religious, or philosophical powers either toward or away from the human. Specifically, if the answer to the second question is "not very much" and the answer to the third is "only insofar as we need to make it suit us," then power shifts considerably onto the shoulders of human beings as we look to make our ways about in the world. Not content with letting it lie here, though, Rorty offers one last upshot to the humanistic rebellion against the philosophical tradition: "We shall become secularists, who let art and politics fill the gap left by God."[5]

The connections between a religion based on fear and a philosophy based on Epistemology seem obvious to Rorty. He makes this explicit when noting the character of the realism/antirealism debate: "That debate is a downmarket version of the nineteenth-century debate between those who did not want to let go of religion and those who thought that, now that we knew how things work, we could forget God. Nowadays the role once played by defenders of religious belief is played by defenders of realism."[6] For Rorty, it is only a matter of time before the debates within contemporary epistemology are dropped much like those in the nineteenth century. The defenders of religion look just as silly to contemporary, scientific, secularized eyes as the defenders of realism will in years to come. Although he would now rather not use the label "antirealist," Rorty recognizes that his position is opposed to such realism because his view denies that "we need to think in terms of a non-human reality at all."[7] The "mind-independent world" of metaphysical realism and Realism with regard to truth is simply a substitute for the transcendent God of religion. On Rorty's account, to be a pragmatist is to have learned to do without the latter or the former and focus on our culturally specific realms of discourse.

Rorty's narrative about religion and his narrative about philosophy have the same theme: they are stories about humanity's learning to come to full maturity. When we reach this stage of full maturity, we will have given up on the notion that we are answerable to some power beyond ourselves, whether God or the world; we will no longer be in fear that we will have done wrong in the eyes of this power, whether fear of punishment or fear of being wrong about everything; and we will no longer abase ourselves before it, whether in praise of God or in praise of science. If we can come to recognize that we are only answerable to ourselves, we will be better off, and we will be liberal humanists.

John McDowell notes the parallels between Rorty's narrative about freeing ourselves from philosophy and John Dewey's narrative about freeing himself from the oppressive religion of his upbringing, "a religious outlook according to which human beings were called on to humble themselves before a non-human authority."[8] For Dewey, freeing himself from this sense of sin helped him come of age and gave him the idea of what it would be for humanity as a whole to do so. On the Rortian narrative, human beings can only achieve maturity if they can, like Dewey, free themselves from "a religion of abasement before the divine Other."[9] Rorty opines that a similar secular emancipation is necessary because "in the period in the development of Western culture during which the God who figures in that sort of religion was stricken . . . with his mortal illness . . . some European intellectuals found themselves conceiving the secular world, the putative object of everyday and scientific knowledge, in ways that paralleled the immature conception of the divine."[10] Philosophy practiced in this vein becomes a secular priestcraft; it is practiced to put us in touch with the wholly other.[11] This leads Rorty to recommend that just as religion was abandoned in the nineteenth century, so too should philosophy as epistemology be abandoned in this century. Only when we rid ourselves of the idea that we are answerable to the world in the same way in which we used to be answerable to God will we reach the maturity for which we were meant.

Such a picture of our relationship to the world is, perhaps self-consciously, partial and parochial. However, McDowell notes that philosophy engaged with this picture of our relationship to the world in mind just is epistemology for Rorty.[12] Because the idea of answerability to the world is caught up in this epistemological project, the discourse of objectivity must be abandoned in favor of the political discussion of solidarity. McDowell rightly diagnoses the problem with this Rortian conception of philosophy as epistemological priestcraft; Rorty identifies the discipline of philosophy with a particular conception of it.[13] The notion that we are answerable to the world is problematic for Rorty because he takes that notion in precisely the sense dictated by philosophy as priestcraft. Nonetheless, McDowell notes that the idea of answerability to the world need not be tied up with such philosophical notions. If we can divorce the idea of answerability to the world from its traditional epistemological trappings, then we ought to be able to find a sense in which reflection on this notion can be useful and epistemological at the same time.

McDowell's suggestion is that the real problem that Rorty identifies in philosophy as epistemological priestcraft is related to a particular conception of God, "the conception of *deus absconditus*, God as withdrawn into a mysterious inaccessibility."[14] The problems with which modern epistemology deals have the urgency they do because of the "frame of mind in which the world to which we want to conceive our thinking as answerable threatens to withdraw out of reach of anything we can think of as our means of access to it."[15] We thus have a *mundus absconditus* to parallel the *deus absconditus*. Getting rid of this conception of our relationship to the world, a world that may be lost, allows us to think reflectively on our relationship to the world without falling prey to either skeptical despair or philosophical hubris. To the extent that they have been successful, the preceding chapters have established that the possibility of a world forever eluding our grasp was never one taken seriously by Peirce or James.

The arguments drawn from Williams and McDowell are worth mentioning here for two reasons. First, they bring to the fore the background of the realist/antirealist debate, a background that, I have argued, is not one against which early American pragmatism is best viewed. Rorty never questions the senses of the terms in which philosophy as epistemology frames the debate and then frames his own position in contrast to these. Of this habit, James Conant remarks that Rorty's responses to realism simply attempt to negate with a logical operator the realist's thesis.[16] Second, these comments on Rortian pragmatism help clarify the religious stakes of the epistemological discussion with which the earlier chapters have dealt. Rorty was certainly not the first philosopher to note the interweaving among scientific, religious, and philosophical discussions, but few contemporary philosophers have argued as boldly and subtly for the intricacies of these entanglements and the rejection of religious discussions in light of them. For Rorty, if the scientific and philosophical discussions can be recast in humanist terms, then humanity can finally be released from the illusion of its need to answer to the non-human—a religious illusion currently recast as a scientific or philosophical one.

McDowell's work does point to a way forward, though he may be unhappy with its application here. Moving beyond the criticisms of Rorty, McDowell suggests that there may be ways in which we conceive of the notions of "answerability" and, with it, of "objectivity" that recast their meanings without the religious overtones Rorty spurns.[17] These suggestions reveal what I take to be the upshot of pragmatism and a true application of the pragmatic method; namely, that the terms in which the debate is framed can be shown not to make sense within certain philosophical contexts, but shown to have yet other senses in other contexts given their conceivable effects. McDowell's rehabilitation of objectivity offers us reason to be non-Rortian pragmatists; by applying the pragmatic method we can attain the clarity of thought necessary to distinguish between sense and nonsense. We can take discourse seriously without thinking it to lead to or stem from philosophical theories.

When it comes to the application of these views to religious belief, the parallel noted above needs to be kept in mind. If the pragmatists never took seriously the notion that the world could somehow recede from us in a way that our answerability to it was questionable—the world itself serving an irreplaceable function within pragmatic inquiry—then asking whether the divine reality might play a similar role seems sensible. This would be an incredibly fruitful area of study, and, certainly, Peirce and James would provide rich fodder for such a discussion. In a future work, I hope to address this question and the question of religious truth more thoroughly than I am able to here. However, a preliminary discussion—a prolegomena to a pragmatic philosophy of religion, if you will—seems necessary. This discussion is necessarily approximate and anticipatory, looking toward further work to be done in the field. Nonetheless, it takes up what I think to be a central concern in thinking about religious belief from the pragmatic perspective, the concern over whether religious beliefs can be subject to the pragmatic method of inquiry.

Pragmatism and Religious Belief

It lies beyond the scope of the current project to compare the results of philosophy of religion, viewed in realist/antirealist light, with those of philosophy of religion, viewed in a pragmatic light. Nonetheless, that pragmatism provides a viable resource for traditional topics in the philosophy of religion seems obvious. Peirce and James both took religion quite seriously, if a tad unorthodoxly. They might have found it disconcerting to see how contemporary discussions of their work have so often neglected or outright scorned their work on religion. In this regard, James fares better than Peirce in that his Gifford Lectures have attained classic status across a variety of fields and much exceptional work has been done on his more religious writings. However, a fuller appreciation of both Peirce's and James's views on religion seems overdue.

My argument here is that the specifically *pragmatic* view of inquiry and investigation outlined in the previous chapter can illuminate matters of religious belief. Although Peirce and James each offered, in their own idiosyncratic ways, discussions regarding the status of religious beliefs, these were often less systematic than one might hope and not infrequently in conflict with other views they espoused. One might, a la Richard Gale, simply choose to separate the scientist pragmatist from the religious believer and allow an inconsistency to remain. One could hold to the kind of non-cognitivist view of religious belief that seems to separate matters of vital importance from science in Peirce or that seems to animate James in *The Varieties* and elsewhere. Doing so would allow religious belief to maintain itself in the face of pragmatically engaged investigation and recognize the deep role that it plays in the lives of believers, often lying beyond the scope of doubt and inquiry.

In arguing as I have that pragmatism lies in the midst of the many notions both Peirce and James articulate, approaching religious belief as lying beyond the reach of pragmatism strikes me as rather unsatisfactory. It seems to make pragmatism a much narrower hall than was intended by its founders. If my earlier assessment that Peirce and James both saw the pragmatic method as having a broader application than to the hypotheses of the empirical sciences and our resultant beliefs were correct, then religious beliefs should be open to elucidation according to the pragmatic method. In order to make this argument, certain objections from Peirce and James themselves will need to be overcome. On the one hand, Peirce denies that philosophy, practiced in the pragmatic vein, should have any role in matters of vital importance, preferring, it seems, to let instinct play the decisive role in ethics and action. On the other hand, James explicitly claims that our passional nature is rightfully invoked in motivating religious belief. Nonetheless, I do want to argue that religious belief can be viewed in the same vein as other beliefs and elucidated through the application of the pragmatic method. Although the full argument for this view cannot be made here, I do want to offer the preliminary sketch of what such a view would be, saving its complete articulation for another volume.

Instinct, passions, and religious belief

In a discussion of the relationship between philosophy and religion that begins some twenty years after his formulation of the pragmatic maxim, Peirce notes that there is a tension between the results that come from philosophy and science and those that bear upon matters of vital importance. Although I have been a bit cavalier throughout the book regarding the historical context of some of the manuscripts and arguments, the discussion in which Peirce engages here needs to be tempered by a brief historical tangent. William James arranged for Peirce to offer a series of lectures at Harvard in 1898. Peirce was at this point rather desperate for employment, having been let go by Johns Hopkins University in 1884 and unable to secure a full-time academic appointment since—despite James's efforts on his behalf. When James learned that he planned to deliver lectures on technical logic, James urged him, in a rather derisive tone, to change topics, and Peirce conceded to speaking on "separate topics of vital importance." Nonetheless, he did so begrudgingly, deriding James's Harvard students for finding "it too arduous a matter to reason exactly."[18] Portions of the lectures are saddled with a tone of sarcasm if not outright scorn, which must be viewed as a result of Peirce's being wounded by James's insistence that he change topics. The lectures thus engage in no small amount of hyperbole as Peirce attempts to create a gulf between the difficult tasks of logic with which he would prefer to occupy himself and the vitally important topic of ethics with which he thinks the Harvard gathering concerned.

Peirce begins by arguing that philosophy in America had largely been the province of those "who have . . . come from the theological seminaries, and have consequently been inflamed with a desire to amend the lives of themselves and others."[19] This leads philosophers to be conservatives by and large, wishing to expound the dogmas of past generations with great fervor but preventing them from any great originality of thought. It is for this reason that Peirce sees the situation in philosophy as "unsettled" and regards "any practical applications of it to religion and conduct as exceedingly dangerous."[20] Philosophy practiced in this vein will be used in attempts to solidify already entrenched theological positions. It will make reason the slave of religion in the interest of maintaining certain practices. The relationship between inquiry and practice will be inverted, and philosophical priestcraft will continue.

As argued in the previous chapter, when we go about our lives in pursuit of goals and ends, we are very much in the realm of pragmatic inquiry. The pursuit of metaphysics, however, is largely the pursuit of theory for its own sake. "In everyday business," Peirce remarks, "reasoning is tolerably successful; but I am inclined to think that it is done as well without the aid of theory as with it."[21] The very idea that we should have to find theories on which our everyday business depends tends to undermine the practices. Peirce offers the following example of the ways in which philosophy in pursuit of theory impedes our practical affairs:

> If, walking in a garden on a dark night, you were suddenly to hear the voice of your sister crying to you to rescue her from a villain, would you stop to reason out the metaphysical question of whether it were possible for one mind to cause material waves of sound and for another mind to perceive them? If you did, the problem might probably occupy the remainder of your days.[22]

When it comes to vitally important topics, practical matters of life or death, Peirce opines that we act in accordance with habit rather than with theory. Attempts to do the latter would lead us to neglect the call of the sister and lead to her demise. To call upon the abstract reasoning of the metaphysician in such situations is entirely out of place.

Peirce considers religion to be a vitally important topic that philosophy in pursuit of theory would do well to avoid. He follows the "sister-in-the-garden" example with the following religious analogue: "[I]f a man undergoes any religious experience and hears the call of his Savior, for him to halt till he has adjusted a philosophical difficulty would seem to be an analogous sort of thing, whether you call it stupid or whether you call it disgusting."[23] No one comes to faith through theory; no one who needs theory to underwrite faith truly has it. Our religious temper, if we have one, is neither a result of reasoning nor a premise for it. To treat it as such is odious.

Likewise, Peirce suggests that moral practices ought not to seek foundations in theoretical sciences; they are objective in and of themselves: "[T]he dicta of common sense are objective facts . . . what the healthy, natural normal democracy thinks."[24] We call upon these in our practices without recourse to ethical theories. This is not to say that reason plays *no* role in matters of belief. Rather it is to recognize that "the man . . . who would precipitately change his code of morals at the dictate of a philosophy of ethics—who would, let us say, hastily practice incest—is a man whom we should consider *unwise*."[25] Because theoretical reasoning is supposed to be independent of the interests we have in our practical affairs, it can lead to conclusions that, if put into practice, would be considered unwise. Our moral practices, and not our ethical theories, should serve as guides for our conduct. To the extent that our moral practices rest on objective facts, they rest on the settled opinions of the culture in which we operate. To think otherwise is to expect of theories a foundation that they cannot provide.

It may indeed seem odd here for Peirce, who is admittedly the most scientistic of the pragmatists, to be arguing for the irrelevance of theory to such vitally important matters. However, he makes clear that the reasons for this are built into certain epistemic considerations regarding belief, opinion, and action. In one of the more hyperbolic moments, Peirce claims that belief "has no place in science at all."[26] This is not to suggest that one comes to propose certain scientific hypotheses *ex nihilo*. It must be remembered that beliefs are habits or rules for action: "We *believe* the proposition we are ready to act upon. *Full belief* is willingness to act upon the proposition in vital crises, *opinion* is willingness to act upon it in relatively insignificant affairs."[27] Opinion is simply that class of propositions none too tightly held that we are willing to expose to the tests and experiments of science because we are willing to go on living without them. What marks the scientist is this willingness to see conclusions falsified, and Peirce tries to make the gap between science and vitally important topics as broad as it can be.

> Nothing is *vital* for science; nothing can be. . . . The scientific man is not in the least wedded to his conclusions. He risks nothing upon them. He stands ready to abandon one or all as soon as experience opposes them . . . There is thus no proposition at all in science which answers to the conception of belief.[28]

This is not to suggest that science is somehow useless or has no bearing on our beliefs or actions. Rather, it is to note that the entertainment of hypotheses in the scientific manner and the belief in propositions in the ordinary manner come to different ends. Insofar as the former are under investigation, they can be falsified without much resistance; the latter are given up only after great struggle. Our beliefs, because they are the rules through which our lives are conducted, ought not to be subjected to scientific investigation unless there are good reasons for us to put them in doubt.

The Peirce of 1898 and the pragmatic Peirce of earlier years may appear to be contradicting each other here. If, as I have been arguing, the pragmatic maxim calls for a broader application of itself and considers logic to be a wider science, then Peirce's separation between the scientific realm, in which reasoning is abstract but useless to common life, and the ordinary realm, in which we operate on belief, would appear to run athwart this earlier argument. Were Peirce to leave us here, this would indeed be the case: the scientific and philosophical but mundane realm of theory would be divorced from the everyday but vital realm of practice. Peirce himself creates this tension: "But the slightest of physical frames might as well attempt to force back a locomotive engine, as for the mightiest of mental giants to try to regulate his life advantageously by a purely reasoned-out theory."[29] When it comes to religion and ethics, matters of vital importance, the disinterested scientific temper is powerless to act as our guide. In spite of this, the attempts to provide purely rational grounds for these matters continue: "When you open the next new book on the philosophy of religion that comes out, the chances are that it will be written by an intellectualist who in his preface offers you his metaphysics as a guide for the soul, talking as if philosophy were one of your deepest concerns."[30] Thus, it seems that Peirce wants to allow philosophy and science their respective places in metaphysics and physics but deny their importance to our everyday lives. This seems a far cry from the Peirce considered in the previous chapter and certainly creates a gulf between Peirce and James that is far greater than I allowed there.

One way to bridge this gulf would be to note that James takes a similar approach to religious belief in "The Will to Believe." His foil is W. K. Clifford, who famously claimed: "'It is wrong always, everywhere, and for anyone, to believe anything on insufficient evidence.'"[31] Against Clifford, James suggests that there are strictly prescribed instances in which believing on insufficient evidence is warranted and that this warranted belief can provide, in some manner, its own verification. James's first point about warrant is a prudential argument. His second point about verification is, clearly, an epistemological argument.[32]

The nature of the decisions or options that are exceptions to Clifford's evidentialist principle are marked by the three criteria James offers for judging "genuine options." In order to be genuine an option must be live, forced, and momentous. An option is considered live if it is between two hypotheses that both make some appeal to us based upon our background beliefs and opinions. James puts this clearly in a religious context: "If I say to you: 'Be a theosophist or be a Mohammedan,' it is probably a dead option, because for you neither hypothesis is likely to be alive. But if I say: 'Be an agnostic or be a Christian,' it is otherwise: trained as you are, each hypothesis makes some appeal, however small, to your belief."[33] An option is live only if it is possible to adopt it into our belief system as a whole with the minimum of jolt and maximum of fit. Second, an option is considered forced if there is no possibility of not choosing. If the options are mutually exclusive and entirely disjunctive, the option between choosing and not choosing is forced: "Every dilemma based on a complete logical disjunction, with no possibility of not choosing, is an option of this forced kind."[34] Third, an option must be momentous if it is to be genuine. The momentous characteristic of a genuine option is its uniqueness, its irreversibility, and the significance of the stake offered: "He who refuses to embrace a unique opportunity loses the prize as surely as if he tried and failed. *Per contra*, the option is trivial when the opportunity is not unique, when the stake is not significant, or when the decision is reversible if it later prove unwise."[35] Momentous options will be significant to the future outcomes in our lives; their impact is great. James marks his distance from the evidentialist Clifford by arguing that in instances of genuine options in which not enough evidence is available, "Our passional nature not only lawfully may but must decide."[36] We are free to abandon strict reasoning and invoke our passions.

The preceding account and the placement of it in the context of James's disagreement with Clifford make clear that there is a fourth criterion for marking the genuineness of the option that is vital to understanding his account of religious belief. In order for an option to be of the sort that James is treating, it must be evidentially ambiguous. This is stated explicitly in James's thesis when he asserts the right to decide "an option between propositions, whenever it is a genuine option *that cannot by its nature be decided on intellectual grounds.*"[37] Although it is not entirely clear what James means by an option qualified by this clause, the examples from his Section II on "matters of fact" provide some clue. There, he cites historical and scientific propositions as propositions that seem settled on purely intellectual grounds. In such instances, our willing nature is inert, incapable of making live contrary propositions regarding "matters of fact, immediate or remote, as Hume said, and relations between ideas, which are either there or not there for us if we see them so, and which if not there cannot be put there by any action of our own."[38] Options by nature decidable on intellectual grounds, then, are those options involving propositions regarding perceptual objects or propositions of formal logic. This is not to say that only genuine options have the character of being indeterminable on intellectual grounds or that no genuine options can involve the intellect. It is, rather, an added restriction to the kinds of decisions with which James is dealing in his will-to-believe doctrine. Combining what we might follow Stephen Davis in calling the "ambiguity criterion" with the three explicitly named by James, it is clear that those decisions that James gives us the right to make are decisions that can be coherently made with reference to our already existing beliefs, that must be made, that provide within their parameters consequences which will have great impact upon our lives, and that are by their very nature indeterminable by purely rational means.[39] We are warranted in making our decision only in those cases in which these specific conditions are met and must indeed decide in a way that is not purely rational. We cannot in such instances strictly proportion our belief to the rationally available evidence.

To see how this functions within the context of James's pragmatism, we must look at what James himself claimed to be doing in subsequent correspondence, a claim also found in the opening paragraph of "The Will to Believe." James claims to be giving "a justification *of* faith, a defence of our right to adopt a believing attitude in religious matters, in spite of the fact that our merely logical intellect may not have been coerced."[40] Unfortunately for us later interpreters of James, he goes on to say, "'The Will to Believe,' accordingly, is the title of my paper."[41] Nonetheless, James's argument is best seen not in terms of his title as a defense of the "will to believe," a defense of voluntarism, but rather in terms of his first statement as a defense of the "right to believe," a defense of warrant. His success and failure should be judged in terms of his establishing this right. We have a right in the cases of genuine options that are ambiguous to invoke our passional nature, but the exercise of this right is constrained by nature of the option: "[F]or to say, under such circumstances, 'Do not decide, but leave the question open,' is itself a passional decision—just like deciding yes or no—and is attended with the same risk of losing truth."[42] This right-turned-obligation is the thrust of James's argument.

James agrees in part with Clifford that one makes one's choice as to what to believe based upon the balance of the evidence on one side or the other: "Free-will and simple wishing do seem, in the matter of our credences to be only fifth wheels to the coach."[43] For James, however, Clifford errs in thinking that it is only cool reason that fixes our belief: "Yet if any one should thereupon assume that intellectual insight is what remains after wish and will and sentimental preference have taken wing, or that pure reason is what then settles our opinions, he would fly quite as directly in the teeth of the facts."[44] James's radical empiricism will not allow him to follow Clifford into thinking that reason alone is operative in belief. We not only can but often do settle our opinions in ways that lie outside the bounds of pure reason, and our previously held beliefs provide the background against which even the most seemingly rational decisions are made.

James's agreement with Clifford may be said to go a bit further. James holds that in a great number of cases, when the facts allow, it is indeed possible to suspend our decisions with few consequences; but he considers incidences of this sort to be trivial and their consequences to be minimal.[45] James's pragmatism comes to bear at this point in that it will not allow him to follow Clifford in thinking that in all cases the suspension of a decision—and thus the suspension of belief—is an option with no real consequences. Clifford takes the second half of the dictum, "know truth—avoid error," too seriously and thus fails to recognize that attempts to avoid error can have significant consequences. James likens Clifford's preference for the avoidance of error to the dictum of a general who advises his soldiers to refrain from battle rather than to risk a single wound. James boldly continues: "Our errors are surely not such awfully solemn things. In a world where we are so certain to incur them in spite of all our caution, a certain lightness of heart seems healthier than this excessive nervousness on their behalf. At any rate, it seems the fittest thing for the empiricist philosopher."[46] In adopting beliefs in trivial cases, such lightness of heart might be warranted; however, in the case of genuine options, their momentousness makes such lightness more difficult. Furthermore, James's pragmatism forces us to recognize that beliefs adopted will be corrected at some point down the road when we are met by some further experience that fails to conform to this belief. Here, the self-correcting nature of the accumulation of beliefs provides a necessary check on both the solemnity and the levity surrounding our decisions. Implicit in this claim on James's part is faith in the regulative constraints on inquiry.

James holds that attempts to suspend one's belief in the case of genuine options that are rationally ambiguous yield two possible outcomes. First, suspending judgment may make unavailable to us the very evidence that would confirm or fail to confirm our hypothesis. Second, because these options are forced, the option to suspend belief with regard to one of the hypotheses *de facto* results in the affirmation of the other.[47] Thus, in these strictly limited cases, evidence is unavailable, and we find it necessary to invoke something other than our rational selves in making the decision between two options. Insofar as James puts religious belief firmly in this camp, it seems that he is offering an account of religious belief that would put it beyond the application of the pragmatic method of inquiry.

We find ourselves here, then, with a view that brings Peirce and James together with regard to religious belief. Both seem to hold religious belief to be the result of something other than the pragmatic method of inquiry, which, I have argued, should apply more broadly than to those cases in which the conceivable effects of beliefs are empirical. If instinct or our passional nature is responsible for our religious beliefs—and in both Peirce and James it appears rightly so—then in what sense might the pragmatic method apply? Furthermore, if the pragmatic method does not apply, then can the pragmatic conception of truth—invoked alongside the method and suggested by Clayton—be useful in cases of religious belief? Clearly, these related issues require some resolution.

Inquiring into religion

The apparent conflict between the pragmatic method and religious belief can be dissolved if we refuse to think of our reasoning, inquiring selves and our passional, instinctive selves as discontinuous entities. Pragmatism applies to beliefs that have been put into doubt by some surprise that arises in our experience. Whether these beliefs arrive initially from instinct or passion matters not. Once put in doubt, the pragmatic method can be applied to help return to a state of belief. Other methods, as Peirce notes, retain their hold upon us. Nonetheless, insofar as our desire is to have beliefs that are largely impervious to future doubt, pragmatism recommends itself as a means through which particular doubts can be settled and truth assessed.

The way to dissolve the apparent conflict between what might seem to be the non-cognitive status of religious belief and the pragmatic method of inquiry comes into clear focus at the end of Peirce's diatribe against regulating one's life according to theory. Here, Peirce makes a singular exception to the rule that science and philosophy are of no use in matters of vital importance "in favor of logic."[48] Logic, because it is the means through which we attain clarity of thought, is separable from the more purely theoretic pursuits of philosophy and science and can be used in matters of vital importance. Philosophy of religion and ethics are both of little value when they are pursued in a purely theoretic vein; but when the broader logic of the pragmatic method is used to attain clarity of thought, we can see that purely theoretic considerations might not make the differences in these fields one would hope.[49] The employment of this broader logic in philosophy of religion and ethics allows them to be rescued from their theoretic entanglements and focused instead on matters of vital importance.

One way forward, then, is suggested by the distinction made in the previous chapter between definition and pragmatic elucidation. It could be argued that when Peirce discusses the theoretic pretensions of metaphysics and the sciences, what he has in mind are those definitional projects with which the pragmatic method is not concerned. On such a reading, the sciences and metaphysics would continue to be pursued in the appropriate ways while we could continue to engage in our everyday practices as we ordinarily would. However, such a reading of the lecture would miss Peirce's point here in two ways. First, such a reading would equate "definition" with "theory" and "elucidation" with "practical" and reopen the difference between theoretical and practical reasoning that I have argued pragmatism wants to avoid. Second, such a reading would neglect the tone Peirce is using here in order to distance his own scientific and logical method from that employed by James's Harvard students in matters of vital importance. To the extent that Peirce is praising science, he is praising it as practiced along pragmatic lines.

Peirce ultimately offers a positive assessment of the possibilities for both philosophy of religion and ethics. The former is "a most interesting study, at any rate, and possibly likely to lead to some useful result."[50] Peirce's ire is reserved for those who would attempt to locate reasons for being religious or explanations of religion in philosophy of religion. At the same time, he allows for the possibility that ethics could be salvaged if it were "merely to signify discussions of what ought to be done in various difficult situations."[51] It is the attempt to pry into "the philosophical basis of morality" that leads ethics astray. Religion and ethics are each better served by the recognition that philosophy cannot come to their aid in order to provide their foundations. Logic, properly applied, reveals this to be the case. When we apply the pragmatic maxim in philosophy of religion and ethics, they can become scientific in the broad sense, as outlined in Chapter 4. We can apply the broad logic of pragmatism to hypotheses in religion and ethics and look for the pragmatic elucidation of our religious and ethical concepts and beliefs. My suggestion here is that Peirce's attacks are to be seen as part of his attack on the foundationalism in which spurious metaphysics engage, and not as a separation of religious belief from inquiry.

In order to unify the views being expressed in this lecture with those expressed in Peirce's earlier series of articles, what is required is some recognition of the status of our beliefs *before* we begin the process of pragmatic inquiry. It is true that beliefs are fallible in the sense that they might individually come to be overturned. In that sense, when we enter pragmatic inquiry, we are dealing with a belief that has become unsettled. We cannot simultaneously believe and inquire into a belief. This would not do justice to the actual state of doubt that begins the process of inquiry. Nonetheless, Peirce offers that the investigator is in what he calls a "double state of mind," about the hypothesis under investigation, "at once ardent in his belief that so it must be, and yet not committing himself further than to do his best to try the experiment."[52] It is not that the pragmatic scientist has no beliefs or has put those he has into free-floating doubt. Rather, it is that the scientific investigator recognizes the instability of the belief currently under investigation. At the same time, the scientific investigator might call some of his or her ideas "*established truths*," which for Peirce would mean those into which inquiry has for the moment ceased. Thus, Peirce offers his colorful description of the procedure of science practiced in the pragmatic vein: "It is walking upon a bog, and can only say, this ground seems to hold for the present."[53] Belief has every bit as much of a place in science as it does in religion and ethics.[54] The point is not to separate belief from the attitude of the scientist so much as it is to show the relationship between inquiry and belief.

If the distance between scientific inquiry and vitally important topics can be mitigated in this way such that the difference between them is not a matter of whether or not they involve *belief* or whether their sources of belief are instinctive or rational, then it seems that vitally important topics could be a subject for pragmatic inquiry. Although Peirce occasionally strays when making this point in the Cambridge Lectures of 1898 when he claims that ethics rests upon instinct or custom rather than reasonable belief, he does hold out hope that matters like these can be open to deliberation and, thus, inquiry.[55] In order to make this claim, though, what is required for Peirce is a distinction between the different sorts of realities or objects of inquiry that might be independent of what any individual might think and yet susceptible to investigation and eventual convergence on truth. That is, an understanding of the differences of the objects of investigation is required—not as metaphysical differences among types of objects but as a functional distinction given their roles in inquiry.

When it comes to inquiry in religion, to settling religious doubts, the differences in the objects of inquiry are vitally important. Peirce allows that functional distinctions are going to exist among the realities into which the pragmatic investigator inquires. We saw this in Chapter 4 with the distinction between empirical and mathematical or logical objects, and again with the consideration of metaphysical objects of the most general nature. Christopher Hookway brings this point to light when he notes that one of the deficiencies of the correspondence theory of truth is in its inability to specify in a satisfactory way how one type of "correspondence with reality" might cover our intuition that mathematical, scientific, and ethical propositions "can all be assessed as true or false."[56] Both the "reality" under consideration and the "correspondence" seem to be different enough in kind that no one specific relation could cover all cases of all types. Nonetheless, insofar as the pragmatic inquirer is motivated by doubt and has formulated a genuine hypothesis, it should be possible to specify the effects of the object of inquiry and investigate.

James offers a similar way forward in thinking about the settlement of religious belief. In his larger discussion invoking our passional nature in asserting the right to believe, James offers the upshot of his pragmatic view of the broadly scientific way in which one might evaluate a belief and settle a doubt as a contrast to the evaluation of a belief based upon its source:

> The strength of [the scholastic's] system lies in the principles, the origin, the *terminus a quo* of his thought; for us the strength is in the outcome, the upshot, the *terminus ad quem*. It matters not to an empiricist from what quarter an hypothesis may come to him: he may have acquired it by fair means or by foul; passion may have whispered or accident suggested it; but if the total drift of thinking continues to confirm it, that is what he means by its being true.[57]

In cases of genuine options, we are faced with a decision that we must make; upon making our decision, our actions bear it out, becoming the context within which the truth or falsity of the belief is assessed. Although James invokes the empiricist temper here, he brings to light the consequences of his pragmatism in the evaluation of the belief. The truth of one option over the other is decided in relation to the consequences that its adoption has for the whole of our lives. Thus, our belief is true only insofar as it remains impervious to further surprise and not as a *direct* result of the method used to arrive at it. Rationality and passionality are not to be equated with truth and falsity, nor does their involvement indelibly stain their products. It is not the clarity of the evidence involved in providing reasons for the decision, nor the way in which the decision is made, that marks it true or false. Errors or affirmations can only be seen in the consequences that the belief has in the life of the believer. An error in belief is the holding of a belief that is highly susceptible to doubt induced by surprises in experience. The absence of error is seen in the way in which the belief holds up to scrutiny and resists correction through future experiences.

This is not to suggest that religious belief, be it tenaciously held in the face of disconfirming experiences, ought to be called "true." If religious belief is to be investigated in the broadly scientific manner specified by the application of the pragmatic method, then it must admit to at least some affinity with other areas of inquiry. In making a parallel point to the one I am making here with regard to religious belief, Peirce offers a view of the relationship among scientific, mathematical, and ethical truths that marks their differences while noting their susceptibility to investigation:

> Now the different sciences deal with different kinds of truth; mathematical truth is one thing, ethical truth is another, the actually existing state of the universe is a third; but all those different conceptions have in common something very marked and clear. We all hope that the different scientific inquiries in which we are severally engaged are going ultimately to lead to some definitely established conclusion, which conclusion we endeavor to anticipate in some measure. Agreement with that ultimate proposition that we look forward to—agreement with that, whatever it may turn out to be, is the scientific truth.[58]

To the extent that we are engaged in genuine inquiry into religious matters, we cling to the regulative nature of the T-I conditional, "If H is true, then, if inquiry relevant to H were pursued as far as it could fruitfully go, H would be believed." The demand that we not block the way of inquiry applies insofar as we seek settled views on beliefs of a religious sort. Nonetheless, the religious inquirer must remain open to the possibility that complete agreement might never be achieved. The T-I conditional is a regulative hope for inquiry and not an assertion.

If we view religious inquiry as a form of inquiry that can be pursued pragmatically, then the regulative nature of the T-I conditional continues to be important much as it is in ethical inquiry and deliberation. Misak points out that viewing the T-I conditional as regulative for inquiry rather than an assertion has consequences for the principle of bivalence that are germane when it comes to those topics about which we might not necessarily expect easy agreement. There might be cases in which inquiry, pursued as far as it could fruitfully go, would fail to reach any agreement. Misak offers the upshot of such a view: "Should it turn out that there is no possibility of accord—should it turn out that the hope or regulative assumption of inquiry would in some case not be fulfilled—then there is no truth of the matter at stake."[59] However, so long as we are engaged in genuine inquiry, we abide by the hope that such a settlement of opinion will be reached while recognizing, on Misak's view, "that bivalence will fail more often in moral inquiry than in chemistry and less often than in deliberation about matters of taste."[60] When it comes to religious matters, it seems that we ought to expect as much variety as we do in ethical ones and that the ultimate settlement of opinion, though desired, might never come. In such instances, we would be forced to say that there is no truth, no belief that would be of such a nature as to be entirely impervious to surprise and, thereby, doubt.

Ultimately, something similar must be said of James's account of the prospect for religious belief and the epistemological argument of "The Will to Believe." Insofar as James allows that immaterial objects are among the objects of inquiry—realities into which we might inquire—objects of religious belief must be susceptible to investigation. In *Pragmatism*, James offers that there are some concepts, *denkmittel*, "means by which we handle facts by thinking them."[61] As noted in the previous chapter, such concepts have a peculiar standing as objects; they can be investigated for their consequences, their abilities to handle the facts of experience. James includes in this class not merely those concepts we use in managing our thinking, but also philosophical or hypersensible realities, "electrons, mind-stuff, God or what not, existing independently of all human thinkers." Such realities can serve as objects of investigation but such investigation is made more difficult by the nature of the object. Nonetheless, the notion of such "final realities, knowledge of which would be absolute truth" forces itself upon us. He claims that although we cannot assert knowledge of them, "They form an inevitable regulative postulate in everyone's thinking."[62] Realities of such a hypersensible sort are objects of investigation despite the fact that agreement as to their exact nature might never be achieved. Thus, it could well be the case here, as it is for Peirce, that there is a reality to such objects without there being a final truth as to their nature, a final belief that is impervious to further surprise and, thereby, doubt.

This is not to suggest, however, that the realities into which the pragmatically inclined religious believer inquires are somehow less real than those into which the chemist inquires. Recall that Peirce's only claim in offering the pragmatic elucidation of "the real" is that it be independent of what any mind or collection of minds happen to think of it. To be real is simply to be capable of impinging upon experience and to be recalcitrant to our expectations while being no less susceptible to discovery and investigation. For Peirce, mathematical and metaphysical objects are real in this sense while not requiring physical instantiation. In "Truth, Falsity, and Error," Peirce argues that mathematical hypotheses are truth-apt while the question of their correspondence to any real thing remains open: "The pure mathematician deals exclusively with hypotheses. Whether or not there is any corresponding real thing, he does not care . . . But whether there is any reality or not, the truth of the pure mathematical proposition is constituted by the impossibility of ever finding a case in which it fails."[63] To take the religious upshot of this, it is entirely possible to inquire into an object whose physical reality is literally immaterial to the investigation. Nonetheless, insofar as the inquiry is genuine and the object "real" it must surprise us sometimes. Religious beliefs can be truth-apt without ever arriving at an ultimate consensus of opinion, a final settlement of belief.

All religious believers might not be engaged in the same kinds of reflective practices in which the pragmatic inquirer in religion is engaged. The believer might be no less a believer for having clung to the beliefs with which she or he was raised. However, if the believer continues to cling to these beliefs in the face of genuine surprise that should motivate doubt and inquiry, then we would merely say that the believer has continued with the method of authority or tenacity rather than having engaged in pragmatic inquiry. Recall that of these methods Peirce says one should "think well." Insofar as we might make this judgment of the believer, though, we are engaged in something other than believing religiously. We are offering an account of the status of that particular religious belief and considering means through which its truth might be assessed. Again, Peirce's concern is to show that belief just is the settlement of doubt and the establishment of a habit for action. Insofar as we want our beliefs to be true—to remain settled—we would do better to embrace the pragmatic method than others, but pragmatism is not a necessary commitment on the part of the religious believer any more than it is on the part of the ethicist.

By introducing the possibility that there might be religious realities without there being final pragmatic truths about these realities, we are noting the ambiguous character of religious belief and religious truth. The religious believer can engage in inquiry in order to settle doubts and enter into a state of belief. The believer does so holding on to the regulative conception of the relationship between truth and inquiry, that the hypothesis, if true, would be believed at the end of inquiry. Nonetheless, given the wide variety of religious beliefs and their susceptibility to doubts of various sorts, we might not expect this kind of final consensus, a final resting place for religious beliefs. The pragmatic method of inquiry seems to leave considerable room for more work on the part of the religious believer.

In offering this account of Peirce's and James's views of religious belief and its prospects for truth, it should be quite clear that I am making an extension that neither make explicitly, although both hint at such an application. Furthermore, it should be clear that the account does not take on the task of looking for all the reasons why religious people might hold religious beliefs. I would argue that these reasons are various and that the fixation of belief comes in many forms. It is also important to note that reference comes in a variety of forms because of this. My purpose in working in detail through Peirce and James here was to overcome their own, occasionally explicit rejections of the application of the pragmatic maxim to religious belief. At worst, I think Peirce and James to be a bit inconsistent here and their explicit statements to be in some tension with the resources actually provided. The historical context of Peirce's begrudging reliance on James when giving the Cambridge Lectures of 1898, in which he makes the more hyperbolic comments cited, explains some of this tension. Even within that lecture, though, Peirce does offer some resolution of the tension between the scientific temper and the ethical or religious one through the application of logic in its broad, pragmatic sense. For James, some of this tension is explicable through the difficulties in separating, as I have tried, his pragmatism from his radical empiricism. In, for example, "The Will to Believe", James opens by stating his attitude in that lecture as bearing just that moniker. In the end, I would argue that for both Peirce and James, religious beliefs are no less susceptible to doubt and inquiry than other beliefs and are, at the very least, capable of being true in the same sense as all other beliefs.

Back to the Hall

The link between the project in epistemology, in which the four main chapters of the book engaged, and the application to religious belief, in which this conclusion has engaged, provide considerable resources for future work. My hope in this conclusion is simply to have argued—against the protestations of Peirce and James—that the pragmatic method can be applied to religious beliefs. Further work will be required in order to make the full application to traditional projects in philosophy of religion, but it should be clear from this that such an application would not be odious or forbidden by either Peirce or James. What tension exists between their protestations regarding the status of religious beliefs and the temper of the pragmatic inquirer can be mitigated, and a richer understanding of religious belief and pragmatism can result.

The anticipated direction of this future work, though, should be clear. It requires embracing a view of pragmatism that sees the main features of the pragmatic hallway as not relying on the resources of contemporary realisms and their counterparts. When either Peirce or James make claims for their own realisms, I have argued that these claims must be tempered by the awareness that the conception of mind and the conception of independence at work in pragmatism are far different from those conceptions in the contemporary debate. Peirce and James each showed the difficulties inherent in making sense of these conceptions within the contexts in which they were originally offered and in which they continue to be used. What emerges from pragmatism is a new way of thinking about philosophical projects, one in which pragmatic elucidation rather than definition is primary. Both Peirce and James are interested in the sense of claims containing the terms "mind" and "independence," which they hold can only be elucidated through reference to the roles these terms may play in genuine hypotheses. In many ways, this loosens the metaphysical grip on truth and points philosophy away from either spurious metaphysics or spurious theology and toward the beliefs people hold and the roles such beliefs and their accompanying doubts actually play. I would suggest that taking this pragmatic understanding into philosophy of religion would illuminate not only Peirce's and James's respective writings on religion and religious belief, but also traditional topics within the field. Insofar as such an undertaking has not been engaged here, I take this conclusion, and the book as a whole, as having engaged in a largely pragmatic project. As James claims, "It appears less as a solution, then, than as a program for more work."[64]

Notes

Introduction

[1] William James, *Pragmatism* (Cambridge, Mass.: Harvard University Press, 1975), 32.
[2] D. Z. Phillips, *Philosophy's Cool Place* (Ithaca, N.Y.: Cornell University Press, 1999), 159.
[3] To Maurice Drury, in M. O'C. Drury "Conversations with Wittgenstein," in *Ludwig Wittgenstein: Personal Recollections*, ed. Rush Rhees (Totowa, N.J.: Rowman and Littlefield, 1981), 121.
[4] Joseph Margolis, *Pragmatism's Advantage: American and European Philosophy at the End of the Twentieth Century* (Stanford, Cal.: Stanford University Press, 2010), 15.
[5] Hilary Putnam, "A Defense of Internal Realism" in *Realism with a Human Face*, ed. James Conant (Cambridge, Mass.: Harvard University Press, 1990), 30. Putnam's "metaphysical realist" foil holds all three of these senses of metaphysical realism to be tenets of the position. In ways that are instructive but not germane to the particular discussion here, Putnam notes that Hartry Field, in many senses Putnam's paradigmatic metaphysical realist, rejects the third proposition regarding truth and favors a redundancy theory. Although Putnam argues that such a position is, at best,unappealing and, at worst, inconsistent, I would argue that this results from Putnam's choosing to view the question of truth as a metaphysical question for Field when Field—perhaps unappealingly but not inconsistently—views the question of truth as being epistemic. (See, ibid., 30ff.)
[6] The terms "metaphysical realism," "metaphysical antirealism," "Realism with regard to truth," and "Nonrealism with regard to truth" mark a number of doctrines in contemporary philosophy, and I do not intend to gloss entirely the variant positions that mark each more general category. For the moment, I take Richard Kirkham's excellent delineation of the general thrust of each to be sufficient. Further explanation will come below in Chapter 1. (See Richard Kirkham, *Theories of Truth: A Critical Introduction* (Cambridge, Mass.: Massachusetts Institute of Technology Press, 1992, 1995), 73–78.
[7] Although examples of such readings are plentiful enough and will be discussed in Chapter 1, it is worth noting here that despite Kirkham's classification of Peirce's pragmaticism as Nonrealist with regard to truth, most commentators seem to accept Richard Rorty's contention that Peirce remained "the most Kantian of thinkers," projecting an "all embracing, ahistorical context" for philosophy, which aligns him far more with the contemporary realist than with the—to Rorty's mind—"good" relativist, antirealist strands of pragmatism in James and Dewey. See Richard Rorty, "Pragmatism, Relativism, and Irrationalism" in *Consequences of Pragmatism* (Minneapolis, Minn.: University of Minnesota Press, 1982), 161ff.

[8] Joseph Margolis, "Peirce's Fallibilism," *Transactions of the Charles S. Peirce Society* 34/3 (Summer 1998), 537–539. As will become clear, I am largely in agreement with Margolis's view that this third theme is vital to understanding pragmatic fallibilism. However, because I construe the metaphysical underpinnings of the pragmatists differently than Margolis, I see Peirce's fallibilism as being more successful than does Margolis, who claims, broadly, that it fails in light of Peirce's inability to overcome his own staunch, if inconsistent, realism about the world and progressive faith in inquiry.

[9] James's interest in religion is well known and fairly obvious in several writings, but Peirce's remains somewhat hidden. Although the entirety of his work is given to showing that Peirce's religious interests are present from very early in his philosophical life, Michael Raposa makes a strong case in his final chapter that Peirce's concerns with the relationship between the teleological role of the divine and the nature of human thought combine toward the end of Peirce's life into the preliminary formulation of a "Theosemiotic." On Raposa's reading of the notes Peirce assembled on this head, "The musing intellect is gently drawn to the truth about nature by the beauty of God's purposes, themselves embodied in natural facts. . . . The universe is God's great poem, a living inferential metaboly of symbols" (Michael L. Raposa, *Peirce's Philosophy of Religion* [Bloomington, Ind.: Indiana University Press, 1989], 144). Joseph A. Brent also notes at several points throughout his excellent study that Peirce's work maintains a religious bent even when it moves in its more scientific and logical directions, and that Peirce's prospectus for his twelve-volume *magnum opus* included one volume dedicated to "The Regeneration of the Church," presumably through its adoption of his contrite fallibilism (Joseph A. Brent, *Charles Sanders Peirce: A Life* [Bloomington, Ind.: Indiana University Press, 1993], 235).

[10] Two of Rorty's essays take up religious issues directly, and neither offers much promise for moving discussion forward regarding religion from a generally philosophical or specifically pragmatic point of view. In both essays, his arguments regarding religion and religious issues are based upon the prevailing assumption that such matters are *private* and ought to remain so. In "Religious Faith, Intellectual Responsibility, and Romance," Rorty argues that religious beliefs only rarely bear the appropriate inferential connections to other beliefs such that they might stand in need of justification or explanation. In this manner, religious notions or beliefs are not properly beliefs but claims to faith, which—citing Paul Tillich—Rorty distinguishes from the more public, propositional, and conversational "beliefs" by noting their vagueness and unanalyzability (Richard Rorty, *Philosophy and Social Hope* [New York, N.Y.: Penguin Books, 1999], 155–160). In "Religion as Conversation-stopper," Rorty takes the more direct and perhaps pragmatic route of simply arguing that the larger philosophical conversation required for democratic deliberation often comes to a halt when religious ideas are introduced as reasons. This too is based on what Rorty takes to be the fact that religious beliefs are inherently private and have no place in conversations about public policy, a conversation that ought to be based on reasons held in common (Rorty, *PSH*, 171). For a rebuttal to Rorty's arguments on the utility of privatizing religious belief, see Jeffrey Stout, *Democracy and Tradition* (Princeton, N.J.: Princeton University Press, 2004), 85–91.

[11] Phillips, *Philosophy's Cool Place*, 161.
[12] Ibid.
[13] Ibid., 160.
[14] Ibid., 163.

Chapter 1

[1] Hilary Putnam, "Realism with a Human Face," in *Realism with a Human Face*, 20 (Emphases in quotations are from the original throughout the text unless otherwise noted.)
[2] James Conant, "Freedom, Cruelty, and Truth," in *Rorty and His Critics*, ed. Robert Brandom (Cambridge, UK: Blackwell Publishers Ltd., 2000), 269.
[3] Michael Dummett, "Realism," in *Truth and Other Enigmas* (Cambridge, Mass.: Harvard University Press, 1978), 145–165.
[4] A. J. Ayer's book on pragmatism treats it largely as a historical curiosity, notable more for its previously unnoticed similarities with other philosophical positions than for its legion of defenders (A. J. Ayer, *The Origins of Pragmatism: Studies in the Philosophy of Charles Sanders Peirce and William James* [San Francisco: Freeman, Cooper and Co., 1968], 1–2). Pragmatism's historical, rather than philosophical relevance, is noted without remorse in George Boas's 1962 "Introduction" to Arthur Lovejoy's *The Thirteen Pragmatisms and Other Essays*: "There can be few living philosophers who would call themselves orthodox followers of this train of thought" (Lovejoy, *The Thirteen Pragmatisms and Other Essays*, ed. George Boas [Cambridge, Mass: Harvard University Press, 1963], vii). Boas further remarks that the essays in that volume are "critical of views taken a generation ago" (Lovejoy, x).
[5] Raymond Boisvert remarks that Rorty's books were one of the main factors sparking the rise of interest in pragmatism in the late 1970s and early 1980s (Boisvert, *Dewey's Metaphysics*, [New York: Fordham University Press, 1988], 1). Rorty himself notes in his "Introduction" to *Consequences of Pragmatism* that interest in pragmatism was hardly piqued by *Philosophy and the Mirror of Nature*: "Among contemporary philosophers, pragmatism is usually regarded as an outdated philosophical movement . . . which has now been either refuted or *aufgehoben*" (Rorty, *Consequences of Pragmatism*, xvii). Despite Rorty's apparent disclaimer regarding the impact of the earlier book and the perceptions of the commentators cited, the two works together are pivotal in that they managed to bring pragmatism back into the philosophical arena by bringing pragmatism into conversation with then-current issues in analytic philosophy.
[6] Although he recognizes that Peirce was a profound thinker in his own right, Rorty distances Peirce from James and Dewey because of his supposed Kantianism. Rorty writes of Peirce: "His main contribution to pragmatism was merely to have given it a name, and to have stimulated James" (Rorty, *Consequences*, 161). Rorty does acknowledge in later works that Peirce had significant insights and that these often align with those he cites appreciatively in Dewey. See Rorty, "Antirepresentationalism, Ethnocentrism, and Liberalism," in *Objectivity, Relativism, and*

Truth: Philosophical Papers, vol. 1 (Cambridge, UK: Cambridge University Press, 1991), 1–17; Rorty, "Is Truth a Goal of Inquiry?" in *Truth and Progress*, 19–20.

7. Richard Rorty, *Contingency, Irony, and Solidarity* (Cambridge, UK: Cambridge University Press, 1989), 73.

8. Richard Rorty, "Universality and Truth," in *Rorty and His Critics*, 2.

9. Rorty, *Contingency*, 74.

10. Rorty, "Universality and Truth," 10–12.

11. By "self-referential" I mean simply that words, phrases, sentences, judgments, and so on, refer only to other words, phrases, sentences, judgments, and so forth, ("marks and noises" in Rortian parlance). By "self-justifying" I mean that, because of this self-reference, only words, phrases, sentences, judgments, and so on, can be cited in the process of justifying our claims, which are expressed in words, phrases, and sentences. The two are related but separate issues.

12. These terms—"realist," "antirealist," "Realist," and "Nonrealist"—will be defined and discussed at greater length below. Often the two questions listed are not distinguished in the literature. However, as both Richard Kirkham and Christopher Kulp have suggested, "metaphysical realism" and "Realism with regard to truth" are distinct positions and are not necessarily related. See Kirkham, *Theories of Truth: A Critical Introduction*, 1–40; Christopher Kulp, "Introduction" in *Realism/Antirealism and Epistemology*, Christopher B. Kulp, ed. (Boulder, Colo.: Rowman and Littlefield Publishers, Inc., 1997), 1–13.

13. Although he was quite happily an "antirealist" when *Consequences* was published, by the publication of the first volume of his *Philosophical Papers* in 1991, Rorty had become an "antirepresentationalist." Compare Rorty's "Introduction," in *Consequences*, xxiiif, with his "Antirepresentationalism" in *Objectivity, Relativism, and Truth*, 2–3. Crediting Donald Davidson, Rorty notes that representationalists "find it fruitful to think of mind or language as containing representations of reality," whereas antirepresentationalists "eschew discussion of realism by denying that the notion of 'representation,' or that of 'fact of the matter,' has any useful role in philosophy" (Rorty, "Antirepresentationalism," 2). This distinction allows Rorty to claim that realism and antirealism are both "representationalist" positions and that neither is "antirepresentationalist." Perhaps unfortunately, many of Rorty's critics have failed to notice this change in his position and this shift in his reading of the pragmatists. Thus, the debate regarding metaphysical realism or antirealism and Realism or Nonrealism with regard to truth in early American pragmatism continues, and much of the debate continues to use Rorty as paradigmatic of the "antirealist" position and the consequences thereof. See H. O. Mounce, *The Two Pragmatisms: From Peirce to Rorty* (London: Routledge, 1997) 11–13 and 210–228; Nicholas Rescher, *Realistic Pragmatism: An Introduction* (Albany, N.Y.: State University of New York Press, 2000), 125–165; and Christopher Hookway, *Truth, Rationality, and Pragmatism: Themes from Peirce* (Oxford, UK: Oxford University Press, 2000), 94–96.

14. Crispin Wright, *Realism, Meaning and Truth*, 2nd ed., (Oxford, UK: Blackwell Publishers, Ltd., 1993), 1.

15. Ibid., 1.

16. Ibid., 2.

17. Ibid., 3.

18. Ibid.

[19] Ibid., 4.

[20] Ibid., 5–8. Wright notes this feature of post-antirealist realism by showing that realism can now be divided into species with regard to three distinct concerns: realism concerned with the objectivity of truth, realism concerned with the objectivity of meaning, and realism concerned with the objectivity of judgment. Although each concern is related to the others and each theory put forward in dealing with each of these concerns can have ramifications for the others, it is important to note that the issues of truth, meaning, and judgment are treated separately. This, again, supports Wright's contention that realism as it exists in its current analytic form must deal piecemeal with the attacks of the antirealist rather than construct theories that cover a broad range of issues. This contention is confirmed when one looks at John Searle's essay "Does the Real World Exist?" Here Searle states: "Realism is the view that there is a way that things are that is logically independent of all human representations. Realism does not say how things are but only that there is a way that they are" (Searle, "Does the Real World Exist?" in Kulp, 20).

[21] Dummett's account of antirealism makes the distinction between metaphysical forms of realism and antirealism and forms bearing on truth only implicitly. His original claim is that the metaphysical dispute between realism and antirealism is in fact a dispute over the truth-values of statements regarding the external world. Although this could be the case for the antirealist, the metaphysical realist is under no obligation to accept this description of his or her position. Michael Devitt, for example, claims that this way of putting the question of metaphysical realism puts the "epistemic cart before the realist horse." For Devitt, the metaphysical nature of realism must be admitted prior to any discussion of truth-values. (See Devitt, *Realism and Truth*, 2nd ed. [Princeton, N.J.: Princeton University Press, 1997], 3 and 40.)

[22] Kirkham, Kulp, Hymers, and Wright each have their own phrasing for the main tenets of metaphysical realism and each recognize that a variety of positions go by the moniker such that specific delineation of the position itself is indeed difficult. However, they are in agreement in the main over the position itself and are largely in agreement with Field regarding the central points of contemporary analytic metaphysical realism.

[23] Hartry Field, "Realism and Relativism," *Journal of Philosophy*, 79 (1982): 553–567, cited in Hilary Putnam, "A Defense of Internal Realism" in *Realism with a Human Face*, 31. Field himself chooses to deny that the third is a necessary tenet of metaphysical realism by offering his redundancy theory of truth, which leads to the division between issues of realism with regard to metaphysics and issues of realism with regard to truth sketched below.

[24] Searle, "World," 18. It is the use of "representation" in claims like this that lead Rorty to identify both "metaphysical realism" and "metaphysical antirealism" with representationalist epistemologies and to distance himself from this tradition completely (Rorty, "Antirepresentationalism," 2).

[25] Devitt, *Realism and Truth*, 40.

[26] Searle, "World," 19.

[27] Hilary Putnam, *Realism with a Human Face*, 23.

[28] Searle, "World," 19. This goes hand-in-hand with Searle's assertion that metaphysical realism is *only* an ontological position.

[29] Michael Hymers, *Philosophy and Its Epistemic Neuroses* (Boulder, Colo.: Westview Press, 2000), 67.
[30] Michael Williams, *Unnatural Doubts: Epistemological Realism and the Basis of Skepticism* (Princeton, N.J.: Princeton University Press, 1995), 233.
[31] According to Lewis, there is a "natural constraint" on the way in which our words and phrases refer to the world, but this constraint continues to allow for several different fixed sets of true sentences. In turn, this natural constraint fixes the reference of natural kind terms to particular "elite classes." These "elite classes" are those sets of sentences in which physical reality insists that our natural kind terms have sets in that family as their extensions. The classes could well be discrete on Lewis's theory, thus giving rise to the possibility of a number of complete descriptions of the world. (Lewis also holds to a theory of multiple possible worlds that further complicates this notion.) The result of this with regard to Tenet 2 is the admission that Tenet 2 can be rejected by the metaphysical realist because there may be any number of "elite classes" to which terms refer such that no one complete true description is necessary. (See Lewis, "Putnam's Paradox," *Australaisian Journal of Philosophy* 62: 221–236; and *On the Plurality of Worlds* [Oxford, UK: Blackwell, 1987].)
[32] Hymers argues cogently that neither Putnam's argument itself nor the metaphysical realist he attacks need be wed to the possibility of an ideal theory. Hymers writes of Putnam's argument: "[T]he notion of an ideal theory does no real work; it is merely an artifact of Putnam's linkage of metaphysical realism with causal theories of reference and of the transitional nature of his views" (Hymers, *Neuroses*, 73.) Hymers is commenting here on the argument Putnam makes in *Reason, Truth, and History*, which is part of a transitional period in Putnam's thinking between the metaphysical realism cum materialism he espoused earlier in his career and the position he now holds, a "modest realism" with affinities to James, Dewey, and the later Wittgenstein. Hymers's argument is simply that the cogency of Putnam's "modest realism" does not depend on the sensibility of the notion of an ideal theory or the possibility of an attack upon it. Rather, the attack is on the notion of reference as an external relation and is effective against such a notion with or without the possibility of an ideal theory. (Hymers, *Neuroses*, 73.) This is not to suggest that the notion of an ideal theory does no work when it is used in the context of *Reason, Truth, and History* in support of Putnam's "internal realism." There, he argues that "the cognitive values of coherence, simplicity, and instrumental efficacy" are entirely "arbitrary considered as anything but a part of a holistic conception of human flourishing" guided by our intentional "idea of the good" (Putnam, *Reason, Truth, and History* [New York: Cambridge University Press, 1981], 136–137.) Here the marks of an ideal theory are simply grounded in our idea of the good, which includes the "standards of rational acceptability" that are explicitly reliant upon the notion of an ideally situated language-user. Even if this language-user is simply a myth or regulative ideal, she does play the role of the possibility of an ideal theory in Putnam's internal realism. Still, I would side with Hymers in thinking that the argument itself can be sustained against external accounts of reference in support of Putnam's modest realism without reliance on the possibility of an ideal theory.

[33] It is important to note here that Putnam thinks that such a position—the acceptance of Tenet 1 and the denial of Tenet 2—empties metaphysical realism of some of its content such that what seemed originally attractive about metaphysical realism was simply an illusion. That is, if metaphysical realism cannot deliver on its promise to tell us something about the way the world really is apart from our representations of it (which would ostensibly occur by showing how our particular descriptions of the world fit into some total description of the way that the world works), then there seems to be little point in being a metaphysical realist from the outset (Putnam, *Realism*, 31).

[34] This rather evasive course of action has the further benefit of reducing what could be an eight-fold confusion to a merely four-fold confusion by eliminating four possible positions comprised of the assent to the truth or falsity of each of these Tenets taken singly. However, one could simply make the divide, which I have suggested need not be made, in the following way. The "strong metaphysical realist" holds Tenets 1 and 2 to be metaphysical and true. The "weak metaphysical realist" holds Tenet 1 to be metaphysical and true but holds that Tenet 2 is epistemic and true. The "minimal metaphysical realist" holds that Tenet 1 is metaphysical and true but that Tenet 2 cannot be given a sense. In turn, the "strong metaphysical antirealist" holds Tenets 1 and 2 to be metaphysical and false. The "weak metaphysical antirealist" holds Tenet 1 to be metaphysical and false but holds that Tenet 2 is epistemic and false. The "minimal metaphysical antirealist" holds Tenet 1 to be metaphysical and false but Tenet 2 to be nonsensical. This way of parsing it demonstrates two important points. First, the truth or falsity of Tenet 2 is independent of the truth or falsity of Tenet 1. Thus, the idealist could—and probably would—claim that Tenet 1 is false while accepting that Tenet 2 is true. Second, the metaphysical realist, qua metaphysical realist, is such only through his or her assent to the truth of Tenet 1. For reasons of simplicity and clarity, then, these different forms of metaphysical realism and metaphysical antirealism are not introduced in the body of the present work, but this second point will be returned to below.

[35] I am here, and will continue to be, cavalier with regard to truth-bearers. Although there is much debate over what sort of thing can be true or false (propositions, beliefs, utterances, sentences, statements, etc.), this need not concern us here. The debate over truth-bearers itself often imports certain assumptions over the ontological status of these truth-bearers, and these assumptions are not shared by the pragmatists with whom this project is concerned. The early American pragmatists were quite content with the notion that those things that most people held to be capable of bearing truth-values were so capable.

[36] Kirkham, *Theories*, 75.

[37] Alston, *A Realist Conception of Truth* (Ithaca, N. Y.: Cornell University Press, 1996), 32–34.

[38] William Alston, "Realism and the Tasks of Epistemology," in Kulp, 54.

[39] Of course it is difficult at times to see what sort of advantage this has. For example, in working out his alethic realism, Alston is at pains to avoid having a correspondence theory of truth given the disrepute such theories currently possess and the host of objections to which they are prone. Unfortunately, this keeps Alston's alethic realism from having any real teeth—his "alethic realism" is

rather anemic. If no satisfactory account (or in Alston's case, no account at all) of the privileged relation that is the truth-granting "correspondence-relation" is given, then we have little reason to go even the little distance that a minimalist account such as Alston's takes us, in spite of his repeated assurances that such an account is somehow philosophically adequate. That is, his "realist conception of truth" is so far from a "theory of truth" that it is incapable of doing the philosophical work for which it is intended. The most that Alston's minimalist project achieves, if successful, is the defense of the idea that only a realist conception of truth can save us from the two-headed monster of radical relativism and subjectivism. The further problems of how we know when we are right to say that a claim is true or how we judge contentious claims are left untouched. Furthermore, there is no account of how our words, as with "truth" itself, acquire the meanings that they do such that they can be used in making either true claims or claims about truth.

[40] Kirkham, *Theories*, 75.

[41] See Alston, *Realist Conception*, 32f, for the relation of his theory to Horwich's and Horwich, *Truth* (Oxford, UK: Blackwell Publishing Ltd., 1990), 25–26, for his assertion that metaphysical projects are not logically necessary to his minimalist or deflationary theory of truth.

[42] Alston, *Realist Conception*, 78, emphasis removed.

[43] It should be noted, however, that Alston does indeed go on to posit his own "minimal" version of Tenet 1 (Alston, *Realist Conception*, 84).

[44] Kirkham, *Theories*, 198. See also Field, "Tarski's Theory of Truth," *Journal of Philosophy* 69: 347–375; "The Deflationary Conception of Truth," in *Fact, Science, and Morality*, eds Graham MacDonald and Crispin Wright (Oxford, UK: Blackwell, 1986), 55–117; and "Realism and Relativism."

[45] Kirkham, *Theories*, 78. Kirkham simply divides the issues as "realism," "antirealism," "Realism," and "Nonrealism," allowing the capitalization to do the work. However, in his brief discussion of the metaphysical issues with which this section opened, he most often pits realism against idealism and leaves current analytic forms of antirealism, like Rorty's, out of the discussion. Kirkham also occasionally uses the terms "epistemological Realism" and "epistemological Nonrealism" as substitutes for the latter pair. Although slightly less cumbersome than my "Realism with regard to truth" and "Nonrealism with regard to truth," these terms would be objectionable to the "Realist" who, like Alston, holds that the entire point of "Realism" is that it is in no way epistemic. Michael Devitt has also suggested the separation of the ontological issues of realism from what he terms the "semantic" issues of realism, which bear on truth (Devitt, *Realism and Truth*, 39–59).

[46] Alston, *Realist Conception*, 84.

[47] Devitt, *Realism and Truth*, 35.

[48] Murray G. Murphey, *The Development of Peirce's Philosophy* (Indianapolis: Hackett Publishing Company, 1993), 40.

[49] Rorty, *Consequences*, 15.

[50] Rorty, "Universality," 12.

[51] Rorty, *Consequences*, 13–14. Rorty's radically epistemic notions here fail to take account of Dewey's own "realism," which, although not metaphysical in the sense discussed above, still holds that "knowledge, even *getting* knowledge, must

rest on facts, or things" and that "psychical things are thus themselves realistically conceived" (John Dewey, "Realism of Pragmatism," *Journal of Philosophy* II [June 1905], 325–326).

[52] Rorty, *Consequences*, 165.

[53] Mounce, *Two Pragmatisms*; Rescher, *Realistic Pragmatism*; Richard Gale, *The Divided Self of William James* (Cambridge, UK: Cambridge University Press, 1999). This is not to suggest that these authors are bound together by finding the same error in Rorty's reading of early American pragmatism or even by arguing directly against Rorty point by point. Rather, it is to suggest that arguing against an antirealist or antimetaphysical reading of American pragmatism—be it Rorty's or some other—binds them together. Rorty's antimetaphysical picture of early American pragmatism is revealed most famously in "Dewey's Metaphysics" (Rorty, *Consequences*, 72–89). Here, he argues that Dewey's project in *Experience and Nature* is best viewed not as metaphysics but "as an explanation of why nobody needs metaphysics" (Rorty, *Consequences*, 72). He then applies this reading retroactively to James.

[54] Mounce, *Two Pragmatisms*, 229; Rescher, *Realistic Pragmatism*, 15–29, 41–47, and 136–138. The criticism that James's position leads necessarily to relativism and subjectivism was made most famously by Bertrand Russell, "William James' Conception of Truth," *Philosophical Essays* (London: Longmans Green, 1910), and "Pragmatism," *Philosophical Essays*, 87–126. The charge of relativism and subjectivism—as well as inconsistency—is leveled against Dewey in Arthur Lovejoy's "Pragmatism vs. the Pragmatist" in *The Thirteen Pragmatisms*, 134–190.

[55] Mounce, *Two Pragmatisms*, 11.

[56] Ibid., 11–12.

[57] Ibid., 12.

[58] Ibid.

[59] Ibid.

[60] Ibid., citing Murphey, *Development*, 360.

[61] Mounce, *Two Pragmatisms*, 31.

[62] Ibid., 13.

[63] Ibid., 30.

[64] Ibid., 231.

[65] Rescher, *Realistic Pragmatism*, 63.

[66] Ibid., 68.

[67] Ibid., 64.

[68] Rescher, *Realism and Pragmatic Epistemology* (Pittsburgh: University of Pittsburgh Press, 2005), 4.

[69] Ibid., 10.

[70] Ibid.

[71] Ibid., 18.

[72] Ibid., 21.

[73] C. J. Misak, *Truth and the End of Inquiry: A Peircean Account of Truth* (Oxford: Oxford University Press, 1991 and 2004), 42.

[74] Charles Sanders Peirce, *Collected Papers*, 8 vols., vols. 1–6, eds Charles Hartshorne and Paul Weiss (Cambridge, Mass.: Harvard University Press, 1934), vols. 7–8, ed. Arthur Burkes (Cambridge, Mass.: Harvard University Press, 1958), 5.407

(cited "volume.paragraph") quoted in Kirkham, *Theories*, 81. Interestingly, both Mounce and Rescher see this "fate" as being Peirce's attempt to reintroduce realism into what is a Nonrealist formulation of the issue (Mounce, *Two Pragmatisms*, 11; and Rescher, *Realistic Pragmatism*, 12). Mounce sees this as a failure to reintroduce realism, which results in Peirce's later rejection of the formulation; Rescher sees this as a sufficient reintroduction of Realism to ground the objectivity of thought. Kirkham's differences with Mounce and Rescher arise from his reading of this constraint as epistemic—coming from the humans involved in the inquiry—as opposed to Mounce's and Rescher's readings of this constraint as metaphysical—coming from the world as the object of inquiry.

[75] Kirkman, *Theories*, 81.

[76] Ibid., 83.

[77] Peirce, *CP*, 8.15, quoted ibid., 84.

[78] Ibid., 84.

[79] Ibid., 86.

[80] See, for example, Ralph Barton Perry's indirect attack along these lines in "Review of Pragmatism as a Philosophical Generalization" in *Journal of Philosophy, Psychology and Scientific Method*, 4 (1907); and Bertrand Russell, "James's Conception," originally printed as "Transatlantic 'Truth,'" *Albany Review*, 2 (1908).

[81] James to C. A. Strong, August 21, 1907, in Ralph Barton Perry, *The Thought and Character of William James*, 2 vols. (Boston: Little, Brown, and Company, 1935), vol. 2, 543.

[82] Although he does not attempt to resolve the tension in a thoroughgoing manner, David Lamberth offers a good summary of it in the closing pages of his book on James. Lamberth keeps his eyes firmly on James's radical empiricism throughout the book but does think that some resolution of the tension could be had through closer attention to James's metaphysics of pure experience and functional account of knowing. See Lamberth, *William James and the Metaphysics of Experience* (Cambridge: Cambridge University Press, 1999), 209–223.

[83] Gale does offer his own resolutions to the aporias he finds deeply embedded in James's thought but admits both that these solutions are "Jamesian-Style" rather than "Jamesian" solutions and that they fail to unify James's Promethean and mystical selves. (See Gale, *Divided Self*, 316–330.)

[84] Gale, *Divided Self*, 195ff.

[85] Ibid., 131–149.

[86] Ibid., 195.

[87] Ibid., 304.

[88] Ibid., 331–332.

[89] Ibid., 261–262.

[90] Lamberth, *James*, 209.

[91] See Rorty, "Solidarity or Objectivity?" and "Putnam and the Relativist Menace," for two clear articulations of his relativist position and his reasons for thinking that such a position is unavoidable (Rorty, *Objectivity, Relativism and Truth*, 21–34; and *Truth and Progress*, 43–62, respectively.)

[92] Peirce, *CP*, 5.525.

Chapter 2

[1] Michael Devitt comes readily to mind here in that he claims that such skepticism is "simply uninteresting" (Michael Devitt, *Realism and Truth*, 2nd ed. [Oxford: Basil Blackwell, 1991], 75).

[2] See Richard Popkin, *The History of Skepticism from Erasmus to Spinoza*, (Berkeley, Calif.: University of California Press, 1979) and Michael Williams, *Unnatural Doubts: Epistemological Realism and the Basis of Scepticism*, (Oxford: Blackwell Publishers Inc., 1991).

[3] Williams, *Unnatural Doubts*, 3.

[4] Ibid., 3.

[5] Ibid., 9.

[6] Descartes is paradigmatic in this sense. While engaging in methodological doubt in the "First Meditation," Descartes sits with an ace up his sleeve, which is pulled out in the "Second Meditation" when he begins his discourse on the true nature of human knowledge through the *cogito* from which he derives all other certain truths. That is, Descartes engages in skepticism only to show how compelling his case against it is (René Descartes, *Meditations on First Philosophy*, in *The Philosophical Writings of Descartes*, 3 vols., ed. John Cottingham, Robert Stoothoff, and Dugald Murdoch [Cambridge: Cambridge University Press, 1984], vol. 2. Hereafter cited as Descartes, *Writings*, according to the standard Adam and Tannery page numbers from their twelve-volume *Oeuvres de Descartes*, rev. edn [Paris: Vrin/C.N.R.S., 1964–1976], volume.page. Thus, here, Descartes, *Writings*, VII.1–90). John Greco sees skepticism as useful in much the same way. It is the compelling nature of skepticism that makes his "externalist, reliabilist epistemology" necessary. (John Greco, *Putting Skeptics in Their Place: The Nature of Skeptical Arguments and Their Role in Philosophical Inquiry* [Cambridge: Cambridge University Press, 2000]). This "duty" is also taken up by G. E. Moore in "Proof of an External World," in *Philosophical Papers* (New York: Humanities Press, 1977). That the conversation has continued in a number of different directions is evidenced by Duncan Pritchard, "Recent Work on Radical Skepticism," *American Philosophical Quarterly*, 39/3 (July, 2002), 215–257.

[7] The purpose here is not to give the most nuanced or charitable reading of Descartes. Some would argue that Descartes' method is not nearly as skeptical as it seems at first blush; in fact, it is only when read in isolation, as it is here, that the "First Meditation" yields the "Cartesian method" of full philosophical skepticism. However, as Richard Popkin makes clear, in spite of Descartes' answers to the skeptical crisis of the seventeenth century, his own foundationalism relies heavily on the skeptical methods of the Pyrrhonists (Popkin, *Skepticism*, Chapters IX and X).

[8] Descartes, *Writings*, VII.12.

[9] Ibid., VII.17.

[10] Ibid., VII.18.

[11] John Clayton, *Religions, Reasons, and Gods: Essays in Cross-Cultural Philosophy of Religion* (Oxford: Oxford University Press, 2006), 64.

[12] Ibid., 64.

[13] Ibid.

[14] Pritchard, "Radical Skepticism," 217.
[15] Popkin, *History*, 179.
[16] Popkin, *History*, 180.
[17] Williams, *Unnatural Doubts*, 1.
[18] Whether or not such skepticism is logically coherent is beyond the scope of this book. Some have called into question whether such doubt can be given any sense whatsoever. They argue that, if not, then we need not concern ourselves with its outcome. (See Hilary Putnam, *Reason, Truth, and History*, for a much-discussed argument along these lines. It should be noted, though, that Putnam still accepts that argument as sound but rejects his own conclusion from that book. He no longer holds that the senselessness of such skepticism forces us into an acceptance of "idealized rational acceptability" as he did then [Putnam, *Realism with a Human Face*, viii–ix]. [See Hymers, *Neuroses*, Chapter 1, for an explanation of this distinction.]).
[19] Akeel Bilgrami, "Is Truth a Goal of Inquiry: Rorty and Davidson on Truth," in *Rorty and His Critics*, ed. Robert Brandom (Oxford: Blackwell Publishers Ltd, 2000), 258 (his italics).
[20] Williams, *Unnatural Doubts*, 2.
[21] Ibid., 6.
[22] Ibid.
[23] Sextus Empiricus, *Outlines of Pyrrhonism*, trans. Sanford G. Etheridge, in *Classics of Western Philosophy*, 7th edn, ed. Steven M. Cahn (Indianapolis: Hackett Publishing Company, Inc., 2006), 337–8.
[24] James Franklin, "Healthy Skepticism," *Philosophy* 66/257 (July, 1991), 309ff.
[25] David Hume, *A Treatise of Human Nature*, ed. L.A. Selby-Bigge, 2nd edn, rev. P.H. Nidditch (Oxford: Oxford University Press, 1978), 268.
[26] Erik J. Olsson, "Not Giving the Skeptic a Hearing: 'Pragmatism and Radical Doubt,'" *Philosophy and Phenomenological Research*, 70/1 (January, 2005), 100.
[27] Hume, *Treatise*, 218.
[28] David Hume, *An Enquiry Concerning Human Understanding in Enquiries Concerning Human Understanding and Concerning the Principles of Morals*, ed. L.A. Selby-Bigge, 3rd edn, rev. P.H. Nidditch (Oxford: Oxford University Press, 1975), 152.
[29] Popkin points out that the malicious demon hypothesis was hardly considered outrageous at the time of Descartes' writing by citing as a possible historical precedent the trial of a priest at Loudun in the 1630s. The priest, Grandier, was accused of "infesting a convent with devils," which "aroused a good deal of interest in the demonic as well as in the standards of evidence by which such matters can be judged." The question arose in the course of the trial as to whether or not the testimony of the supposed victims could be true given that they were infected by devils and so under Grandier's complete control. Because these victims could be lying without knowing that they were, great debates ensued over whether or not they were perjuring themselves by testifying and whether or not any testimony they offered could be trusted (Popkin, *History*, 180–181).
[30] Daniel Dennett is the only philosopher I know of who would dissent from my assessment of the brains-in-a-vat hypothesis as simply an unusual assemblage of readily available parts. (See Daniel Dennett, *Consciousness Explained* [Boston: Little, Brown, and Co., 1991], 5–7.) Michael Devitt, on the other hand, underwrites my assessment. (See Devitt, *Realism and Truth*, 63–65.)

[31] Stroud, *Significance*, 82.
[32] Descartes is again paradigmatic in this regard. Although the appearance of the *cogito* is simple enough, there is an entire epistemological framework in which this idea appears. The *cogito* itself only makes a difference within Descartes' foundationalist epistemology. As Hume notes, it does little to refute the skeptic who does not already hold a developed epistemology in which such an idea can be foundational. Thus, Descartes' later meditations are the development of a theory to counter skepticism whereas the original skepticism is supposed to be intuitive. What Descartes asks Hume cannot grant: that we defeat intuition with theory.
[33] Williams, *Unnatural Doubts*, 6.
[34] Ludwig Wittgenstein, *On Certainty*, ed. G. E. M. Anscombe and G.H. von Wright, trans. Denis Paul and G. E. M. Anscombe (New York: Harper Torchbooks, 1972), 481.
[35] Williams, *Unnatural Doubts*, 7.
[36] Ibid., 9–10.
[37] Peter van Inwagen, "On Always Being Wrong," in *Midwest Studies in Philosophy XII: Realism and Antirealism*, ed. Peter A. French, Theodore E. Uehling, Jr., and Howard K. Wettstein (Minneapolis: University of Minnesota Press, 1988), 99. Van Inwagen's comment is directed against the brains-in-a-vat hypothesis, but he acknowledges that this is simply a twentieth-century derivative of Descartes' malicious-demon hypothesis.
[38] Hume, *Enquiry*, 158–159.
[39] Hume, *Treatise*, 218.
[40] Williams, *Unnatural Doubts*, 9.
[41] James, *Pragmatism*, 27.
[42] Ibid., 27.
[43] Ibid.
[44] Olsson, "Hearing," 101ff. Olsson takes H. O. Mounce's reading of James's "Will to Believe" as his starting point for James's response to skepticism. Although I find James's essay provocative and recognize its relationship to belief formation and, thereby, skepticism, neither Mounce nor Olsson seem particularly interested in seeing this essay in the larger light of James's emerging pragmatism and radical empiricism. Chapter 4 will investigate the prospect for doing so, albeit in a slightly tangential manner. Interestingly, three other recent and excellent works on James barely even take up James's reproach to the skeptic. See, for example, Richard Gale, *Divided Self*; David Lamberth, *William James*; and Wesley Cooper, *The Unity of William James's Thought* (Nashville: Vanderbilt University Press, 2002).
[45] Mounce, *Two Pragmatisms*, 101.
[46] Mounce offers a surprisingly Humean reading of James on this point, saying: "[T]here is no incompatibility between the perspective adopted by the sceptic and that of ordinary practice, *just so long as neither is taken as absolute*" (ibid., 101).
[47] Olsson, "Hearing," 112.
[48] Ibid., 114.
[49] Ibid., 113–114.
[50] From rather different perspectives, both H. O. Mounce and Christopher Hookway view Peirce's response to skepticism against the background of a philosophy of common sense along the lines of Thomas Reid's. Both recognize that Peirce went further than Reid, which makes Peirce's common sensism "critical"; but both

hold that Peirce's response is, in the end, to show the primacy of the practical over the theoretical in responding to the skeptic. See, Mounce, *Two Pragmatisms*, 12–16 and Hookway, *Truth, Rationality, and Pragmatism*, 202–205. This reading of Peirce will be taken up more directly in Chapter 4.

[51] Williams takes these first three to be the positions of Barry Stroud, P. F. Strawson, and Stanley Cavell, respectively, with regard to definitively refuting skepticism (Williams, *Unnatural Doubts*, 32–33; Stroud, *Significance*, 273–274; P. F. Strawson, *Skepticism*, 10; Stanley Cavell, *The Claim of Reason* [Oxford: Oxford University Press, 1979], 223). The final position is that of Hilary Putnam in *Reason, Truth, and History*. There, Putnam argues that radical skepticism of the brains-in-a-vat sort is nonsensical because it relies upon our ability as brains-in-vats to refer to brains-in-vats with which we have no causal interaction and to which we cannot therefore refer (Putnam, *Reason, Truth, and History*, 1–21). However, Putnam later recognizes that this refutation relies upon at least two theoretical commitments that are unnecessary to the skeptic's own position, which would give the skeptic the upper hand again. (See Putnam, *Realism with a Human Face* [Cambridge, Mass.: Harvard University Press, 1990], viii–ix, for his disavowal of the notion of an ideal theory and Putnam, *Renewing Philosophy* [Cambridge, Mass.: Harvard University Press, 1992], 160–179, for his disavowal of a purely causal theory of reference. Although he claims in the latter never to have held a causal theory of reference [160, n. 4], Michael Hymers points out that Putnam gives his critics plenty of reasons for thinking that he does hold such a theory in *Reason, Truth, and History* [Hymers, *Neuroses*, 74–76].)

[52] Each of those cited by Williams admit as much. See Williams, *Unnatural Doubts*, 32–33.

[53] Ibid., 12.

[54] Ibid.

[55] Ibid.

[56] Ibid.

[57] Although Williams often assumes Rorty's account to have been philosophically effective against the early moderns and their accounts of skepticism, this thesis of Rorty's has been challenged often on historical grounds. Popkin and Stroud both challenge Rorty's claim that skepticism of the Cartesian sort is necessarily tied to foundationalism and look elsewhere for its theoretical roots. Popkin looks to the religious crisis of the Reformation, and Stroud contends that there is no philosophical context for such skepticism other than that of general reflection (Popkin, *Skepticism*, 172; Stroud, *Significance*, 39). Margaret Wilson has also challenged Rorty's reading, arguing that Cartesian skepticism is related more to the early modern scientific picture of the world than to any particular set of philosophical commitments (Margaret Wilson, "Skepticism without Indubitability," *The Journal of Philosophy* 81 [1984]: 537–544). However, Wilson's position fails to take skepticism seriously in that she sees it as an historical artifact left over from relatively primitive scientific views and unrelated to philosophical problems that have persisted long after the demise of early modern science. That is, Wilson fails to recognize that radical skepticism remains the epistemological problem *par excellence*.

[58] John Locke, *An Essay Concerning Human Understanding*, I.i.8, quoted in Rorty, *PMN*, 48.

[59] Rorty, *PMN*, 50.
[60] Ibid., 51.
[61] Ibid., 139–140.
[62] Descartes, *Writings*, VII.79–80.
[63] Rorty, *PMN*, 140.
[64] Ibid., 139. Williams and I differ from Rorty in that we would not suppose, as Rorty does in *Philosophy and the Mirror of Nature*, that the problem of skepticism is confined to Cartesian or foundationalist epistemologies. Rather, what Hume makes clear in pointing to the asymmetry between the intuitive skeptical hypothesis and any philosophical theories arrayed against it is that radical skepticism plagues even those theories of knowledge that would take up theories of meaning or language as their starting points. The notion that ideas can be identified and individuated is the root of the skeptical problem identified by the pragmatists, and their denial of such a doctrine moves them in a quite un-Cartesian direction.
[65] Stroud, *Significance*, 82.
[66] It is worthwhile to note here that Williams does not find any affinities between his own views and those of the early American pragmatists. He occasionally seems to think that they are "bluff pragmatists," particularly when addressing Rorty's view of Dewey (Williams, *Unnatural Doubts*, 363–366). At other points, he seems to find their views to be more coherentist in nature and thus to be thrown out with Rorty's and Davidson's because coherentist views presuppose that there is something to be contained over and against the world that is uncontained. This admits of the divide that leads to the epistemologist's paradox. The difference between Rorty and the epistemologist is that Rorty tells us not to worry about our inability to "get outside" our language and our beliefs whereas the epistemologist laments it (Williams, *Unnatural Doubts*, 269). However, because Williams does not directly address the early American pragmatists, it seems entirely likely that he would be sympathetic to the view I am about to give of their work and would find this form of pragmatism much more agreeable than the Rortian pragmatism he derides.
[67] Peirce, *CP*, 5.416.
[68] James, *Pragmatism*, 13.
[69] Williams and Hymers both argue that this is the case (Williams, *Unnatural Doubts*, 237–238; Hymers, *Neuroses*, 72–79). Williams is particularly pointed in his criticism, referring to the view that bequeaths skepticism as both "foundationalism" and "epistemological realism" at different points. In its early modern form, it is indeed a form of foundationalism—particularly Cartesian foundationalism—that gives us the problem of skepticism. In its more contemporary form, it is epistemological realism, the view that reference and truth require a relationship to the world that exists mind-independently. We will return to this in Chapters 3 and 4.
[70] Charles S. Peirce, *Writings of Charles S. Peirce: A Chronological Edition*, 8 vols., ed. Max Fisch (Bloomington, Ind.: Indiana University Press, 1982), vol. 2, 193–211. Hereafter, cited as Peirce, *CE*, volume.page.
[71] The Cartesian criteria of clarity and distinctness are derived directly from the recognition that the *cogito* is clear and distinct and independent of other cognitions. These become the marks of certainty. (See Descartes, *Writings*, VII.33–34.)
[72] Peirce, *CE*, 2.195–199.
[73] Ibid., 2.200.

[74] The conception of self-consciousness is covered by the second of Peirce's seven questions (ibid., 2.200–204).

[75] Ibid., 2.204.

[76] Ibid.

[77] Ibid.

[78] Ibid. Both Murphey and Hookway note that Peirce's conception of "inference" from these early papers undergoes significant revision in the years that follow. Whereas Peirce views this inference as being involuntary in the papers of 1868, by the drafts of the 1878 papers, which are produced as early as 1873, Peirce has begun to move from this position. Hookway notes that Peirce's more mature position regarding the ineluctable conclusions of common sense from 1898 onward places his "critical common sensism" at some distance from Reid's. Although *how* such inferences are drawn changes, I would argue that the basic conception of such conclusions as *inferences* does not. See Murphey, *Development*, 108 and 166; and Hookway, *Truth, Rationality, and Pragmatism*, 201 and 205–206.

[79] Peirce, *CE*, 2.205; and Immanuel Kant, *Critique of Pure Reason*, trans. Norman Kemp Smith, (New York: St. Martin's Press, 1965), B274–275 (cited according to Kemp Smith's pagination of editions).

[80] Peirce, *CE*, 2.205–206.

[81] Ibid., 2.206.

[82] Ibid. For Peirce, this points directly to the necessity of signs, which are external to particular thoughts but bound to thought in general.

[83] Ibid., 2.211–212.

[84] Ibid., 2.212.

[85] D. Z. Phillips writes: "For example, if someone could convince you now that you are not where you are, reading these words, but are actually at the other end of the world, reading something quite different, you would not say, 'I made a rather big mistake today.' Think of it actually happening to you. You would be terrified. Your world would be falling apart. If you had made a mistake, you would need correction. But what you would actually need is treatment" (D. Z. Phillips, *Philosophy's Cool Place*, 162). In other words, to have the philosopher's doubts arise in common life would not simply be to doubt that one were right; it would be to doubt that one were sane.

[86] Lamberth, *James*, 71ff.

[87] William James, *A Pluralistic Universe* (Cambridge, Mass.: Harvard University Press, 1977), 106 (hereafter cited as "James, *PU*").

[88] James, *PU*, 107.

[89] Ibid., 109.

[90] Lamberth, *James*, 24–25.

[91] William James, *Essays in Radical Empiricism: The Works of William James*, eds. Frederick Burkhardt and Fredson Bowers (Cambridge, Mass.: Harvard University Press, 1976), 4 (hereafter cited as "James, *ERE*"). Interestingly, if James's account is to be trusted, this dates his doubts about "consciousness" to the mid-1880s and his "pragmatic" working out of its equivalent to the late-1890s, which suggests both that Lamberth is correct to identify the strains of James's radical empiricism prior to the publication of the *Principles* and that James's turn to pragmatism and development of his radical empiricism occur together. As will become clear,

although pragmatism and radical empiricism are separable doctrines, in the broader sense in which this book is concerned with pragmatism, the two notions could be considered as being, at the very least, complementary.

[92] James, *ERE*, 5. The more substantive elements of James's criticisms of Kant and neo-Kantians will be taken up in Chapter 3.

[93] Ibid., 6.

[94] Ibid.

[95] I am indebted here to Lamberth's account of "cognitive" as being less important than "relation" in identifying the function of "knowing" in "Does Consciousness Exist?" See Lamberth, *James*, 33–34.

[96] James, *ERE*, 22 and 7.

[97] Ibid., 13.

[98] Ibid.

[99] The issue of how a relationship might be verified as one of "knowing" is complicated in James but will be taken up in Chapter 4. The issue hinges on James's dual understanding of the relationship as being either of "direct acquaintance" or "knowledge about," depending upon the proximity of the knower to the known.

[100] Clearly, this lands pretty near the heart of pragmatism and cannot be taken up in depth here. It will be addressed in Chapter 4.

[101] Richard Rorty, "Response to Putnam," in *Rorty and His Critics*, 88.

Chapter 3

[1] The capitalization of "Epistemology" and "Philosophy" is Rorty's way of marking the difference between the early modern conceptions of this project and the ancient. I will continue to use it for simplicity's sake. Rorty, *PMN*, 132.

[2] Ibid., 137.

[3] Ibid., 139 and 144.

[4] Ibid., 137.

[5] Williams, *Unnatural Doubts*, 11–12.

[6] Rorty, *PMN*, 137.

[7] Ibid., 137–138.

[8] Ibid., 161.

[9] Because the definition of the "noumena" that Kant works out means that anything noumenal is also undetermined as an object, I will try to be more consistent than Kant in using the singular when giving neutral account of the noumenon. Only as determined objects of intellectual intuition could there really be "noumena." Thus, it is only if we take the noumenon to be in some sense differentiated, as some do through Kant's conception of noumena in the positive sense, that we arrive at noumena rather than a single noumenon.

[10] Ibid., 154–155.

[11] Immanuel Kant, *Prolegomena to Any Future Metaphysics*, trans. Paul Carus, (New York: The Bobbs-Merrill Company, Inc., 1950), 13.

[12] J. E. Tiles, "Dewey's Realism: Applying the Term 'Mental' in a World without Withins," *Transactions of the Charles S. Peirce Society*, XXXI (1995): 137.

[13] Mounce attributes the former view to both Peirce and James, seizing on Peirce's triadic theory of signs as a metaphysical notion, and James's use of "pure experience" as the underlying stratum of the world. (See Mounce, *Two Pragmatisms*, 63–65.) This possibility will be more directly addressed in Chapter 4.

[14] Kant attributes this view to Locke, whom he terms a "transcendental realist." (See Kant, *Critique of Pure Reason*, A 271/B 327.)

[15] Hilary Putnam, *Renewing Philosophy*, (Cambridge, Mass.: Harvard University Press, 1992), 2. Although Paul Churchland and Steven Stich certainly fall into this category, Putnam cites Bernard Williams as the leading proponent of this view. (See Paul Churchland, *Matter and Consciousness: A Contemporary Introduction to the Philosophy of Mind*, [Cambridge, Mass.: Massachusetts Institute of Technology Press, 1988] and *A Neurocomputational Perspective: The Nature of Mind and the Structure of Science*, [Cambridge, Mass.: Massachusetts Institute of Technology Press, 1989]; Stephen Stich, *From Folk Psychology to Cognitive Science* [Cambridge, Mass.: Massachusetts Institute of Technology Press, 1983] and *Deconstructing the Mind* [New York: Oxford University Press, 1996]; and Bernard Williams, *Ethics and the Limits of Philosophy* [Cambridge, Mass.: Harvard University Press, 1985].)

[16] Hilary Putnam, *Realism with a Human Face*, 3.

[17] Of the debt to Kant owed by contemporary philosophy in both its Continental and Anglo-American forms, Rorty writes: "Even those with the gravest doubts about most Kantian doctrines never doubted that something like his 'transcendental turn' was essential . . . On the Anglo-Saxon side, the so-called 'linguistic turn' was thought to do the job . . . while freeing one of any vestiges of, or temptation to, 'idealism' (which was thought the besetting sin of philosophy on the Continent)" (Rorty, *PMN*, 162).

[18] Henry E. Allison, *Kant's Transcendental Idealism: An Interpretation and Defense* (New Haven: Yale University Press, 1983), 27 (his italics; hereafter cited as "Allison, *KTI*").

[19] Allison, *KTI*, 27–28.

[20] Ibid., 242–246. When referring to the noumenon as transcendental objects, I will break my practice of using the singular in order to make clearer the reading being given here. That is, Kant uses the terms "noumenon" and "noumena" with what can seem to be rather reckless abandon, but there are at least two senses to the concept itself. The first is simply the undifferentiated manifold, which I will continue to call "noumenon." The second is the differentiated world of "things-in-themselves" or "transcendental objects" for which I will use "noumena."

[21] Kant, *Critique of Pure Reason*, A 253.

[22] Ibid., A 255/B 311.

[23] One sees the notion of an object or set of objects "out there" somewhere beyond our ken in the works of H. A. Prichard, P. F. Strawson, and A. J. Ayer—each of whom has a connection with the analytic tradition that gives us the dichotomies of metaphysical realism/metaphysical antirealism and Realism/Nonrealism with regard to truth that were raised in Chapter 1. Although these might be considered rather poor readings of Kant, they seem to have enshrined what one scholar of modern philosophy referred to as the "received view" of Kant's project and what another referred to as a "rather silly" reading of Kant. (See H. A. Prichard, *Kant's Theory of Knowledge* [Oxford: Clarendon Press, 1909]; P. F. Strawson, *The Bounds of*

Sense: An Essay on Kant's Critique of Pure Reason [London: Methuen & Co., Ltd., 1966]; and A. J. Ayer, *Language, Truth, and Logic* [New York: Dover, 1946] and *Origins of Pragmatism* for various expressions of this reading of Kant. See Note 33 below for James Conant's opinion of such readings of Kant and Note 48 below for a brief synopsis of Henry Allison's argument against this reading of Kant.)

[24] One may see this conception of noumena as the "real" or "objective" world as an important piece in Kant's attempt to bring philosophy into line with Newtonian physics, while avoiding both skepticism and absolute idealism.

[25] Kant, *Critique of Pure Reason*, A 51/B 75.

[26] Ibid., A 238/B 298. Note that here and in the following quote the term "objects" is being used not in the transcendental sense, but in the weighty sense pointed to above. (See Allison, *KTI*, 27–28.)

[27] Kant, *Critique of Pure Reason*, A 240/B 299.

[28] Ibid., B 307.

[29] Ibid., B 308.

[30] Ibid.

[31] Ibid., B 307.

[32] Ibid., A 255/B 310.

[33] Ibid., B 307. In a footnote, James Conant offers a reading of Kant that nearly completely discounts the reading of "noumena in the positive sense" given here. Conant notes that it is Kemp Smith's confusing use of "things-in-themselves" in his translation that gives the reading of Kant that I present credence. Furthermore, Conant claims that it is the purpose of the substantial revisions in the B edition to the chapter "The Ground of the Distinction of All Objects in General into Phenomena and Noumena" to overcome the misunderstandings of the notion of noumena in the positive sense presented here. Kant's B edition revisions are made to emphasize the importance of the noumenon in the negative sense for his theoretical philosophy and to downplay, or perhaps negate, the possibility of noumena in the positive sense. Of this Conant writes: "He denies that we can assign sense or reference to the notion of a reality which is utterly screened off from us by the conditions of knowledge . . . It is only in the context of characterizing the content of the positive concept of the noumenon—whose content derives entirely from the doctrines of Kant's *practical* philosophy B that it remains permissible, in the light of the B edition revisions, to employ the locution 'things *as* they are in themselves.' Within the theoretical philosophy, the only role that the notion of a noumenon has to play is to signal the emptiness of such a notion and to warn against the philosophical confusion of thinking that such a notion can be put to work in theoretical philosophy" (James Conant, "Freedom, Cruelty, and Truth: Rorty versus Orwell," in *Rorty and His Critics*, 318). However, in the very same footnote Conant is quick to point out that metaphysical realism and metaphysical antirealism, with which we are concerned here, can both be credited with assuming that "noumena in the positive sense" as it is presented here is a Kantian thesis. Furthermore, Conant remarks that Rorty is one among "a great many philosophers" to assume that it is a Kantian thesis and to see its persistence in the contemporary debates among analytic philosophers regarding metaphysical realism as being directly attributable to Kant. Thus, even if Conant is correct regarding the status of this doctrine in the first *Critique* (and we have every reason

to believe that he is), the reading offered here of "noumena in the positive sense" presents to us the conception of "things-in-themselves" that pervades the notion of the mind-independent world present in these contemporary discussions. That is, it is this particularly inelegant reading of the *Critique of Pure Reason* that is of import. (See Notes 23 above and 48 below.)

[34] The "transcendental realist" is, for Kant, any philosopher who mistakes appearances for things-in-themselves. Although the arguments surrounding this are not germane here, this concept is important for Kant in that it allows him to make strange bedfellows of Berkeley, Locke, and Descartes, and to group their mistakes under one head. (See Allison, *KTI*, 33–56.)

[35] Kant, *Critique of Pure Reason*, A 254/B 309.

[36] Ibid.

[37] Ibid., A 249–250. Kant's use of "knowledge" to describe the outcome of such non-sensible intuition and his use of the qualifiers "merely" and "only" gives the silly reading of Kant further credence. As Allison notes, it is passages such as this that give the received view some philosophical weight (Allison, *KTI*, 16).

[38] Karl-Otto Apel, *Charles Sanders Peirce: From Pragmatism to Pragmaticism*, trans. John Michael Krois, (Atlantic Highlands, N.J.: Humanities Press International, 1995), 36f.

[39] Kant, *Critique of Pure Reason*, A 252.

[40] As with the first occurrence of "objects" in this sentence, Kant here means objects in the "weighty" sense.

[41] As with the second occurrence of "objects" in this sentence, Kant here means objects in the "transcendental" sense. Again, Kant's rather confusing use of the term lends credence to poor readings of his work. See Note 48.

[42] Ibid., A 258/B 313–314.

[43] Causality is one of the categories of relation. As such, it can only be applied to appearances and never to things-in-themselves or to the relationship between appearances and things-in-themselves. (See ibid., A 80/B 106.)

[44] Ibid., B 274–275.

[45] Ibid., B 275 and B 277.

[46] Ibid., B 277–278.

[47] This is not to suggest that the forms of sensible intuition or the categories are themselves dependent upon human minds. Kant is clear that because these are the very conditions for human knowledge, they cannot be said to depend upon individual minds. Rather, they form the synthetic unity of apperception, which is the transcendental condition for the material extension of human knowledge. This is all simply to say that the forms and the categories do not depend on individual minds. To ask whether or not they would "exist" if there were no minds would be nonsensical to Kant. To put it into the parlance adopted at the beginning of this section, we should say that they are objects in the first sense, objects of possible judgment, but not objects in the second or third senses, "weighty" objects or "transcendental" objects. To ask whether or not they would "exist" independently of human minds is to ask whether they would meet the conditions for being objects in the third sense when Kant is fairly clear that they cannot because they simply are not that kind of object.

[48] Henry Allison notes that this problem of knowledge plagued Kant's pre-critical philosophy. Allison goes on to claim that such a model is "theocentric" in that

"a hypothetical God's-eye view of things is used as a standard in terms of which the 'objectivity' of human knowledge is analyzed" (Allison, *KTI*, 19). Thus, skepticism enters when we recognize that no such standard of objectivity can be approached by our own finite minds. Our experience is mediated by the forms of sensible intuition and the categories and, as such, cannot provide immediate knowledge of the mind-independent world. Furthermore, it is impossible to "peal back" the layers of subjectivity to arrive at the core of the appearance, some thing-in-itself, because these forms and categories are the very conditions for all possible experience. This may simply be seen as another way of putting the contention that the thing-in-itself is incognizable. However, Kant has a rather cavalier solution to this thorny problem. If, as he claims, all human knowledge is conditioned by the forms of sensible intuition and the application of the categories such that all knowledge is merely knowledge of appearances, then we have no reason for postulating that another form of knowledge is possible or somehow more objective than the knowledge that we do indeed possess. That is, Kant throws out the notion of a "God's-eye view" as a model for knowledge and with it the notion that immediate knowledge of the mind-independent world would be objective knowledge. As Allison notes, the appeal to a divine knowledge from Kant's earlier works "fulfills much the same function as does the appeal to the human intellect in the *Critique*" (Allison, *KTI*, 25). Objective knowledge, for Kant, *is* knowledge of "mere appearances," or "objects in the weighty sense." Thus, truth, on a Kantian account, is not and cannot be correspondence between a claim and a mind-independent object. If he were to make this suggestion, then his position would be as odd as that of Kirkham's "odd but not inconsistent" idealist. Kant's claim would be equivalent to the suggestion that one condition for truth is never met because there is no means for the application of claims to mind-independent objects. Instead, our claims apply to appearances, and our knowledge is objective knowledge of appearances. In fact, Part 3 of Allison's book is a complete explanation of this very premise. Unfortunately, few others have recognized this redefinition of knowledge and even fewer have taken up Allison's view in this regard. Allison himself recognizes that Kant leaves himself open to the standard interpretation, which is the one I have given above, by referring often "to the objects of human experience not as 'appearances' but also as 'mere representations.' The latter locution, which is extremely frequent in Kant, is mainly responsible for the standard picture" (Allison, *KTI*, 26). That is, by his use of the term "mere representations," Kant seems to be implying that there is something more robust to which our claims should apply if they are going to have objective truth-values. Furthermore, Allison notes that Kant's very title of "transcendental idealism" for his position lent itself to the standard reading by carrying with it the connotation that there was something to be "transcended" in the application of critical philosophy. This is why Kant himself later attempts to circumvent these misunderstandings with the renaming of his position as "formal" or "critical" idealism (Allison, *KTI*, 26; and Kant, *Critique of Pure Reason*, B 519). Kant's change in terminology seems to have had little impact.

[49] Rorty, *PMN*, 162. Again, I am willing to accept that the Rortian version of this story may not give the best reading of Kant or of the history of philosophy. However,

Rorty's work is helpful in that it points out the way in which the conception detailed above has worked its way into the contemporary discussion.

[50] Devitt, *Realism and Truth*, 72.
[51] Ibid.
[52] Ibid., 157.
[53] Ibid., 3–4, 73.
[54] Ibid., 15. These dual dimensions keep idealism of any sort from being associated with Devitt's Realism. (See ibid., 16.)
[55] Ibid., 17.
[56] Ibid., 238. Devitt sees the notion of "different conceptual schemes" as a doctrine of Constructivism—the idea that we in some way help constitute the known world. This, in a way, presupposes the kind of Realism that he himself espouses in that there has to be one world, which can be known, in order for there to be the kind of difference noted among various conceptual schemes. Given that Rorty, Davidson, and Kuhn, three of the Constructivists cited, reject both the notion of different conceptual schemes and the notion of a world that is "carved up" by our concepts, it seems likely that Devitt has created something of a straw man here.
[57] Ibid., 19–20. Of course, Devitt posits this and then immediately points out that the realist committed to such a view of objects being dependent upon science holds out the possibility "that our current science *might be* massively wrong in its ontology, so that realism (now) would be false" (ibid., 20). In accordance with the notion of metaphysics that Kant gives, one can see Devitt's conception of science as simply our new metaphysics.
[58] Richard Rorty, "The World Well Lost," in *Consequences of Pragmatism*, 14.
[59] It must be remembered that Devitt admits as much but continues to find such skepticism "uninteresting." (See Devitt, *Realism and Truth*, 75.)
[60] Rorty, *Consequences*, 16.
[61] Ibid., 12.
[62] Ibid., 17. It is these conclusions that turn out to be unwarranted under the view that the notion of "the world" cannot be given a sense outside its "Kantian" context.
[63] Conant, "Freedom, Cruelty, and Truth," 272. This is followed immediately by the footnote cited above.
[64] Ibid., 272.
[65] Ibid.
[66] See Murray G. Murphey, *The Development of Peirce's Philosophy*; Karl Otto Apel, *Peirce*; Thomas Carlson, "James and the Kantian Tradition," in *The Cambridge Companion to William James*, ed. Ruth Anna Putnam, (Cambridge: Cambridge University Press, 1997), 363–383 for but three examples. Certainly, a fruitful study could be made simply of their dealings with Kant's philosophy, but this lies beyond the mission here.
[67] Peirce, *CP*, 4.2.
[68] James, *Pragmatism*, 84.
[69] Rorty, "Pragmatism, Relativism, and Irrationalism" in *Consequences*, 161.
[70] Ibid., 160.
[71] Karl-Otto Apel offers perhaps the most compelling Kantian reading of Peirce (Apel, *Peirce*, 19–53); and Nicholas Rescher offers another (Nicholas Rescher, *Realistic Pragmatism*, 11–12).

[72] Peirce, *CE*, 199 n. 4.
[73] Peirce, *CP*, 5.452.
[74] Apel, *Peirce*, 10–11. Apel counts F. C. S. Schiller and George Herbert Mead among those from whom Peirce was trying to distance himself in his later work. Christopher Hookway argues quite effectively that thinking of Peirce along Kantian lines leads to a misunderstanding of his mature metaphysics, particularly if one views Peirce's project (as Apel does) as being "transcendental." The divide between Peirce and Kant on both Apel's and Hookway's views is that Peirce's categories are not constitutive, as they are in Kant, but regulative. Hookway sees this as a favorable development in Peirce's thought; Apel sees it as an embarrassment. (See Hookway, *Truth, Rationality, and Pragmatism*, 186–187.)
[75] Peirce, *CP*, 6.96.
[76] Ibid., 6.96.
[77] Ibid., 5.553.
[78] Ibid., 5.525.
[79] Ibid., 8.30.
[80] Christopher Hookway offers an excellent discussion of the determination of objects by inquiry when he turns to the problem of "lost facts" in Peirce's conception of inquiry. See Hookway, *Truth, Rationality, and Pragmatism*, 52–59.
[81] Peirce, *CP*, 5.525.
[82] Ibid.
[83] Peirce, *CE*, 3.208.
[84] Ibid.
[85] Ibid.
[86] Peirce, *CE*, 3.238.
[87] Ibid.
[88] Peirce, *CE*, 3.31–32.
[89] Peirce, *CP*, 5.525.
[90] Peirce, *CP*, 5.452.
[91] In the "Transcendental Deduction" Kant writes: "There can be in us no modes of knowledge, no connection or unity of one mode of knowledge with another, with that unity of consciousness which precedes all data of intuitions, and by relation to which representation of objects is alone possible. This pure original unchangeable consciousness I shall name *transcendental apperception*" (Kant, *Critique of Pure Reason*, A 107). Kant continues, "The numerical unity of this apperception is thus the *a priori* ground of all concepts" (Kant, *Critique of Pure Reason*, A 107). Thus "transcendental apperception" guarantees the possibility of consciousness, and the "transcendental unity of apperception" guarantees the possibility of knowledge through concepts.
[92] Hookway makes this point in his discussion of his distance from Apel in reading Kant. See Hookway, *Truth, Rationality, and Pragmatism*, 181–187.
[93] Carlson, "James," 363.
[94] This is not to suggest that James did not *want* to deal with Kant more directly or a philosophical audience more explicitly. James's peers knew well of his intentions to write a systematic metaphysic in the last ten years of his life, but these intentions were often frustrated by the need to offer "popular" lectures to larger audiences. See Lamberth, *James*, 10f.

⁹⁵ Carlson, "James," 363. It is worth noting that Carlson actually does argue that James can be read "as a sort of Kantian" (Carlson, "James," 363). He does so by arguing that James's distinction between theoretical and practical reason is in line with that of Kant and that James's criticisms of metaphysics also align with those of Kant. As will become clear, I disagree.
⁹⁶ William James, *Essays in Philosophy* (Cambridge, Mass.: Harvard University Press, 1978), 139; hereafter "James, *Philosophy*."
⁹⁷ James, *Philosophy*, 139.
⁹⁸ James, *PU*, 101.
⁹⁹ Ibid., 105.
¹⁰⁰ Ibid.
¹⁰¹ Ibid.
¹⁰² Ibid.
¹⁰³ Ibid., 107.
¹⁰⁴ Ibid.
¹⁰⁵ Ibid.
¹⁰⁶ Ibid., 108. Recall here Kant's criticisms of the "transcendental realists" who mistake "appearances" for "things-in-themselves" (Kant, *Critique of Pure Reason*, A 378).
¹⁰⁷ Elsewhere, James puts the point this way: "Throughout the history of philosophy the subject and its object have been treated as absolutely discontinuous entities; and thereupon the presence of the latter to the former, or the 'apprehension' by the former of the latter, has assumed a paradoxical character which all sorts of theories had to be invented to overcome" (William James, *ERE*, 27).
¹⁰⁸ James, *PU*, 109.
¹⁰⁹ Ibid.
¹¹⁰ Ibid.
¹¹¹ Ibid.
¹¹² Ibid.
¹¹³ Ibid., 111.
¹¹⁴ Ibid., 113.
¹¹⁵ James, however weakly, addresses this objection in a footnote at the end of the lecture (ibid., 122–124).
¹¹⁶ Ibid., 131–132.
¹¹⁷ Ibid., 131. James distinguishes between "talking" and "showing" or "pointing" in this passage to indicate the differences between his position and that of the intellectualist of either the transcendental or the empirical type.
¹¹⁸ Lamberth, *James*, 166 n. 69.
¹¹⁹ James, *PU*, 111.

Chapter 4

¹ Lars Hertzberg, "The Sense Is Where You Find It," in *Wittgenstein in America*, eds Timothy McCarthy and Sean C. Stidd (Oxford: Clarendon Press, 2001), 93.
² Ibid., 92–93.

[3] Devitt, Alston, and Rorty make strange bedfellows here in that they all note the close relationship between metaphysical realism and "correspondence truth." Peirce notes this as well when arguing against a version of correspondence truth in which true claims are in agreement with the thing-in-itself (Peirce, *CP*, 5.416).

[4] As noted previously, Rorty makes much of Peirce's Kantianism in his earlier works but seems to have tempered his view considerably since. Comparing his comments on Peirce in "Pragmatism, Relativism, and Irrationalism" with those in "Universality and Truth" reveals Rorty to have become slightly more sympathetic to Peircean pragmatism (Rorty, "Pragmatism," 161; Rorty, "Universality and Truth," 6–9).

[5] Rorty, "World," 15; and Rorty, "Universality and Truth," 20–21.

[6] Rorty, "World," 16.

[7] Conant, "Freedom, Cruelty, and Truth," 274.

[8] James, *Pragmatism*, 29. As noted in the Introduction, the pragmatic theory of truth is really just a special application of the pragmatic method to the concept of truth. My suggestion that pragmatism itself is metaphysically neutral is not a suggestion that the method of pragmatism cannot be applied to metaphysical views. Clearly, Peirce and James both thought that the method could be so applied and that certain metaphysical views might be ruled out as a result and others endorsed. This is, however, a result of the investigation and not a presupposition of it or a necessary outcome.

[9] John Dewey, "The Realism of Pragmatism," 326.

[10] Peirce, *CP*, 5.14.

[11] Ibid., 5.412 (his italics).

[12] Peirce, *CE*, 3.254.

[13] Ibid.

[14] See Hookway, *Truth, Rationality, and Pragmatism*, 74.

[15] Nicholas Rescher seems to have something like this in mind when he offers his pragmatic argument for realism as a regulative principle in inquiry: "We could not form our existing conceptions of truth, fact, inquiry, and communication without presupposing the independent reality of an external world." (Nicholas Rescher, *Realism and Pragmatic Epistemology* [Pittsburg: University of Pittsburg Press, 2005], 21). There are two difficulties with Rescher's reading here. The first is that he fails to limit his pragmatic argument to scientific inquiry when Peirce was, it will be argued below, interested in inquiry more generally conducted along scientific lines. The second and more serious difficulty is that Rescher quickly moves from this pragmatic argument in which the independent reality of objects in the external world is a regulative principle to a "transcendental argument" for accepting this particular regulative requirement.

[16] Peirce, *CE*, 3.246.

[17] A. J. Ayer, *Origins of Pragmatism*, 55.

[18] Peirce, *CE*, 3.254.

[19] Ibid., 3.264.

[20] Ibid., 3.266.

[21] Ibid., 3.321ff.

[22] Ibid., 3.307.

[23] Ibid., 3.322.

24 A. J. Ayer, *Language, Truth, and Logic* (New York: Dover Publications, Inc., 1946), 119.
25 See, for example, Cheryl Misak's construal of logical positivism. Misak, *TEI*, 9.
26 Peirce, *CP*, 6.5.
27 Ibid., 6.2.
28 Ibid., 6.3.
29 Peirce, *CE*, 3.255.
30 In offering a descriptive account of Peirce's view of inquiry, Cheryl Misak shows the extent to which metaphysical and theistic hypotheses are taken up by Peirce as hypotheses the truth of which might be ascertained by the application of the pragmatic principle. She notes, however, that when it comes to the theistic hypothesis, each of Peirce's attempts at drawing out its testable consequences "breaks off just as he tries to carry out this task" (Misak, *TEI*, 32).
31 Ibid., 175–177.
32 Peirce, *CP*, 4.530; and Misak, *TEI*, 22.
33 Peirce, *CP*, 1.240; and Misak, *TEI*, 23.
34 Misak, *TEI*, 23–24.
35 Ibid., 28.
36 H. O. Mounce moves in this direction, claiming that we find in Peirce an idealism that is "objective and is compatible with the most thoroughgoing Realism." Such idealism "holds that the world is constituted by an order which is mental in character but which is quite independent of the *human* mind" (Mounce, *Two Pragmatisms*, 9).
37 In aligning Peirce's view with Thomas Reid's, for example, Mounce makes this exact claim without seeing it as problematic for Peirce's account of inquiry. (See Mounce, *Two Pragmatisms*, 12.) Mounce thus preserves two common sense realist intuitions about truth: that truths are true independent of our thoughts about them and that all hypotheses in investigation are subject to the principle of bivalence. Misak rightly notes that these two intuitions about truth were not viewed by Peirce in quite the way Mounce suggests; Peirce saw them as regulative assumptions regarding inquiry and not "logical truths or even assertions" (Misak, *TEI*, 157).
38 Peirce, *CP*, vol. 5, 223, note.
39 Misak, *TEI*, 35.
40 See ibid., 37.
41 Peirce, *CP*, 1.135.
42 The four methods considered are "tenacity," "authority," "the *a priori*," and "the scientific." Clarity of thought and settlement of opinion are necessary because these settled opinions are beliefs and these beliefs are "guiding principles" or "habits" for action. (Peirce uses these nearly interchangeably. See Peirce, *CE*, 3.245 and 3.247.) Peirce clarifies the role of belief in action in the second of his 1903 lectures at Harvard: "Belief does not make us act at once, but puts us into such a condition that we shall behave in some certain way, when the occasion arises" (Peirce, *CP*, 5.373). It is important to note that Peirce later (1905) reformulates claims like this from the conditional to the subjunctive conditional; for example, "Belief . . . puts us into such a condition that we *would* behave in some certain way *if* the occasion *were to arise*." (For this distinction, see Peirce, *CP*, 5.453

and 5.457; for the importance of this distinction, see Misak, *TEI*, 10 and 13; and Hookway, *Truth, Rationality, and Pragmatism*, 52.)

[43] Peirce, *CE*, 3.257.

[44] Ibid., 3.266. Although Peirce turns immediately in the essay to a sensible example when he considers the diamond and offers an interpretation of the example that seems to support a kind of verificationist reading, Misak shows that Peirce's later writings correct this error by emphasizing the importance of the subjunctive conditional in the statement of hypotheses. That is, rather than having said that the proper form of the hypothesis was indicative ("If the diamond is hard, then it will resist scratching"), Peirce admits that he should have said that the proper form of the hypothesis was subjunctive conditional ("If the diamond *were* hard, it *would* resist scratching.") Such a formulation allows us to maintain the truth of the claim without requiring *actual* testing. (See Peirce, *CP*, 5.453 and 5.457, both from 1905. See also Misak, *TEI*, 10–12.)

[45] Peirce, *CE*, 3.260.

[46] Misak, *TEI*, 12.

[47] Peirce, *CE*, 3.273.

[48] Peirce, *CP*, 5.423.

[49] Misak notes this neglect with regard to truth and inquiry. I am consciously extending this account to include Peirce's conception of the objects of inquiry. See Misak, *TEI*, 14.

[50] Peirce, *CE*, 3.273.

[51] Peirce, *CE*, 3.274.

[52] Ibid.

[53] Misak, *TEI*, 43.

[54] Ibid., 46.

[55] Ibid., 43.

[56] Ibid., 156–157.

[57] Peirce, *CE*, 3.247.

[58] Misak, *TEI*, 59.

[59] Metaphysical questions regarding the character of God, the "essence" of truth, or a non-experiential understanding of objects would be such inquiries. They could be pursued, but not fruitfully.

[60] Misak notes that when Peirce criticizes Kant's view of truth, he does so because it seems not to express a view of truth that is pragmatically significant and not because it expresses a view contrary to the pragmatic view. (See Misak, *TEI*, 128–129.)

[61] Peirce does seem to think, though, that at least one conception of objects fails the test of pragmatic elucidation. An idealism that holds that "the only objects of possible experience [are] our own ideas," is "without exaggeration the very epitome of *all* falsity" (Peirce, *CP*, 6.95). If our ideas were the only objects of experience, we would never have the sorts of surprises that are the starting points of inquiry.

[62] Misak notes this important feature of Peirce's conception of the real: "So when Peirce says that dispositions, generals, possibilities, etc. are real, he does not mean that they actually exist as objects or entities" (Misak, *TEI*, 135). Thus, "real objects" are any objects represented in the final opinion, whether they are actually existent or not.

63. Misak, *TEI*, 37.
64. Christopher Hookway argues persuasively that allowing for a formal definition of truth as correspondence is not the same as allowing for a full-blown "correspondence theory of truth." Insofar as the latter notion entails a conception of truth according to which truth outruns inquiry and then attempts to spell out the connections that nonetheless remain between inquiry and truth, the correspondence theory violates the restrictions on genuine inquiry. See Hookway, *Truth, Rationality, and Pragmatism*, 96.
65. David Lamberth, for one, sees deriving a consistent pragmatism from James without the functional account of knowing offered in his radical empiricism as being difficult, if not impossible. See Lamberth, *James*, 220–223.
66. See, for example, James's responses to Marcel Hébert and Bertrand Russell, "Professor Hébert on Pragmatism" and "Two English Critics," both collected in *The Meaning of Truth*, 126–133 and 146–153, respectively.
67. See Richard J. Bernstein, "Introduction," in James, *PU*, xi.
68. Lamberth, *James*, 163.
69. James, *PU*, 45.
70. Ibid., 46.
71. Ibid., 48–49. Although it is important to offer a more nuanced view of Hegel than that offered by James here, James's view derives from the ways in which Hegel's project was taken up by then-contemporary idealists, most especially Josiah Royce. We can recognize, then, that this reading of Hegel is not entirely accurate while allowing that it is pragmatically acceptable, given the aims of this chapter.
72. Ibid., 50.
73. Ibid., 54.
74. Ibid., 55.
75. Ibid.
76. Ibid.
77. Ibid., 56. Just before the passage quoted, James quotes at length from Royce's "effulgent" description of self-transcendence achieved through the fulfillment of temporal aims in the eternal world in *The World and the Individual* as one such example.
78. James, *PU*, 56.
79. Ibid., 57
80. Ibid., 57.
81. Ibid., 59.
82. Ibid., 56–57.
83. Ibid., 31.
84. Ibid., 32.
85. Ibid.
86. Ibid.
87. Lamberth, *James*, 166n.
88. It is only "relatively" unproblematic, though. James still accuses Hegel of vicious intellectualism, but it is not quite the same critique that he levels at then-contemporary idealists.
89. James, *PU*, 90.

[90] Ibid.
[91] Lamberth makes a similar argument through a more detailed analysis of "The Compounding of Consciousness" than is possible here. See Lamberth, *James*, 179–185.
[92] James, *PU*, 91.
[93] Ibid., 95. James had approached this trilemma in other places, as early as the *Principles of Psychology*, but he was philosophically unsatisfied with the solution there, despite it being adequate for empirical psychology. Between 1895 and 1905, the trilemma occupies several articles—usually in the form of the problem of co-consciousness, the knowledge of one thing by two minds simultaneously. Lamberth offers an excellent overview of the development of James's views in this period. See Lamberth, *James*, 175–179.
[94] Again, Peirce does seem to hold that absolute idealism is logically problematic in holding that our only objects of experiences are concepts—the combination of idealism with rationalism to which James points—but he does not, so far as I am aware, marshal the sort of argument against it that James provides. See Peirce, *CP*, 6.95.
[95] See Lamberth, *James*, 154 ff., for a discussion of James's philosophical typology in *A Pluralistic Universe* that indicates the extent of his sympathies with idealism, only some of which have been mentioned above.
[96] James is one of the sources of the confusion. In "The Experience of Activity" in *Essays in Radical Empiricism*, James claims that "if radical empiricism be good for anything, it ought, with its pragmatic method and its principle of pure experience," to be able to settle the psychological, metaphysical, and epistemological questions regarding activity. James, *ERE*, 81.
[97] James, *Pragmatism*, 6.
[98] William James, *Essays in Philosophy* (Cambridge: Harvard University Press, 1978), 123.
[99] In offering this view, it might seem that I am glossing intentionally over James's use of the word "sensations" in this early statement of the pragmatic method. Much like Peirce, though, James's later statements of the method or maxim use this word to elucidate the conceivable effects, which may or may not be sensory. This may be one instance in which I am in agreement with Lamberth that reading James's pragmatism in light of his radical empiricism becomes necessary, lest we wind up with the verificationist sort of account of pragmatism discussed in the prior section. Suffice it to say that "sensations" must encompass this larger notion and not merely "raw feels" to borrow from Quine. This seems to be one of the points at which Gale sees a conflict between James's Promethean self, which would be wed to the sensationalism here and allow a kind of pragmatism, and his mystic self, which would allow for unmediated contact with the world and disallow pragmatism.
[100] James, *Meaning of Truth*, 101.
[101] See Lamberth, *James*, 215.
[102] James, *Meaning of Truth*, 100.
[103] Ibid., 101.
[104] Ibid., 101–102.
[105] Ibid., 109.
[106] Ibid., 108–109.

[107] Ibid., 111.
[108] Ibid., 112.
[109] Ibid.
[110] Ibid., 113.
[111] Ibid., 142.
[112] Ibid., 143.
[113] Ibid., 142
[114] Ibid., 143.
[115] Ibid.
[116] Ibid.
[117] Ibid., 144.
[118] Ibid., 144–145.
[119] See Lamberth, *James*, 220.
[120] Ibid., 220.
[121] James, *Meaning of Truth*, 118.
[122] Ibid.
[123] Ibid.
[124] Peirce, *CE*, 3.208.
[125] James, *PU*, 107.

Conclusion

[1] Clayton, *Religions, Reasons and Gods*, 3.
[2] Ibid.
[3] Richard Rorty, "Response to Michael Williams," in *Rorty and His Critics*, 214.
[4] Ibid., 215.
[5] Ibid.
[6] Ibid., 217.
[7] Ibid.
[8] John McDowell, "Towards Rehabilitating Objectivity," in *Rorty and His Critics*, 109.
[9] Ibid., 109.
[10] Ibid.
[11] Ibid., 110.
[12] Ibid., 109.
[13] Ibid., 110.
[14] Ibid.
[15] Ibid.
[16] Conant, "Freedom, Cruelty, and Truth," 274.
[17] McDowell notes that Dewey himself offers an example of this in that his own coming to maturity with regard to religion did not require that he give up religion entirely. Likewise, he does not call for humanity to do so in order to reach maturity. Liberating ourselves from the "religion of abasement" is "not the same as liberating ourselves from religion *tout court*" (McDowell, "Rehabilitating," 121).

[18] Charles S. Peirce to William James, 18 December 1897, quoted in Brent, *Peirce*, 264.
[19] Peirce, *CP*, 1.620.
[20] Ibid.
[21] Ibid., 1.623.
[22] Ibid., 1.654.
[23] Ibid., 1.654.
[24] Ibid.
[25] Ibid., 1.633.
[26] Ibid., 1.635.
[27] Ibid.
[28] Ibid.
[29] Ibid., 1.653.
[30] Ibid., 1.654.
[31] William James, *The Will to Believe and Other Essays in Popular Philosophy* (Cambridge, Mass.: Harvard University Press, 1979), 18.
[32] In a recent article on James's "The Will to Believe," Rose Ann Christian distinguishes clearly, as others have, between these two strands of James's argument, which have not been clearly distinguished in the above. Christian, as have others before her, finds the prudential argument largely successful but the epistemological argument definitively not so. On Christian's account, the epistemological argument in which James engages at the end of "The Will to Believe" is, at best, a reinforcement of the prudential argument in that it shows that accepting a certain ontological vision changes the character and relative value of the evidence under consideration. We might, in light of one ontological vision, consider the same evidence differently than those who hold alternative ontological visions. Recognizing this, we might then realize that our own conception of the evidence influences our conception of the veracity of that ontological vision. However, the shift in character and relative value "does not constitute evidence of the truth of such a vision, but only of the value of embracing it." Thus, on Christian's account, James's epistemological argument cannot help but collapse back into his prudential argument. See Rose Ann Christian, "Truth and Consequences in James 'The Will to Believe,'" *International Journal for Philosophy of Religion* [2005] 58: 2f. Edward Madden reads both a "weak" right-to-believe doctrine according to which one might be justified in believing what one's "affective and volitional needs require" and a "stronger" claim that "willingness to believe without adequate evidence is a condition for obtaining that very evidence" in James's essay. See Edward Madden, "Introduction," in *The Will to Believe*, xv–xvi.
[33] Ibid., 14.
[34] Ibid., 15.
[35] Ibid.
[36] Ibid., 20 (italics deleted).
[37] Ibid (my italics).
[38] Ibid., 16.
[39] Stephen T. Davis, "Wishful Thinking and 'The Will to Believe,'" in *Transactions of the Charles S. Peirce Society*, 8/4 (Fall 1972): 234.
[40] James, *Will*, 13.

[41] James, *Will*, 13. Gail Kennedy argues persuasively that the first statement regarding our "right to believe" is in fact James's real intent in authoring the essay, and that the later statement of the title of the paper as "the will to believe" points us in the wrong direction for the interpretation of the essay. See Gail Kennedy, "Pragmatism, Pragmaticism, and the Will to Believe—A Reconsideration," *The Journal of Philosophy*, 55/14 (3 July 1958): 578–588.

[42] James, *Will*, 20 (italics deleted).

[43] Ibid., 18.

[44] Ibid.

[45] Ibid., 24–25.

[46] Ibid., 25.

[47] If we look closely at Clifford's example of the ship-owner, we see that it is precisely an example of this type. The ship-owner cannot make a decision as to the seaworthiness of his vessel on rational grounds, but if he were to suspend belief in the way recommended by Clifford, he would not send the ship to sea. Thus, he would have *de facto* decided that his ship was not sea-worthy.

[48] Peirce, *CP*, 1.672. It must be remembered that Peirce's conception of formal logic is triadic, involving abduction (the creative development of new hypotheses), induction, and deduction, unlike what is now considered formal logic. If Peirce conceived of formal logic as simply the formalization of deduction, then his pragmatic maxim could hardly be considered a logical maxim.

[49] Ibid., 1.665–666.

[50] Ibid., 1.665.

[51] Ibid., 1.666.

[52] Quoted in Misak, *TEI*, 181–182.

[53] Peirce, *CP*, 5.589.

[54] For further discussion of the application of this view to ethics, see Misak, *TEI*, Chapter 5.

[55] Misak is again instructive here. When she wrote *Truth, Politics, Morality*, Misak presented a cognitivist view of ethics "on Peirce's behalf—as one which he ought to have held, not as one that he actually held" (Misak, *TEI*, 169). Nonetheless, in the second edition of *Truth and the End of Inquiry*, published some four years later, Misak defends a cognitivist position on ethics by working within the Peircean corpus. That is, she offers that Peirce did hold beliefs on vitally important matters to be open to deliberation, which opens them to investigation through pragmatic inquiry.

[56] Hookway, *Truth, Rationality, and Pragmatism*, 97.

[57] James, *Will*, 24. James's appeal to the case of the bachelor who hesitates indefinitely to ask a certain woman to marry him is an example of this type (ibid., 30).

[58] Peirce, *CP*, 7.188.

[59] Misak, *TEI*, 185.

[60] Ibid., 186.

[61] James, *Pragmatism*, 84.

[62] James, *Meaning of Truth*, 130–131.

[63] Peirce, *CP*, 5.567.

[64] James, *Pragmatism*, 32.

Bibliography

Allison, Henry E., *Kant's Transcendental Idealism: An Interpretation and Defense.* New Haven, Connecticut: Yale University Press, 1983.
Alston, William P., "Realism and the Tasks of Epistemology." In *Realism/Antirealism and Epistemology*, edited by Christopher B. Kulp, pp. 53–94. New York: Rowman & Littlefield Publishers, Inc., 1997.
—. *A Realist Conception of Truth.* Ithaca, New York: Cornell University Press, 1996.
Anderson, Victor, *Pragmatic Theology: Negotiating the Intersections of an American Philosophy of Religion and Public Theology.* Albany, New York: State University of New York Press, 1998.
Apel, Karl-Otto, *Charles S. Peirce: From Pragmatism to Pragmaticism*, trans. John Michael Krois. Amherst, Massachusetts: University of Massachusetts Press, 1981.
Ayer, Alfred J., *Language, Truth, and Logic.* New York: Dover, 1946.
—. *The Origins of Pragmatism: Studies in the Philosophy of Charles Sanders Peirce and William James.* San Francisco: Freeman, Cooper and Company, 1968.
Bernstein, Richard J., "Action, Conduct, and Self-Control." In *Perspectives on Peirce: Critical Essays on Charles Sanders Peirce*, edited by Richard J. Bernstein, pp. 66–91. New Haven, Connecticut: Yale University Press, 1965.
Bilgrami, Akeel, "Is Truth a Goal of Inquiry?: Rorty and Davidson on Truth." In *Rorty and His Critics*, edited by Robert B. Brandom, pp 242–262. Oxford: Blackwell Publishers Ltd., 2000.
Boisvert, Raymond D., *Dewey's Metaphysics.* New York: Fordham University Press, 1988.
Brandom, Robert B., "Vocabularies of Pragmatism: Synthesizing Naturalism and Historicism." In *Rorty and His Critics*, edited by Robert B. Brandom, pp. 156–183. Oxford: Blackwell Publishers Ltd., 2000.
Brent, Joseph, *Charles Sanders Peirce: A Life.* Revised and enlarged edition. Bloomington, Indiana: Indiana University Press, 1998.
Brown, Hunter, *William James on Radical Empiricism and Religion.* Toronto: University of Toronto Press, 2000.
Buchler, Justus, *Charles Peirce's Empiricism.* New York: Harcourt, Brace, and Company, 1939.
Butchvarov, Panayot, *Skepticism about the External World.* Oxford: Oxford University Press, 1998.
Carlson, Thomas, "James and the Kantian Tradition." In *The Cambridge Companion to William James*, edited by Ruth Anna Putnam, pp. 363–383. Cambridge, UK: Cambridge University Press, 1997.
Cavell, Stanley, *The Claim of Reason: Wittgenstein, Skepticism, Morality, and Tragedy.* Oxford: Oxford University Press, 1979.

Chisholm, Roderick, "Why the Theory of Knowledge Has to Be Realistic." In *Realism/Antirealism and Epistemology*, edited by Christopher B. Kulp. New York: Rowman & Littlefield Publishers, Inc., 1997.

Churchland, Paul, *Matter and Consciousness: A Contemporary Introduction to the Philosophy of Mind.* Cambridge, Mass.: Massachusetts Institute of Technology Press, 1988.

—. *A Neurocomputational Perspective: The Nature of Mind and the Structure of Science.* Cambridge, Mass.: Massachusetts Institute of Technology Press, 1989.

Clayton, John, *Religions, Reasons, and Gods: Essays in Cross-Cultural Philosophy of Religion*, prepared for publication by Anne M. Blackburn and Thomas D. Carroll. Cambridge, UK: Cambridge University Press, 2006.

Conant, James, "Freedom, Cruelty, and Truth: Rorty versus Orwell." In *Rorty and His Critics*, edited by Robert B. Brandom, pp. 268–342. Oxford: Blackwell Publishers Ltd., 2000.

Cooper, Wesley, *The Unity of William James's Thought.* Nashville, Tenn.: Vanderbilt University Press, 2002.

Davaney, Sheila Greeve, *Pragmatic Historicism: A Theology for the Twenty-First Century.* Albany, New York: State University of New York Press, 2000.

Davidson, Donald, "Indeterminism and Antirealism." In *Realism/Antirealism and Epistemology*, edited by Christopher B. Kulp, pp. 109–122. New York: Rowman & Littlefield Publishers, Inc., 1997.

—. "Truth Rehabilitated." In *Rorty and His Critics*, edited by Robert B. Brandom, pp. 65–74. Oxford: Blackwell Publishers Ltd., 2000.

Dennett, Daniel C., "The Case for Rorts." In *Rorty and His Critics*, edited by Robert B. Brandom, pp. 91–101. Oxford: Blackwell Publishers Ltd., 2000.

—. *Consciousness Explained.* Boston: Little, Brown, and Company, 1991.

Descartes, René, *The Philosophical Writings of Descartes*, translated by John Cottingham, Robert Stoothoff, and Dugald Murdoch, volume II. Cambridge: Cambridge University Press, 1984.

Devitt, Michael, *Realism and Truth*, second edition. Oxford: Blackwell Publishers, Ltd., 1991.

Dewey, John, "The Control of Ideas by Facts I." *Journal of Philosophy* IV (April 1907): 197–203.

—. *Essays in Experimental Logic.* Chicago: The University of Chicago Press, 1916.

—. *Experience and Nature.* Chicago: Open Court Publishing, 1925.

—. *The Quest for Certainty.* New York: Milton, Balch, and Company, 1929.

—. "The Realism of Pragmatism." *Journal of Philosophy* II (8 June 1905): 324–327.

—. *Reconstruction in Philosophy.* Enlarged edition with new introduction. Boston: The Beacon Press, 1957.

Drury, Maurice O'Connor, "Conversations with Wittgenstein." In *Ludwig Wittgenstein: Personal Recollections*, edited by Rush Rhees. Totowa, N.J.: Rowman and Littlefield, 1981.

Dummett, Michael, *Truth and Other Enigmas.* Cambridge, Mass.: Harvard University Press, 1978.

—. "What Does the Appeal to Use Do for the Theory of Meaning?" In *Meaning and Use: Papers Presented at the Second Jerusalem Philosophical Encounter, April 1976*, edited by Avishai Margalit, pp. 123–135. Boston: D. Reidel Publishing Company, 1979.

Empiricus, Sextus, "Outlines of Pyrrhonism," translated by Sanford G. Etheridge. In *Classics of Western Philosophy*, seventh edition, edited by Steven M. Cahn. Indianapolis: Hackett Publishing Company, Inc., 2006.

Feibleman, James, *An Introduction to Peirce's Philosophy Interpreted as a System*. New York: Harper and Brothers Publishers, 1946.

Field, Hartry, "Realism and Relativism." *Journal of Philosophy* 79 (1982): 553–567.

—. "Tarski's Theory of Truth." *Journal of Philosophy* 69 (1972): 347–375.

—. "The Deflationary Conception of Truth." In *Fact, Science, and Morality*, edited by Graham MacDonald and Crispin Wright. pp. 55–117. Oxford, UK: Blackwell, 1986.

Ford, Marcus, *William James's Philosophy: A New Perspective*. Amherst, Massachusetts: University of Massachusetts Press, 1982.

Forster, Paul, "The Logical Foundations of Peirce's Indeterminism." In *The Rule of Reason: The Philosophy of Charles Sanders Peirce*, edited by Jacqueline Brunning and Paul Forster, pp. 57–80. Toronto: University of Toronto Press, 1997.

Franklin, James, "Healthy Skepticism." *Philosophy* 66/257 (July 1991): pp. 305–324.

Gale, Richard, *The Divided Self of William James*. Cambridge, UK: Cambridge University Press, 1999.

Goodman, Nelson, "The Fabrication of Facts." In *Relativism: Cognitive and Moral*, edited by Jack W. Meiland and Michael Krause, 18–29. Notre Dame, Indiana: University of Notre Dame Press, 1982.

Greco, John, *Putting Skeptics in Their Place: The Nature of Skeptical Arguments and Their Role in Philosophical Inquiry*. Cambridge, UK: Cambridge University Press, 2000.

Greenwood, David, *Truth and Meaning*. New York: Philosophical Library, Inc., 1957.

Haack, Susan, "The First Rule of Reason." *The Rule of Reason: The Philosophy of Charles Sanders Peirce*, edited by Jacqueline Brunning and Paul Forster, pp. 241–261. Toronto: University of Toronto Press, 1997.

Habermas, Jürgen, "Richard Rorty's Pragmatic Turn." In *Rorty and His Critics*, edited by Robert B. Brandom, pp. 31–56. Oxford: Blackwell Publishers Ltd., 2000.

Harman, Gilbert, "Pragmatism and Reasons for Belief." In *Realism/Antirealism and Epistemology*, edited by Christopher B. Kulp, pp. 123–148. New York: Rowman & Littlefield Publishers, Inc., 1997.

—. *Skepticism and the Definition of Knowledge*, edited by Robert Nozick. New York: Garland Publishing, 1990.

Hausman, Carl R., "Charles Peirce and the Origin of Interpretation." In *The Rule of Reason: The Philosophy of Charles Sanders Peirce*, edited by Jacqueline Brunning and Paul Forster, pp. 185–200. Toronto: University of Toronto Press, 1997.

Heal, Jane, "Pragmatism and Choosing to Believe." In *Reading Rorty: Critical Responses to "Philosophy and the Mirror of Nature" (and Beyond)*, edited by Alan R. Malachowski, pp. 101–114. Oxford: Basil Blackwell Ltd., 1990.

Hertzberg, Lars, "The Sense is Where You Find It." In *Wittgenstein in America*, edited by Timothy McCarthy and Sean C. Stidd, pp. 90–103. Oxford: Oxford University Press, 2001.

Hildebrand, David, *Beyond Realism and Antirealism: John Dewey and the Neopragmatists*. Nashville, Tenn.: Vanderbilt University Press, 2003.

Hintikka, Jaakko, "The Place of C. S. Peirce in the History of Logical Theory." In *The Rule of Reason: The Philosophy of Charles Sanders Peirce*, edited by Jacqueline Brunning and Paul Forster, pp. 13–33. Toronto: University of Toronto Press, 1997.

Hookway, Christopher, *Peirce*. London: Routledge and Kegan Paul, 1985.
—. *Truth, Rationality, and Pragmatism: Themes from Peirce*. Oxford: Clarendon Press, 2000.
Hornsby, Jennifer, "Descartes, Rorty and the Mind-Body Fiction." In *Reading Rorty: Critical Responses to "Philosophy and the Mirror of Nature" (and Beyond)*, edited by Alan R. Malachowski, pp. 41–57. Oxford: Basil Blackwell Ltd., 1990.
Horwich, Paul, *Truth*. Oxford, UK: Blackwell Publishing, Ltd., 1990.
Houghton, David, "Rorty's Talk-About." In *Reading Rorty: Critical Responses to "Philosophy and the Mirror of Nature" (and Beyond)*, edited by Alan R. Malachowski, pp. 156–170. Oxford: Basil Blackwell Ltd., 1990.
Hume, David, *A Treatise of Human Nature*, second edition, edited by L. A. Selby-Bigge, revised by P.H. Nidditch. Oxford, UK: Oxford University Press, 1978.
—. *An Enquiry Concerning Human Understanding*, third edition, edited by L.A. Selby-Bigge, revised by P.H. Nidditch. Oxford, UK: Oxford University Press, 1975.
Hymers, Michael, *Philosophy and Its Epistemic Neuroses*. Boulder, Colorado: Westview Press, 2000.
James, William, *Essays in Radical Empiricism*. Cambridge, Massachusetts: Harvard University Press, 1976.
—. *Essays in Philosophy*. Cambridge, Massachusetts: Harvard University Press, 1978.
—. *The Meaning of Truth*. Cambridge, Massachusetts: Harvard University Press, 1975.
—. *A Pluralistic Universe*. Cambridge, Massachusetts: Harvard University Press, 1977.
—. *Pragmatism: A New Name for Some Old Ways of Thinking*. Cambridge, Massachusetts: Harvard University Press, 1975.
—. *The Varieties of Religious Experience*. New York: Penguin Books, 1982.
—. *The Will to Believe and Other Essays in Popular Philosophy*. Cambridge, Massachusetts: Harvard University Press, 1979.
Kant, Immanuel, *Critique of Pure Reason*. Translated by Norman Kemp Smith. New York: St. Martin's Press, 1965.
—. *Prolegomena to Any Future Metaphysics*, translated by Paul Carus with an Introduction by Lewis White Beck. New York: The Bobbs-Merrill Company, Inc., 1950.
Kirkham, Richard L., *Theories of Truth: A Critical Introduction*. Cambridge, Massachusetts: Massachusetts Institute of Technology Press, 1992.
Kripke, Saul A., "A Puzzle about Belief." In *Meaning and Use: Papers Presented at the Second Jerusalem Philosophical Encounter, April 1976*, edited by Avishai Margalit, pp. 239–283. Boston: D. Reidel Publishing Company, 1979.
Kuklick, Bruce, "American Philosophy and Its Lost Public." In *Pragmatism: From Progressivism to Postmodernism*, edited by David Depew and Robert Hollinger, pp. 142–152. Westport: Praeger Publishers, 1995.
Kulp, Christopher B., "Introduction." In *Realism/Antirealism and Epistemology*, edited by Christopher B. Kulp, pp. 1–14. New York: Rowman & Littlefield Publishers, Inc., 1997.
Lamberth, David, *William James and the Metaphysics of Experience*. Cambridge: Cambridge University Press, 1999.
Lewis, David, *On the Plurality of Worlds*. Oxford, UK: Blackwell Publishing, Ltd., 1987.

—. "Putnam's Paradox." *Australasian Journal of Philosophy* 62 (1984): 221–236.
Lovejoy, Arthur O., *The Thirteen Pragmatisms and Other Essays*. Baltimore: The Johns Hopkins Press, 1963.
Margolis, Joseph, "Peirce's Fallibilism." *Transactions of the Charles S. Peirce Society* XXXIV, no. 3 (1998): 535–569.
—. *Pragmatism without Foundations: Reconciling Realism and Relativism*. New York: Basil Blackwell, 1986.
—. *Pragmatism's Advantage: American and European Philosophy at the End of the Twentieth Century*. Stanford, Cal.: Stanford University Press, 2010.
McDermid, Douglas, *The Varieties of Pragmatism: Truth, Realism, and Knowledge from James to Rorty*. London: Continuum Publishing, Inc., 2006.
McDowell, John, *Mind and World*. Cambridge, Massachusetts: Harvard University Press, 1994.
—. "Towards Rehabilitating Objectivity." In *Rorty and His Critics*, edited by Robert B. Brandom, pp. 109–123. Oxford: Blackwell Publishers Ltd., 2000.
Misak, Cheryl J., *Truth and the End of Inquiry: A Peircean Account of Truth*. Oxford, UK: Oxford University Press, 1991 and 2004.
—. *Truth, Politics, Morality: Pragmatism and Deliberation*. London: Routledge, 2000.
Moore, George E., *Philosophical Papers*. New York: Humanities Press, 1977.
Mounce, Howard O., *The Two Pragmatisms: From Peirce to Rorty*. London: Routledge, 1997.
Murphey, Murray G., *The Development of Peirce's Philosophy*. Cambridge, Massachusetts: Harvard University Press, 1961.
Murphy, John P., *Pragmatism: From Peirce to Davidson*. San Francisco: Westview Press, 1990.
Nagel, Thomas, *The Last Word*. Cambridge, Massachusetts: Harvard University Press, 1997.
—. "Subjective and Objective." In *Post-Analytic Philosophy*, edited by John Rajchman and Cornel West, pp. 31–47. New York: Columbia University Press, 1985.
—. *The View from Nowhere*. Oxford: Oxford University Press, 1986.
O'Connell, Robert J., S J. *William James on the Courage to Believe*. New York: Fordham University Press, 1984.
Olssson, Erik J., "Not Giving the Skeptic a Hearing: 'Pragmatism and Radical Doubt.'" *Philosophy and Phenomenological Research* 70/1 (January 2005): 98–126.
Peirce, Charles S., *Chance, Love, and Logic*, edited by Morris R. Cohen. New York: Harcourt, Brace, and Company, Inc., 1923.
—. *Collected Papers*, edited by Charles Hartshorne, Paul Weiss, and Arthur W. Burks, volumes 1–8. Cambridge, Massachusetts: Harvard University Press, 1931–1958.
—. *Pragmatism as a Principle and Method of Right Thinking*, edited with commentary by Patricia Ann Turrisi. Albany, New York: State University of New York Press, 1997.
—. *Reasoning and the Logic of Things: The Cambridge Conferences Lectures of 1898*, edited by Kenneth Laine Ketner with an Introduction by Kenneth Laine Tanner and Hilary Putnam. Cambridge, Massachusetts: Harvard University Press, 1992.
—. *Selected Writings: Values in a Universe of Chance*, edited by Philip P. Wiener. New York: Dover Publications, Inc., 1958.
—. *Writings of Charles Sanders Peirce: A Chronological Edition*, edited by Max H. Fisch, 8 volumes. Bloomington, Indiana: Indiana University Press, 1982.

Perry, Ralph Barton, "Review of Pragmatism as a Philosophical Generalization." *Journal of Philosophy, Psychology, and Scientific Method* 4 (1907).
—. *The Thought and Character of William James.* Boston: Little, Brown, and Co., 1935.
Phillips, Dewi Z., *Philosophy's Cool Place.* Ithaca: Cornell University Press, 1999.
Popkin, Richard H., *The History of Skepticism from Erasmus to Spinoza.* Berkeley: University of California Press, 1979.
Prichard, Harold A., *Kant's Theory of Knowledge.* Oxford: Clarendon Press, 1909.
Pritchard, Duncan, "Recent Work on Radical Skepticism." *American Philosophical Quarterly* 39/3 (July 2002): 215–257.
Putnam, Hilary, "Comments." In *Meaning and Use: Papers Presented at the Second Jerusalem Philosophical Encounter, April 1976*, edited by Avishai Margalit, pp. 284–288. Boston: D. Reidel Publishing Company, 1979.
—. *The Many Faces of Realism: The Paul Carus Lectures.* LaSalle, Illinois: Open Court Publishing Company, 1987.
—. *Pragmatism: An Open Question.* Cambridge: Blackwell Publishers, 1995.
—. *Realism with a Human Face*, edited by James Conant. Cambridge, Massachusetts: Harvard University Press, 1990.
—. *Reason, Truth, and History.* New York: Cambridge University Press, 1981.
—. "Reference and Understanding." In *Meaning and Use: Papers Presented at the Second Jerusalem Philosophical Encounter, April 1976*, edited by Avishai Margalit, pp. 199–217. Boston: D. Reidel Publishing Company, 1979.
—. *Renewing Philosophy.* Cambridge, Massachusetts: Harvard University Press, 1992.
—. "Reply to Dummett's Comment." In *Meaning and Use: Papers Presented at the Second Jerusalem Philosophical Encounter, April 1976*, edited by Avishai Margalit, pp. 226–228. Boston: D. Reidel Publishing Company, 1979.
—. *Representation and Reality.* Cambridge, Massachusetts: Massachusetts Institute of Technology, 1988.
—. "Richard Rorty on Reality and Justification." In *Rorty and His Critics*, edited by Robert B. Brandom, 81–87. Oxford: Blackwell Publishers Ltd., 2000.
Ramberg, Bjørn, "Post-Ontological Philosophy of Mind: Rorty versus Davidson." In *Rorty and His Critics*, edited by Robert B. Brandom, pp. 351–370. Oxford: Blackwell Publishers Ltd., 2000.
Raposa, Michael L., *Peirce's Philosophy of Religion.* Bloomington, Ind.: Indiana University Press, 1989.
Rescher, Nicholas, *Realistic Pragmatism: An Introduction to Pragmatic Philosophy.* Albany: State University of New York Press, 2001.
—. *Realism and Pragmatic Epistemology.* Pittsburgh: University of Pittsburgh Press, 2005.
Robin, Richard S., "Classical Pragmatism and Pragmatism's Proof." In *The Rule of Reason: The Philosophy of Charles Sanders Peirce*, edited by Jacqueline Brunning and Paul Forster, pp. 139–152. Toronto: University of Toronto Press, 1997.
Rorty, Richard, *Achieving Our Country: Leftist Thought in Twentieth Century America.* Cambridge, Massachusetts: Harvard University Press, 1998.
—. *Consequences of Pragmatism.* Minneapolis, Minnesota: University of Minnesota Press, 1982.
—. *Contingency, Irony, and Solidarity.* New York: Cambridge University Press, 1989.
—. *Objectivity, Relativism, and Truth: Philosophical Papers, Volume 1.* Cambridge: Cambridge University Press, 1991.

—. *Philosophy and the Mirror of Nature.* Princeton: Princeton University Press, 1979.
—. *Philosophy and Social Hope.* New York: Penguin Books, 1999.
—. "Realism, Antirealism, and Pragmatism: Comments on Alston, Chisholm, Davidson, Harman, and Searle." In *Realism/Antirealism and Epistemology,* edited by Christopher B. Kulp, pp. 149–171. New York: Rowman & Littlefield Publishers, Inc., 1997.
—. "Response to Bilgrami." In *Rorty and His Critics,* edited by Robert B. Brandom, pp. 262–267. Oxford: Blackwell Publishers Ltd., 2000.
—. "Response to Brandom." In *Rorty and His Critics,* edited by Robert B. Brandom, pp. 183–190. Oxford: Blackwell Publishers Ltd., 2000.
—. "Response to Conant." In *Rorty and His Critics,* edited by Robert B. Brandom, pp. 342–349. Oxford: Blackwell Publishers Ltd., 2000.
—. "Response to Davidson." In *Rorty and His Critics,* edited by Robert B. Brandom, pp. 74–80. Oxford: Blackwell Publishers Ltd., 2000.
—. "Response to Dennett." In *Rorty and His Critics,* edited by Robert B. Brandom, pp. 101–108. Oxford: Blackwell Publishers Ltd., 2000.
—. "Response to Habermas." In *Rorty and His Critics,* edited by Robert B. Brandom, pp. 56–64. Oxford: Blackwell Publishers Ltd., 2000.
—. "Response to McDowell." In *Rorty and His Critics,* edited by Robert B. Brandom, pp. 123–128. Oxford: Blackwell Publishers Ltd., 2000.
—. "Response to Putnam." In *Rorty and His Critics,* edited by Robert B. Brandom, pp. 87–90. Oxford: Blackwell Publishers Ltd., 2000.
—. "Response to Ramberg." In *Rorty and His Critics,* edited by Robert B. Brandom, pp. 370–377. Oxford: Blackwell Publishers Ltd., 2000.
—. "Response to Williams." In *Rorty and His Critics,* edited by Robert B. Brandom, pp. 213–219. Oxford: Blackwell Publishers Ltd., 2000.
—. *Truth and Progress: Philosophical Papers, Volume 3.* New York: Cambridge University Press, 1998.
—. "Universality and Truth." In *Rorty and His Critics,* edited by Robert B. Brandom, pp. 1–30. Oxford: Blackwell Publishers Ltd., 2000.
Rosenthal, Sandra B., *Charles Peirce's Pragmatic Pluralism.* Albany, New York: State University of New York Press, 1994.
—. "Pragmatic Experimentalism and the Derivation of the Categories." In *The Rule of Reason: The Philosophy of Charles Sanders Peirce,* edited by Brunning and Paul Forster, pp. 120–137. Toronto: University of Toronto Press, 1997.
—. *Speculative Pragmatism.* Amherst, Massachusetts: University of Massachusetts Press, 1986.
Ruf, Frederick J., *The Creation of Chaos: William James and the Stylistic Making of a Disorderly World.* Albany, N.Y.: State University of New York Press, 1991.
Russell, Bertrand, *Philosophical Essays.* London: Longmans Green, 1910.
Searle, John R., "Does the Real World Exist?" In *Realism/Antirealism and Epistemology,* edited by Christopher B. Kulp, pp. 15–52. New York: Rowman & Littlefield Publishers, Inc., 1997.
Seigfried, Charlene Haddock, *William James's Radical Reconstruction of Philosophy.* Albany, N.Y.: State University of New York Press, 1990.
Sheriff, John K., *Charles Peirce's Guess at the Riddle: Grounds for Human Significance.* Bloomington: Indiana University Press, 1994.

Short, Thomas L., "Hypostatic Abstraction in Self-Consciousness." In *The Rule of Reason: The Philosophy of Charles Sanders Peirce*, edited by Jacqueline Brunning and Paul Forster, pp. 289–308. Toronto: University of Toronto Press, 1997.

Smith, John E., "Community and Reality." In *Perspectives on Peirce: Critical Essays on Charles Sanders Peirce*, edited by Richard J. Bernstein, pp. 92–119. New Haven, Connecticut: Yale University Press, 1965.

—. *Purpose and Thought: The Meaning of Pragmatism*. New Haven, Connecticut: Yale University Press, 1978.

Sorell, Tom, "The World from its Own Point of View." In *Reading Rorty: Critical Responses to "Philosophy and the Mirror of Nature" (and Beyond)*, edited by Alan R. Malachowski, pp. 11–25. Oxford: Basil Blackwell Ltd., 1990.

Stich, Stephen, *From Folk Psychology to Cognitive Science*. Cambridge, Mass.: Massachusetts Institute of Technology Press, 1983.

—. *Deconstructing the Mind*. New York: Oxford University Press, 1996.

Stout, Jeffrey, *Democracy and Tradition*. Princeton, N.J.: Princeton University Press, 2004.

Strawson, Peter F., *The Bounds of Sense: An Essay on Kant's "Critique of Pure Reason."* London: Methuen and Company, Ltd., 1966.

Stroud, Barry, *The Significance of Philosophical Skepticism*. Oxford: Clarendon Press, 1984.

Suckiel, Ellen Kappy, *Heaven's Champion: William James's Philosophy of Religion*. South Bend, Ind.: University of Notre Dame Press, 1996.

Taylor, Charles, "Rorty in the Epistemological Tradition." In *Reading Rorty: Critical Responses to "Philosophy and the Mirror of Nature" (and Beyond)*, edited by Alan R. Malachowski, pp. 257–275. Oxford: Basil Blackwell Ltd., 1990.

Tiles, James E., "Dewey's Realism: Applying the Term 'Mental' in a World without Withins." *Transactions of the Charles S. Peirce Society* XXXI, no. 1 (1995): pp. 137–163.

van Inwagen, Peter, "On Always Being Wrong." In *Midwest Studies in Philosophy Volume XII: Realism and Antirealism*, edited by Peter H. French, Theodore E. Uehling, Jr., and Howard K. Wettstein, pp. 95–111. Minneapolis, Minnesota: University of Minnesota Press, 1988.

Weiss, Paul, "Biography of Charles S. Peirce." In *Perspectives on Peirce: Critical Essays on Charles Sanders Peirce*, edited by Richard J. Bernstein, pp. 1–12. New Haven, Connecticut: Yale University Press, 1965.

—. "Charles S. Peirce, Philosopher." In *Perspectives on Peirce: Critical Essays on Charles Sanders Peirce*, edited by Richard J. Bernstein, pp. 120–140. New Haven, Connecticut: Yale University Press, 1965.

Wells, Rulon, "Charles S. Peirce as an American." *Perspectives on Peirce: Critical Essays on Charles Sanders Peirce*, edited by Richard J. Bernstein, pp. 13–41. New Haven, Connecticut: Yale University Press, 1965.

Wennerberg, Hjalmar, *The Pragmatism of C. S. Peirce*. Lund: CWK Gleerup, 1962.

Wernham, James C. S., *James's Will-to-Believe Doctrine: A Heretical View*. Montreal: McGill-Queen's University Press, 1987.

West, Cornell, *The American Evasion of Philosophy: A Genealogy of Pragmatism*. Madison: University of Wisconsin Press, 1989.

—. "The Politics of American Neo-Pragmatism." In *Post-Analytic Philosophy*, edited by John Rajchman and Cornel West, pp. 259–272. New York: Columbia University Press, 1985.

Will, Frederick L., *Pragmatism and Realism*, edited by Kenneth R. Westphal. New York: Rowman and Littlefield Publishers, Inc., 1997.
Williams, Bernard, "Auto-da-Fé: Consequences of Pragmatism." In *Reading Rorty: Critical Responses to "Philosophy and the Mirror of Nature" (and Beyond)*, edited by Alan R. Malachowski, pp. 26–37. Oxford: Basil Blackwell Ltd., 1990.
—. *Ethics and the Limits of Philosophy*. Cambridge, Mass.: Harvard University Press, 1985.
Williams, Michael, "Epistemology and the Mirror of Nature." In *Rorty and His Critics*, edited by Robert B. Brandom, pp. 191–213. Oxford: Blackwell Publishers Ltd., 2000.
—. *Unnatural Doubts: Epistemological Realism and the Basis of Skepticism*. Oxford: Blackwell Publishers Inc., 1991.
Wilson, Margaret D., "Skepticism Without Indubitability." *The Journal of Philosophy* LXXI, no. 10 (1984): 537–544.
Wittgenstein, Ludwig, *Culture and Value*, edited by G. H. von Wright and Heikki Nyman. Translated by Peter Winch. Chicago: The University of Chicago Press, 1980.
—. *On Certainty*, edited by G. E. M. Anscombe and G. H. von Wright. Translated by Denis Paul and G. E. M. Anscombe. San Francisco: Harper and Row, Publishers, 1969.
—. *Philosophical Investigations*, translated by G. E. M. Anscombe. Englewood Cliffs, New Jersey: Prentice-Hall, 1958.
Wright, Crispin, *Realism, Meaning and Truth*. second edition. Oxford: Blackwell Publishers, 1993.
Yolton, John W., "Mirrors and Veils, Thoughts and Things: The Epistemological Problematic." In *Reading Rorty: Critical Responses to "Philosophy and the Mirror of Nature" (and Beyond)*, edited by Alan R. Malachowski, pp. 58–73. Oxford: Basil Blackwell Ltd., 1990.

Index

a priori method   115, 118, 196
Allison, Henry E.   190–1
Alston, William   19–22, 177, 195
antirealism   16–23, 175
   and classical pragmatism   30–4, 67–8, 110
   and Richard Rorty   24–9, 149–50, 174, 189
Apel, Karl-Otto   82, 91
authority (method of)   118, 167, 196
Ayer, Alfred Jules   113, 115, 173

belief   15, 87, 148
   and inquiry   112–15, 118, 122, 134, 138, 142–3
   and justification   38, 41, 45, 52, 136, 183
   and truth   20–1, 122–4, 140
   as habit for action   111, 196
   religious   9, 148, 152–69
Bergson, Henri   63

Carlson, Thomas   98f, 194
Clayton, John   41, 43, 198
Clifford, W.K.   157–60, 202
Conant, James   11, 88–9, 94, 105–6, 110, 152, 189

Descartes, René   4, 39, 40ff, 119, 181, 183
Devitt, Michael   17, 22, 85–90, 175, 178, 192
Dewey, John   3, 12, 24, 27, 35, 53, 90, 97, 111, 147, 150, 173, 176, 178–9, 185, 200
doubt (genuine)   52, 119, 123–4, 135, 157, 161, 163–8
Dummett, Michael   12, 15, 175

Empiricus, Sextus   38, 45
epistemology   3, 7, 10, 13, 48, 53–8, 73–5, 87–8, 99, 110, 136, 149–53, 181, 183, 187
Essays in Radical Empiricism   63–7, 135
   passim   194, 199

Field, Hartry   15–17, 19, 21, 23, 171, 175
Franklin, James   45

Gale, Richard   25, 31–4, 153, 180, 199

Hegel, G. W. F.   25–6, 80, 117, 127, 132, 198
Hertzberg, Lars   107
Hookway, Christopher   112, 117, 125, 164, 183, 186, 193, 198
Horwich, Paul   21
Hume, David   38–40, 44–50, 52–5, 59, 62–3, 71–3, 100, 158, 183, 185
Hymers, Michael   17, 176

idealism   14–16, 60, 67, 74, 90, 137, 143, 178, 191
   absolute   25, 84, 92, 126–35, 197, 199
   objective   26, 30, 84, 117, 196
inquiry   2–5, 24, 26–9, 52, 89, 103, 106, 111, 148, 153, 155, 160–1
   and C.S. Peirce   112–25, 193, 195–8
   and religious beliefs   161–8
   and William James   125, 135–43

James, William   1f, 9–13, 90, 135f, 173
   and idealism   99, 131–3, 198
   and intellectualism   98–105, 126–32, 134, 141ff, 144, 194
   and realism   31–6, 100, 137, 151, 188
   and Richard Rorty   22–5, 109–10, 143, 147, 166, 176, 179
   and skepticism   51–2, 58, 62–7, 69–72, 183

Kant, Immanuel   4, 23, 60, 64, 73ff, 108, 110, 126, 144, 187–90
Kirkham, Richard L.   20–2, 29–31, 110, 124, 171, 175, 178, 191

Lamberth, David C.   34, 63, 103, 127, 130, 132, 135, 142, 180, 186, 198–9

Index

logic 5, 34, 63, 96, 98–103, 104ff, 111, 113–14, 118, 126, 130, 132, 134–9, 143–5, 154, 157, 161–2, 168, 202
Lovejoy, Arthur O. 7

Margolis, Joseph 2, 4, 172
Meaning of Truth, The 136ff, 166
metaphysics 2, 3, 5, 10, 13, 24, 29, 31, 34, 63, 74ff, 87ff, 99, 102, 110, 114ff, 120, 124–5, 128, 132–5, 155–7, 162
Misak, C. J. 116–19, 122–5, 165–6, 196–7, 202
Montaigne, Michel de 38
Moore, G. E. 48, 65–6, 181
Mounce, H. O. 25–7, 28–9, 51–2, 80, 147, 180, 183, 188, 196
Murphey, Murray G. 23, 186

Nagel, Thomas 38
Natorp, Paul 65–6
neo-pragmatism 23–4, 109–11, 185, 195
Nonrealism with regard to truth 14, 22–5, 30–2, 110, 171, 174, 178
noumena 77–85, 88, 187–9
noumenon 25–6, 74, 76–86, 92–3, 96, 187–9

object 3, 4, 8, 23, 30, 35, 37, 46, 55–7, 60, 64–8, 74–96, 108, 112–22, 124, 130–2, 139–44, 163–7, 187–91, 195, 197
objective 13, 66, 117, 151–2, 175, 180, 191
Olsson, Erik J. 45, 51–2, 183

Peirce, Charles Sanders 3, 91–3, 172
  and idealism 23, 74, 93, 95, 111–12, 117, 121 *passim*, 134, 183, 188, 199
  and realism 25–9, 94, 108–9, 112–14, 147, 169, 180, 196
  and religion 5–7, 154ff, 161, 165–6
  and Richard Rorty 35, 90, 94, 171, 173, 195
  and skepticism 40, 49, 51–3, 58–63, 67–72, 93, 95, 111–12, 117, 121 *passim*, 134, 183, 188
phenomena 74, 76, 82, 115, 189
Phillips, D. Z. 7–9, 186
Popkin, Richard H. 43, 181–2, 184

pragmatic elucidation 4, 112, 117–21, 123–5, 128, 131, 133–6, 138–45, 149, 162, 169, 197
pragmatism 14, 23–34, 39, 49, 52–3, 55, 58, 64, 67–71, 75, 90–1, 97, 103, 105, 108, 111, 116, 120, 124–5, 135–45, 147–9, 152–3, 159–69, 171, 173, 179, 183, 185–6, 195, 198–9
Pragmatism 1–2 , 34, 50f, 58, 108, 135f, 195
Pritchard, Duncan 42, 45, 181
Putnam, Hilary 3, 11, 17–18, 42, 75, 171, 176, 182, 184

radical empiricism 34, 63, 67, 70, 135, 143, 160, 168, 180, 183, 186, 199
Raposa, Michael 172
rationality 41, 103, 128–30, 134–7, 143
realism 3–4, 14ff, 67, 85ff, 90, 109–10, 124, 137, 147, 149–50, 152, 171–2, 174–8, 180, 185, 188–9, 192, 195–6
Realism with regard to truth 3, 14, 22ff, 31ff, 147, 150, 171, 174, 178
Reality 99, 102, 105, 112, 121–2, 134, 137–8, 142, 148, 164–7, 174, 176, 189, 195
relativism 13, 25–7, 31–2, 35, 140, 147, 178–9
religion 5, 111, 114–15, 149–69, 172, 200
Rescher, Nicholas 25, 27–30, 147, 180, 195
Rorty, Richard 6, 11–13, 23–5, 34–5, 55–7, 72–3, 85–91, 109ff, 147, 149–52, 171–4, 178–9, 184–5, 188–9, 192, 195
Royce, Josiah 198
Russell, Bertrand 19, 179, 198

science 20, 29, 73, 75, 82, 86, 89, 111–18, 149–50, 154, 156–7, 161–3, 184, 192
skepticism 14–16, 37ff, 73, 103–4, 108, 181–5, 189, 191

tenacity (method of) 118, 167, 196
truth 3–6, 8, 13, 14ff, 27ff, 42, 59, 99, 109–10, 147, 150, 152, 160–1, 164–8, 171, 175, 185

coherence 129–30
correspondence 125, 148, 164, 177, 191, 195, 198
pragmatic 112, 121, 122ff, 126, 136ff, 140ff, 163, 195, 196

Will to Believe and Other Essays in Popular Philosophy, The 12, 34, 51, 157ff, 166, 183, 201–2

Williams, Michael 18, 38, 44ff, 54ff, 72 149, 184–5
Wittgenstein, Ludwig 1, 3, 8, 19, 48
world 12–16, 18–21, 24, 26–9, 31–4, 38, 43, 53, 56–7, 60–4, 73–4, 83, 85–90, 96, 100ff, 105, 109, 114–16, 120, 127–9, 134, 150ff, 175–7, 184–5, 189, 191–2, 195, 199
Wright, Crispin L. 14f, 175